ERRATA
THE TARGUM OF EZEKIEL

The following lines, printed in Bold, were omitted:

- *page 117, line 6:*

they may humble themselves for **their sins; and let them measure its design. 11. And if they humble themselves for**

- *page 123, Chapter 46, line 7:*

closed until the evening. **3. The people of the land shall bow down[a] before the Lord at the entrance of that gate on the Sabbaths and the new moons.**

The Targum of Ezekiel

THE ARAMAIC BIBLE
• THE TARGUMS •

PROJECT DIRECTOR
Martin McNamara, M.S.C.

EDITORS
Kevin Cathcart • Michael Maher, M.S.C.
Martin McNamara, M.S.C.

EDITORIAL CONSULTANTS
Daniel J. Harrington, S.J. • Bernard Grossfeld
Alejandro Díez Macho, M.S.C.†

The Aramaic Bible

Volume 13

The Targum of Ezekiel

Translated, with a Critical Introduction,
Apparatus, and Notes

BY

Samson H. Levey

Michael Glazier, Inc.
Wilmington, Delaware

About the Translator:

Samson H. Levey received his doctorate from the University of Southern California. He is Professor Emeritus of Rabbinics and Jewish Religious Thought, Hebrew Union College—Jewish Institute of Religion in Los Angeles. His publications include *The Messiah: An Aramaic Interpretation.*

First published in 1987 by Michael Glazier, Inc., 1935 West Fourth Street, Wilmington, Delaware 19805.
©Copyright 1987 by Michael Glazier, Inc. All rights reserved.

Library of Congress Cataloging in Publication Data

Bible. O.T. Ezekiel. English. Levey. 1987.
The Targum of Ezekiel.

(The Aramaic Bible ; v. 13)
Translation of the Aramaic Targum of Ezekiel, which is itself a translation from Hebrew.
Bibliography: p.
Includes indexes.
1. Bible. O.T. Ezekiel. Aramaic—Translations into English. 2. Bible. O.T. Ezekiel. Aramaic—Criticism, Textual. I. Levey, Samson, H. II. Title. III. Series: Bible. O.T. English. Aramaic Bible. 1986 ; v. 13.
BS895.A72 1986 Vol. 13   220.5,2 s   85-45546
[BS1543]   [224,.4052]
ISBN 0-89453-482-3

Logo design by Florence Bern.
Printed in the United States of America.

Table of Contents

TO
ROSALIND SLADE LEVEY
B'ḤIBBAH YETERAH

AND
TO THE MEMORY OF
NATHAN H. LEVEY
NISHMATO EDEN

Editors' Foreword

While any translation of the Scriptures may in Hebrew be called a Targum, the word is used especially for a translation of a book of the Hebrew Bible into Aramaic. Before the Christian era Aramaic had in good part replaced Hebrew in Palestine as the vernacular of the Jews. It continued as their vernacular for centuries later and remained in part as the language of the schools after Aramaic itself had been replaced as the vernacular.

Rabbinic Judaism has transmitted Targums of all books of the Hebrew Canon, with the exception of Daniel and Ezra-Nehemiah, which are themselves partly in Aramaic. We also have a translation of the Samaritan Pentateuch into the dialect of Samaritan Aramaic. From the Qumran Library we have sections of a Targum of Job and fragments of a Targum of Leviticus, chapter 16, facts which indicate that the Bible was being translated in Aramaic in pre-Christian times.

Translations of books of the Hebrew Bible into Aramaic for liturgical purposes must have begun before the Christian era, even though none of the Targums transmitted to us by Rabbinic Judaism can be shown to be that old and though some of them are demonstrably compositions from later centuries.

In recent decades there has been increasing interest among scholars and a larger public in these Targums. A noticeable lacuna, however, has been the absence of a modern English translation of this body of writing. It is in marked contrast with most other bodies of Jewish literature for which there are good modern English translations, for instance the Apocrypha and Pseudepigrapha of the Old Testament, Josephus, Philo, the Mishnah, the Babylonian Talmud and Midrashic literature, and more recently the Tosefta and Palestinian Talmud.

It is hoped that this present series will provide some remedy for this state of affairs.

The aim of the series is to translate all the traditionally-known Targums, that is those transmitted by Rabbinic Judaism, into modern English idiom, while at the same time respecting the particular and peculiar nature of what these Aramaic translations were originally intended to be. A translator's task is never an easy one. It is rendered doubly difficult when the text to be rendered is itself a translation which is at times governed by an entire set of principles.

All the translations in this series have been specially commissioned. The translators have made use of what they reckon as the best printed editions of the Aramaic Targum in question or have themselves directly consulted the manuscripts.

The translation aims at giving a faithful rendering of the Aramaic. The introduction to each Targum contains the necessary background information on the particular work. In general, each Targum translation is accompanied by an apparatus and notes. The former is concerned mainly with such items as the variant readings in the Aramaic texts, the relation of the English translation to the original, etc. The notes give what explanations the translator thinks necessary or useful for this series.

Not all the Targums here translated are of the same kind. Targums were translated at different times, and most probably for varying purposes, and have more than one interpretative approach to the Hebrew Bible. This diversity between the Targums themselves is reflected in the translation and in the manner in which the accompanying explanatory material is presented. However, a basic unity of presentation has been maintained. Targumic deviations from the Hebrew text, whether by interpretation or paraphrase, are indicated by italics.

A point that needs to be stressed with regard to this translation of the Targums is that by reason of the state of current targumic research, to a certain extent it must be regarded as a provisional one. Despite the progress made, especially in recent decades, much work still remains to be done in the field of targumic study. Not all the Targums are as yet available in critical editions. And with regard to those that have been critically edited from known manuscripts, in the case of the Targums of some books the variants between the manuscripts themselves are such as to give rise to the question whether they have all descended from a single common original.

Details regarding these points will be found in the various introductions and critical notes.

It is recognised that a series such as this will have a broad readership. The Targums constitute a valuable source of information for students of Jewish literature, particularly those concerned with the history of interpretation, and also for students of the New Testament, especially for those interested in its relationship to its Jewish origins. The Targums also concern members of the general public who have an interest in the Jewish interpretation of the Scriptures or in the Jewish background to the New Testament. For them the Targums should be both interesting and enlightening.

By their translations, introductions and critical notes the contributors to this series have rendered an immense service to the progress of targumic studies. It is hoped that the series, provisional though it may be, will bring significantly nearer the day when the definitive translation of the Targums can be made.

Kevin Cathcart   Martin McNamara, M.S.C.   Michael Maher, M.S.C.

Acknowledgements

I am indebted to Fr. Martin McNamara, and his Editorial Board, for the invitation to contribute this volume on the Targum of Ezekiel as part of the Aramaic Bible, and to Michael Glazier, Inc. for the herculean task of publication of the entire project.

The readiness of President Alfred Gottschalk to promote scholarship, and the enthusiastic support of Dr. Uri D. Herscher, Executive Vice President of the Hebrew Union College—Jewish Institute of Religion, have been of inestimable value.

Prof. Willis W. Fisher, who for decades was the head of the Department of Old Testament at the University of Southern California and Claremont School of Theology, Professor of Bible *par excellence*, has had a profound influence on the direction of my academic life.

Prof. Bernard Grossfeld of the University of Wisconsin has been most helpful in an exchange of views on our Targumic studies.

From my students at Hebrew Union College—Jewish Institute of Religion, Los Angeles, I have gained more than I have given.

To the Targum of Ezekiel itself I owe an enduring debt of gratitude for its electrifying challenge and for giving me no rest, day or night.

B'ezrat Hashem Adon Olme Olamim.

List of Principal Abbreviations

AB   Greenberg, M., *Ezekiel 1-20*, The Anchor Bible, Garden City, N.Y., 1983.

BDB   Brown, Driver, and Briggs, *Hebrew and English Lexicon of the Old Testament*, Oxford, 1952.

Churgin   Churgin, P., *Targum Jonathan to the Prophets*, New Haven, Conn., 1927.

EJ   *Encyclopaedia Judaica*, Jerusalem, 1971.

HUCA   Hebrew Union College Annual

IB   May, H. G., and Allen, E. L., *The Book of Ezekiel*, The Interpreter's Bible, vol. VI, Nashville, 1980.

ICC   Cooke, G. A., *The Book of Ezekiel*, International Critical Commentary, Edinburgh, 1960.

Jastrow   Jastrow, M., *A Dictionary of the Targumim, etc.*, 2 vols., London and New York, 1903.

JE   *The Jewish Encyclopedia*, New York, 1903.

JPS (N) *The Prophets, A New Translation*, The Jewish Publication Society, Philadelphia, 1978.

Ket.   *Ketib*, the written form of a word in the Masoretic Text of Scriptures.

K-B   Koehler, L., and Baumgartner, W., *Lexicon in Veteris Testamenti Libros*, Leiden, 1958.

Levy   Levy, J., *Chaldäisches Wörterbuch über die Targumim*, Darmstadt, 1966, 2 volumes (in one).

LXX   Greek, Septuagint, Göttingen, 1952.

MT   The Masoretic Text of the Hebrew Scriptures (Kittel).
(Targum's departures from MT are in italics.)

Q   *Qere*, the form of a word as read, not written, in the Masoretic Text.

RSV   *The Holy Bible, Revised Standard Version*, N.Y., 1953 (IB).

S   Syriac, Peshitta, London, 1823-1826.

S-A   Smolar, L., and Aberbach, M., *Studies in Targum Jonathan to the Prophets*, N.Y. and Baltimore, 1983, (with a reprint of Churgin).

Tg.   Aramaic, Targum(im).

V   Latin, Vulgate, Rome, 1959.

VT   *Vetus Testamentum.*

RABBINIC SOURCES CITED

TALMUDIC

m. - Mishnah   (London, 1951-63, Hebrew and English)

t. - Tosefta   (Pasewalk, 1880)

b. - Babylonian Talmud   (Wilno, 1913-14. English, Soncino, London)

y. — Jerusalem Talmud (Krotoshin, 1866)

Ab.	'Abot	*Mid.*	Middot
Arak.	'Arakin	*M.K.*	Mo'ed Kaṭan
A.Z.	'Abodah Zarah	*Pes.*	Pesaḥim
B.B.	Baba' Batra'	*R.H.*	Roš Haššanah
Ber.	Berakot	*Sanh.*	Sanhedrin
Ed.	'Eduyot	*Šab.*	*Šab.*
		Šeq.	Šeqalim
Erub.	'Erubin	*Sot.*	Sotah
Git.	Giṭṭin		
Ḥag.	Ḥagigah	*Suk.*	Sukkah
Kel.	Kelim	*Ta'an.*	Ta'anit
Ket.	Ketubot	*Tam.*	Tamid
Kid.	Kiddušin	*Yeb.*	Yebamot
Mak.	Makkot	*Yom.*	Yoma'

Meg.   Megillah   *Zeb.*   Zebaḥim
Men.   Menaḥot

TANNAITIC MIDRASHIM

Mek. - Mekilta (on Exodus, Philadelphia, 1933. Hebrew and English)
Sifra (on Leviticus, New York, 1956)

Sifre (on Numbers and Deuteronomy, Breslau, 1935)

MINOR TRACTATES OF THE TALMUD

Ab. de R. Nat.   Abot de Rabbi Natan, London, 1887. English, Soncino,
London, 1965; Goldin, (A), New Haven, 1955; Saldarini, (B),
Chico, 1982.

Kal. R.   Kallah Rabbati, N.Y., 1936. English, Soncino, London, 1965.

Der. Er. Zuṭ   Derek Ereṣ Zuṭa, N.Y., 1935. English, Soncino,

MIDRASH RABBAH   Wilno, 1878.   English, Soncino, London, 1951.

Gen. R.	Genesis Rabbah	*S. S. R.*	Song of Songs Rabbah
Ex. R.	Exodus Rabbah	*Ruth R.*	Ruth Rabbah
Lev. R.	Leviticus Rabbah	*Lam. R.*	Lamentations Rabbah
Num. R.	Numbers Rabbah	*Eccl. R.*	Ecclesiastes Rabbah
Deut. R.	Deuteronomy Rabbah	*Est. R.*	Esther Rabbah

OTHER SOURCES

Bet HaMidraš,   (Jellinek), Jerusalem, 1967.

Mek. de R. Šim.   Mekilta de Rabbi Šim'on, Frankfurt-am-Main, 1905.

Mid. Teh.   Midraš Tehillim (Šoḥar Ṭob), Wilno, 1891. English, Braude.

Pes. R.   Pesiqta Rabbati, Vienna, 1880. English, Braude.

Pirq. de R. El.   Pirqe de Rabbi Eliezer, Warsaw, 1852. English, Friedlander.

Tanh.	Midraš Tanḥuma, Wilno, 1913.
Yal. Šim.	Yalquṭ Šimʻoni, Wilno, 1898.
Zohar,	Amesterdam, 1805. English, Soncino, London, 1949.

THE APPARATUS

The apparatus employed in this work is that of Alexander Sperber, *The Bible in Aramaic*, vol. III *The Latter Prophets According to Targum Jonathan*, Leiden, Brill, 1962, pp. v ff. However, I did not use Sperber's siglia, in the belief that his would be rather difficult to cope with in the process of reading the translation of the Targum. I have simplified the indications to correspond more closely to the work indicated, providing one for the Sperber manuscript along with the others. In some instances, where it was necessary for me to discuss an item of the Apparatus at some length, I have placed this in the notes in addition to the Apparatus.

In alphabetical order, rather than classification:

A — ʻAruk of R. Nathan (ed. Kohut)

AP — The Antwerp Polyglot Bible, 1569/73

BM — One or another of the MSS., British Museum

CR — Codex Reuchlinianus

K — Kimḥi's Commentary in the Rabbinic Bible

MM — Ms. of the Montefiore Library, Jews' College, London

R — Rashi's Commentary in the Rabbinic Bible

RB — One or another of the Rabbinic Bibles

SP — The Sperber manuscript, printed in vol. III of *The Bible in Aramaic*, which is the basic text used in this work.

Introduction

Targum of Ezekiel in the Framework of the Targum on the Prophets

The Targum of Ezekiel is an intriguing exegetical vehicle, which, critically analyzed, provides us with a vivid insight into an area of Jewish theological speculation which stretches far back into the history of Jewish religious thought.

The Book of Ezekiel itself is a complex literary document which challenges the most incisive Biblical analysts.[1] The severe nature of this complexity is compounded by a difficult Mosoretic text, abundant grammatical and syntactical problems, an infusion of strange language and linguistic peculiarities.[2] Additionally, Torrey's argument and the Qumran material have aroused some speculative questions and problems regarding the date and substantive elements in Ezekiel.[3]

The Targum of Ezekiel is a challenging version which is worthy of consideration, not alone for its illumination of the biblical text, but for its intrinsic value for Targumic study *per se.* It, too, like the Book of Ezekiel, is a complex literary document posing problems of different kinds, literary, exegetical and theological.

In general, the Targum of Ezekiel belongs to the same genre as the other official Targumim, designated in Jewish Tradition as Onqelos on the Pentateuch and Jonathan on the Prophets. Its language is basically Palestinian Aramaic, revised and edited in Babylon. Its vocabulary, idiom, grammatical form, and rendering of the Hebrew text are essentially the same as we find in the official Targumim on the other books, and follows their characteristic pattern of explanation and interpretation. The exegetical complement is used to enlarge upon terse passages in the Hebrew text; paraphrase is employed where the text is obscure; prose renderings simplify the biblical poetry; and similar devices are designed to make Scripture intelligible to the Aramaic-speaking Jews. Beyond this, the Targum of Ezekiel has some peculiarities distinctively its own.

---

[1] Among the most cogent discussions of the subject are the arguments and counterarguments between C.C.Torrey and S. Spiegel most recently reprinted in the Library of Biblical Studies, edited by Prof. Harry M. Orlinsky: *Pseudo-Ezekiel and the Original Prophecy and Critical Articles*, N.Y., 1970.

[2] See C.G. Howie, *The Date and Composition of Ezekiel*, J.B.L. Monograph Series, v. VII, Phil. 1960, especially pp. 47-68.

[3] C.C.Torrey in *Pseudo-Ezekiel and the Original Prophecy and Critical Articles*, p. 99 dates the prophecy at c. 230. M.D. Cassuto, *Yehezkel*, Tel Aviv, 1959, Introduction. M. Burrows, *More Light on the Dead Sea Scrolls*, N.Y., 1958, p. 304, a.e.

The Date of the Targum of Ezekiel

Modern scholars differ widely in their attempt to date the various Targumim, relating them linguistically to such literary strata as the Qumran scrolls and the Jerusalem Talmud.[4] Regardless of the date of their origin, what is certain is that being a vernacular rendering delivered orally, they were subject to some modification from time to time, but only by the Rabbinic authorities who guided the synagogue ritual, including the readings from the Torah and the Prophets. There was censorial control to assure adherence to Rabbinic halakah and ideology.[5] This prevailed until their final redaction, which I maintain was probably the work of Saadia Gaon during the early part of the tenth century.[6] This is significant especially for the Ezekiel Targum, which bears evidence of the redactive hand of R. Johanan b. Zakkai at Yavneh.

The process by which the official Targum originally came into being may not have applied to Ezekiel. That process involved the use of Scripture in the original Hebrew as integral to Jewish worship, and the practice of translation into Aramaic of the biblical text by a Meturgeman.[7]

The wary approach to Ezekiel by the religious authorities[8] and the specific prohibition against reading chapter 1 for the Haftarah,[9] must have militated against rendering the prophet into Aramaic in the usual manner. The caveat undoubtedly is connected with Merkabah Mysticism, based in some measure on Ezekiel's account of the celestial chariot. *m. Hag.* 2:1 issues an interdict against expounding the Merkabah even for one singular person, "unless he is a sage who understands it with his own mind." i.e. one who is so brilliant that he needs no teacher to expound it for him. The very wording of the Mishnah seems to imply that there was a mystical tradition by which one might appropriate a knowledge of the Merkabah through other than the usual channels of learning and transmission. In any case, Ezekiel's portrait of the divine throne and the speculative mysticism which it evoked surely must have been a matter which the authorities sought to conceal, especially from the masses;[10] hence the Targum, the vehicle of popular exposition, had to be carefully worded, esoteric, and comprehended with caution.

The Book of Ezekiel and the Merkabah Tradition

To understand the Targum of Ezekiel we must look to the association of Merkabah Mysticism with the prophecy of Ezekiel. We must also recognize the historical

---

[4]There is an excellent summation of the current literature on the subject in *Studies in Targum Jonathan to the Prophets*, by Leivy Smolar and Moses Aberbach, pp. xi ff.

[5]Cf. M. McNamara, *The New Testament and the Palestinian Targum*, p. 64; *S–A*, p. xvii.

[6]S.H. Levey, "The Date of Targum Jonathan to the Prophets," *VT*, 21 (1971), p. 193 f.

[7]*m. Meg.* 4:4.

[8]*b. Šab.* 13b; *Men.* 45a; *Hag.* 13a. "Were it not for Hananiah b. Hezekiah, the Book of Ezekiel would have been withdrawn, because its words contradict the words of the Torah (Mosaic Law)."

[9]*m. Meg.* 4:10.

[10]Cf. *b. Pes.* 119a.

situation when Merkabah Mysticism becomes the instrumentality for the preservation of the ego-structure of the Jewish people in the face of critical threats to its survival. Immediately apparent are the crises of 586 B.C.E. and 70 C.E., the destruction of the two Temples of Jerusalem. These Sanctuaries had been symbols of the faith of Israel and the validity of the Jewish God-concept. The two situations had much in common in terms of the indispensable need to establish a surrogate for the demolished Sanctuary. If this had not been done, the Jewish religion might have perished in the conflagrations set by Nebuchadnezzar and Titus, and with it the people who believed in the Omnipotent Presence of the God of Israel.

Viewed from the perspective of history, the prophecy of Ezekiel is a masterpiece of religio-political philosophy which enabled the Jew to weather the crisis of the fall of Jerusalem, the destruction of Judah as a political entity, and the Babylonian Exile. This was in defiance of the usual process of history which would normally indicate the complete disappearance of any nation so ravaged. Jeremiah could be characterized as the greatest of the literary prophets because of his personal xperiences and his visions of impending doom and subsequent deliverance,[11] but to Ezekiel belongs the credit for delivering the Jewish people from total oblivion and for insuring that they would not vanish from the face of the earth. He accomplished this by the religio-psychological expedient of the vision of the Merkabah, stressing that though the earthly Temple was destroyed there was a heavenly throne of YHWH beyond the reach of Babylonian might, or for that matter, inaccessible to any mundane military power. YHWH was still supreme both as deity and as the providential protector of His people. The justification of the tragic fate of Judah (chs. 4-24), the oracles against the nations (chs. 25-32), the vision of a restored nation and its final vindication (chs. 33-39) and a reconstructed Temple and cult (chs. 40-48) all emanate logically from the central focus of a supermundane Power, enthroned on high, respelendent in glory, awesome to contemplate, imperceptible to the mere mortal. Only the prophet who is endowed with penetrating perception is qualified to get a glimpse of the divine throne and its mysteries and to convey his experiences to the initiated who might understand.

The Targum senses the supreme drama enacted in the Book of Ezekiel as none of the other versions do because those who formulated it lived in the mainstream of the historical processes which were operative among the Jews in the land of Israel. Targum of the Prophets especially reflects actual historical events incorporated and perserved in the body of its exegetical interpretations, probably as eyewitness accounts of the great men and movements in Jewish life.[12] In the case of the Targum

---

[11]M. Buttenwieser, *The Prophets of Israel*, N.Y., 1914, and by implication, S.H. Blank, *Jeremiah, Man and Prophet*, Cincinnati, 1961. But even Ezekiel, torn to shreds and denigrated by some authorities, is recognized for his genius and greatness by others. Thus, C.G. Howie, *The Date and Composition of Ezekiel*, concludes: "Contrary to a growing belief, Ezekiel was not a schizophrenic ... On the other hand, he would not fit the mould of normality even in his day. Therein lies his greatness; he was a sensitive spirit who was caught up in the cross-currents of history. Torn from his native land and transplanted to a strange place, he turned inward and became perhaps the outstanding visionary of the Old Testament. Our prophet may correctly be classed with the world's best known mystics ... In all, Ezekiel was one of the greatest spiritual figures of ancient Israel." pp. 101-2. Cf. also Y. Kaufmann, *The Religion of Israel*, p. 436 ff.

[12]For illustrative examples see P. Churgin, *Targum Jonathan to the Prophets*, p. 26, and S.H. Levey, *The Messiah*, p. 67; cf. also Ps.-J. to Gen. 49:10-12.

of Ezekiel, I venture to suggest that its historico-theological thrust reflects the situation in Palestine immediately following the catastrophe of 70 C.E. The destruction of Jerusalem and the Temple by the Romans was a re-enactment of Jewish history six centuries earlier, which Ezekiel had witnessed. Ezekiel's response, the psychological impact of the Merkabah concept, proved to be effective, as was borne out by the return from exile, the rebuilding of the Temple and the re-establishment of the nation in the Judean state. Perhaps it was no mere coincidence that the same formula for survival was imposed by Rabban Johanan b. Zakkai in his effort to salvage the Jewish people from total collapse when he established Yavneh and its Sages as the rallying point of a resurgent Jewish community.

Messianic Activism and Merkabah Mysticism

Uri D. Herscher has demonstrated that the predominance of Merkabah Mysticism in the post destruction era under R. Johanan b. Zakkai was a deliberate effort to preserve the disciples whom he had gathered around him from being decimated by the Roman authorities. [13] Johanan's reasoning must have been rather simple. Messianic activism was regarded by Rome as treason against the emperor. It had resulted in the execution of a number of Jewish Messianic figures and their followers, including the Nazarene, who was accused by the Romans of being "King of the Jews," i.e., traitor to Rome. Christianity subsequently took the approach that "My kingdom is not of this world" (John 18:36), that is, it is not political activism and hence no threat to Rome. Johanan, too, had to suppress open Messianic activity in order to protect his followers from the charge of treason, but at the same time he had to keep alive their faith in God and their hope for national restitution and restoration of their sovereignty, all symbolized by the Temple. This he did by substituting Merkabah Mysticism for Messianic activism. As in Ezekiel, this placed the divine throne in heaven out of reach of the adversary, in this instance, Rome. This accounts for such vivid passages of Merkabah as found in *b. Ḥag.* 14b and *t. Ḥag.* 2:1, in which Johanan and his disciples play such a dominant role. [14] Neusner and Rivkin significantly observe that Johanan b. Zakkai ignores the doctrine of the Messiah. [15]

There is evidence that the Targum of Ezekiel may be a document reflecting the views of R. Johanan, emphasizing the Merkabah instead of the Messianic. I have demonstrated [16] that the Targum of Ezekiel is unique in that unlike the Targum on

---

[13] Uri Herscher, "Yochanan ben Zakkai: Acrobatics at Yavneh," a paper submitted in partial fulfillment of a minor in Rabbinics for his doctoral, Hebrew Union College - Jewish institute of Religion, Los Angeles, CA., 1973.

[14] The praise of Eleazar b. Arakh as *na'eh doreš wena'eh meqayyem* seems to imply that he was not only adept at the exposition of Merkabah, but was observant in following Johanan's appeal, to refrain from overt Messianic activity.

[15] Ellis Rivkin, "The Meaning of Messiah in Jewish Thought," *Union Seminary Quarterly Review*, vol. 26, no. 4, 1971, p. 395. Cf. also J. Neusner, *A Life of Yohanan ben Zakkai*, Leiden, 1970, pp. 3-4, 49. However, Johanan's deathbed admonition to his disciples, "Prepare a throne for Hezekiah, King of Judah, who is coming," *b. Ber.* 28b, cannot be construed as being anything but Messianic. But note the double entendre, the hidden meaning to be understood only by the initiated.

[16] S.H. Levey, *The Messiah*, pp. 78-79, 85-87.

the other prophetic books, nowhere in it is the outright designation *mešiḥa'* to be found, though there is ample opportunity for Messianic interpretation. Illustrative of this, Ezek. 17:22 is rendered by the Targum, "I will bring near a child from the kingdom of the House of David;" and in 37:24, "My servant David" is translated literally. Nor is the *nasi'* in chs. 44, 45, 46 and 48 interpreted as the Messiah, as it is understood by some Rabbinic Commentaries, on the strength of 34:24.[17] In these instances the Ezekiel Targum translates *nasi'* simply as "prince," although in 34:24 and 37:25 it is translated as "king." Compare this with the context of Jer. 33:12-26, where David comes into the prophecy, and Targum still finds room for the designated Messiah, vv. 13 and 15. Similarly in Jer. 23:5. Even more boldly, in Jer. 30:9, Tg. renders the Hebrew, "David their king" as "the Messiah, son of David, their king." I have pointed out further that the phrase in Ezek. 21:32, "until he comes, to whom judgment belongs," which lends itself naturally to a Messianic interpretation, is applied by the Targumist to the historical picture of the final days of the Kingdom of Judah, specifically to Ishmael the son of Nethaniah, the murderer of Gedaliah. Furthermore, Ezekiel should lend itself more readily to Messianic exegesis by virtue of its Gog passages in chapters 38 and 39, which had become intimately associated with the advent of the Messiah in Rabbinic thought, and yet even these the Targum renders without Messianic reference.

There were historical interludes in Palestine under Roman rule when Messianic activism, or even articulation, carried the death penalty with it.[18] We can best explain our Targum's exegesis as adhering to the Merkabah rather than the Messianic approach, and in all likelihood expressing the political posture of R. Joḥanan b. Zakkai at Yavneh.

Allusions to Merkabah Mysticism in the Targum of Ezekiel

Throne mysticism and its concomitants are not limited to the primary Merkabah chapters 1 and 10. There is sufficient sprinkling of the theme throughout the entire Targum. Ezek. 3:12 ff.; 8:3; 11:1; 24; 43:5, instances where the prophet is lifted by the spirit, have overtones of the mystic ascent of the Merkabah devotee. The introduction to the Temple vision 40:1-4 likewise is interpreted by the Targum in such a manner as to equate prophecy with strange mystic powers of locomotion; and the mysterious figure whom the prophet sees standing at the gate is a divine being who addressed him even as he is customarily addressed by the deity. In 43:1 ff. the prophet himself draws a comparison between the vision of the glory of YHWH in the Temple with the vision that he saw on the river Chebar. Thus the Temple-to-be is a replica of the heavenly Merkabah.[19] In language that echoes the parlance of the Merkabah mystic, the Targum translates Ezek. 43:7[20] in such a manner as to make

---

[17]Cf. Kimḥi and Metzudat David to Ezek. 34:23.

[18]S.H. Levey, *The Messiah*, p. 86.

[19]Cf. W. Eichrodt, *Ezekiel*, Phila., 1970, p. 542: "The Temple makes its appearance as a heavenly reality created by Yahweh himself and transplanted to stand on earth."

[20]Cf. the poetic figure of the throne and the footstool with Is. 66.1.

the Sanctuary an *eternal* abode of God, possibly an indestructible edifice. Note that in the new Sanctuary there will be a palace housing God's throne of glory and His Shekinah in the midst of Israel eternally.

Further attestation to the eschatological, divine nature of the reconstructed city of Jerusalem, which will contain the Sanctuary of the future is found in the very last verse of the prophecy, 48:35b, which the Targum paraphrases, "And the name of the city shall be designated from the day that He makes His Shekinah rest (upon it), 'The Lord is there.'"[21] A possible implication of this could be that the new worldly Jerusalem will be a replica of the heavenly city superimposed on the ruins of the old.[22] In this, too, Merkabah Mysticism is the dominant motif, and the absence of the Messianic in the Targumic exegesis of Ezekiel is clear and unmistakable.

Son of Adam

The key to a proper understanding of the exegesis of the Ezekiel Targum is its interpretation of the designation *ben 'adam* (2:1 a.e.) by which God addresses the prophet, and which occurs 87 times in the biblical book. The Septuagint, the Vulgate, and the Syriac all render the phrase "son of man." Some Rabbinic interpretation attributes the appellation to the fear that Ezekiel might think of himself as a superior being of angelic status by virtue of the heavenly vision which he had seen; hence he is reminded that he is only human, a "son of man," Rashi and Kimḥi, *ad loc.* The English versions including the *Revised Standard Version*, following the King James, and the *New American Bible*, are content with "son of man;" the *American Translation* (Gordon), "mortal man;" the *New English Bible* and *Anchor Bible* render it simply as "man;" *JPS* (N), "O mortal." *ArtScroll* leaves it untranslated, "*Ben Adam.*" Of the modern commentators, the most prevalent opinion is that the appellation suggests the mortal unworthiness of the prophet Ezekiel, with an implied transcendence of YHWH. Eichrodt, Stalker, Taylor, and Cassuto all express this thought in one way or another.[23]

Eichrodt's comment is typical: "The choice of this particular man as prophet in itself runs counter to practically every human presupposition. The title 'son of man' by which he is addressed is frequently employed in this book. But it is found nowhere else in the Old Testament except Dan. 8:17, which is derived from the present passage. Now that title already expresses, in the same words and manner as Ps. 8:5 the weakness of the creature to whom the mighty Lord shows such condescension."[24]

---

[21]The version is that of A. Sperber, *The Bible in Aramaic*, Leiden, 1962, vol. III, p. 384. However, compare the versions of Rashi, Kimḥi, and the Rabbinic Bibles: "The name of the city shall be designated from the day when the Lord makes His Shekinah dwell there."

[22]Cf. Rev. 3:12.

[23]W. Eichrodt, *Ezekiel*, Phila., 1952, p. 61; D.M.G. Stalker, *Ezekiel*, London, 1968, p. 50; J.B. Taylor, *Ezekiel*, Downers Grove, Ill., 1969, p. 60; M.D. Cassuto, *Yeḥezkel*, p. 13.

[24]W. Eichrodt, *Ezekiel*, p. 61.

The Targum's rendering of the phrase goes contrary to the accepted notions. For instead of translating *ben 'adam* by the Aramaic *bar 'enaša'* or its variants, which would imply the idea of a mere mortal, and occurs in Targum to Ps. 8:5, 146:3; Num. 23:19; Is. 51:12, 56:2; Jer. 49:18, 33; 50:40; 51:43 and Mic. 5:6, it consistently, without exception, renders it *bar 'adam* in Ezekiel. The Targumic phrase can only mean "son of Adam" or "Adamite." *'Adam* is a proper noun in the Aramaic (Gen. 2:7, 8, 15, 16, 18, etc.).[25]

Kimḥi seems to sense a deliberately construed exegetical design in the Targum's rendering. His initial comment is the prevalent traditional explanation, as found in Rashi, but his own view is worthy of note, since he recognizes the unique phraseology of the Targum's translation.

Kimḥi: "The commentators have explained that He (God) called him (Ezekiel), *Ben 'Adam* so that he should not magnify himself and consider himself as one of the angels by virtue of his having seen this great vision. But it properly sems to me, that because he saw the face of a man in the chariot, He made known to him that he is upright and good in His eyes, and that he is a son of man, not the son of a lion, nor the son of an ox, nor the son of an eagle in the manner in which we have explained it. Therefore, Jonathan translates the phrase *bar 'adam* not *bar 'enaša'*, even though he translates *pene 'adam* as *'ape 'enaša'*, with reference to the likeness (Ezek. 1:10)."

Kimḥi's citing of the Targum to support his explanation that the prophet is man and not one of the other figures in the chariot may be admissible, but I do not believe that Kimḥi was aware of the full force of the phrase *bar 'adam*.

It is my contention that there may be something more esoteric in the Targum's *bar 'adam*, perhaps in opposition to the Septuagint and to those who see in *ben 'adam* a denigration of Ezekiel. While it seems evident that the intent is deliberate, we can only conjecture as to the purpose of the phrase. The Targumist may have detected a problem if he translated it as *bar 'enaša'* in view of Daniel's designation of the Messianic cloud-man or angelic figure by *bar 'enaš* (7:13), a concept which figures prominently in the Book of Enoch, (45:3, 46:2, a.e.), IV Ezra, and in the New Testament. His *bar 'adam* may be his way of elevating Ezekiel to the most exalted level of prophecy, since Adam was regarded in some Rabbinic opinion as a prophet who foresaw all that was to happen in the entire course of human history, generation by generation, until the resurrection of the dead.[26] It also may be a subtle ploy relating to the mystery of the Merkabah which is integral to Ezekiel's role in Rabbinic Mysticism.

The association of Adam with the celestial Temple, the divine abode, and the throne of the deity is established in recognized strata from which the Targum could draw. The Merkabah tradition itself is preserved in the Intertestamental Literature, specifically in the Enoch books, 1 Enoch xiv, 2 Enoch xx and xxi, and in the Testament of Levi v. There is a striking passage in which Adam relates to Seth, his vision of the Merkabah, after his expulsion from the Garden of Eden. "When we were at prayer there came to me Michael the archangel, a messenger of God. And I

[25]See Hasting's *Dictionary of the Bible*. N.Y., 1902, vol. IV, p. 580.
[26]*b. A.Z.* 5a; *Sanh.* 38b; *Mid. Teh.* 139:6. Cf. also R. Judah b. R. Simon's statement in *Gen. R.* 24:5; "Adam was worthy to have the Torah revealed by him ..."

saw a chariot like the wind and its wheels were fiery and I was caught up in the Paradise of Righteousness, and I saw the Lord sitting and His face was flaming fire that could not be endured. And many thousands of angels were on the right and the left of the chariot."[27] This is from the Vita Adae et Evae, the Jewish origin and characteristics of which Ginzberg had demonstrated, and assigned to an early period antedating the destruction of 70 C.E.[28]

In the Vita the Second Temple is still in its prime, bearing out the pre-destruction antiquity of the document. And, perhaps of even greater relevance to this study, the eschatological structure is one in which the doctrine of the Messiah is totally absent.[29] The inclusion of the vision of the divine chariot, and the non-Messianic picture of the future marks the Vita as an ideal source for or parallel to the exegetical thrust of the Targum of Ezekiel. It supports the idea of the Merkabah as a surrogate for the Messianic, and provides an existential rationale for the eschatology of our Ezekiel Targum as an exception to the rest of Targum on the Prophets in this respect.

The Adamite-Temple-Merkabah motif is found in Rabbinic sources as well. A Baraita lists those things that are pre-mundane: "It was taught, seven things were created before the world was created, and these are Torah and repentance; the Garden of Eden (paradise) and Gehenna (hell); the Throne of Glory and the Temple; and the name of the Messiah."[30] Note the wording, "the Throne of Glory and the Temple," the two are coupled, linked together. This could point to the mystery of the divine nature of the Sanctuary as the abode of God. A homily in the Midrash also attributes pre-existence to Adam: "Thou didst form me after and before... R. Simeon b. Lakish says, after the work of the last day and before the work of the first day of Creation."[31] The implication is that there is a pre-existent celestial as well as a mundane aspect of Adam,[32] the former intimately associated with premundane creations, including God's throne and the Temple. But even the earthly Adam is a reflection of the Sanctuary, since he was created out of dust taken from the site of the Temple. "R. Berekiah and R. Helbo in the name of R. Samuel b. Naḥman said, He (Adam) was created from the place of his atonement."[33]

The link between Adam and the Merkabah in Judaic esoteric speculation is clearly descernible. The Targum of Ezekiel sees in the Prophet Ezekiel a counterpart of Adam, unmistakable in its designation of him as *bar 'adam*. Rabbinic lore further reinforces this portrait of Ezekiel by insisting that God need not have revealed the secrets of the Merkabah at all, except that when the children of Israel said *na'aseh*

[27]R.H. Charles, *Apocrypha and Pseudepigrapha*, vol. II, "Vita Adae et Evae," XXV, p. 139.

[28]L. Ginzberg, "Book of Adam," *JE*, vol. I, p. 179 f.

[29]"Vita Adae et Evae," XXIX, Charles II, p. 140. The vision of the chariot of splendor also appears to Eve when Adam is about to die. Apocalypse of Moses XXXIII, XXXIV, Charles II, p. 149.

[30]*b.Ned.* 39b; *Pes.* 54a. There is variant in *Gen.R.* 1:4 — "Six things preceded the creation of the world. Some were actually created, some God thought of creating. The Torah and the Throne of Glory were actually created ... The Patriarchs, Israel, the Temple, and the name of the Messiah He thought of creating ... R. Ahavah b. R. Zera says, also repentance." Cf. *Mid. Teh.* 90:12; *Pir. de R. El.*, III.

[31]*Gen. R.* 8:1, according to L. Ginzberg, article, "Adam Kadmon," *JE*, I, 181.

[32]Cf. The Assumption of Moses, 1:14, Charles II, p. 415 which declares Moses to be pre-existent. This book, too, is non-Messianic.

[33]*Gen. R.* 14:8.

venisma‘ God felt impelled to make known to them those matters hidden in His chambers.[34] There is also an eschatological interpretation to the effect that in the future Ezekiel will come again to unlock for Israel the hidden chambers of the Merkabah.[35]

There is yet another possibility. If Ezekiel is regarded as a *bar 'adam*, "Adamite," the Targumist may be implying an indirect polemical thrust against the Pauline view that Jesus was the eschatological Adam (I Cor. 15:45).[36] The implicit Targumic argument might be that the Christian contention that Jesus is the unique Adamite who alone could raise the dead (John 11:1ff.) is fallacious, since Ezekiel was an Adamite long before Jesus, and he did more than revive one man; he resurrected an entire multitude of the dead as depicted in chapter 37.[37] Then, too, Adam is seen as the ultimate personification of goodness.[38] This, too, might be construed as a polemic against the Pauline position that Adam was evil, the culprit whose sin brought death into the world (I Cor. 15:21, 22).

Ezekiel's legacy from Adam, and the Merkabah tradition associated with it, help explain this aspect of our Targum's exegesis.

Historical Allusions

While the non-Messianic Merkabah theme is of major significance, there is another current of exegetical interest in the Targum of Ezekiel. That is its emphatic historical interpretations, interpolating the names of historical personages and events of historical importance. This is probably stimulated by the nature of Eze-kiel's prophecy, the historical scene out of which it emerges, and the destruction and the exile which enlarged Israel's role on the international scene. In the case of the Targum, the historical factors involved in the destiny of Israel were multiplied many times over after the era in which Ezekiel lived. Some historical allusions will demon-strate the point.

The Targum injects the picture of the exile of Seraiah, the High Priest, and King Zedekiah, the appointment of Gedaliah, and his assassination by Ishmael the son of Nethaniah, all of which are historical facts. This is done exegetically, where the Hebrew text is merely unspecified poetic expression. There are other applications of

---

[34] *Songs of Songs Rabbah* 1:14.

[35] Ibid. K. Kohler, "Merkabah," *JE* vol. VIII, p. 499. For further detailed treatment of Merkabah Mysticism and the antiquity of the tradition in the literary strata, see G.G. Scholem, *Major Trands in Jewish Mysticism*, N.Y., 1954, pp. 40-79 and his *Jewish Gnosticism, Merkabah Mysticism, and Talmudic Tradition*, N.Y., 1965.

[36] J. Bowker holds that the Targum regularly counters Christian theology, *The Targums and Rabbinic Literature*, Cambridge University Press, 1969, p. xi. Cf. S.H. Levey, *The Messiah - An Aramaic Interpretation*, p. 152.

[37] Rabbinic opinion differs as to whether Ezekiel's prophecy in chapter 37 is mere poetic symbolism for a restored Jewish nation or a literal revival of the dead. Many prominent Sages believed that Ezekiel actually brought the dead back to life, *b. Sanh.* 92b. Both the Hebrew text and more so the Targum Ezek. 37:7-10 indicate that the prophet, as an agent of God, had a hand in the revival of the dry bones. Cf. *Lev. R.* 27:4. the incident of Elijah is absorbed into the Messianic picture both by Judaism and Christianity. Mal. 3:23 (4:5 in the Versions); Matt. 11:13-14; Mark 8:27, 28.

[38] *Gen. R.* 8:5. In *Gen. R.* 9:12, on Gen. 1:31, *tob me'od* and *'adam* are equated.

this principle in the same chapter 21:13-22, where the Targum interprets the poetic imagery in the light of vv. 23 ff. It explains 21:15 as referring to the rejoicing of the tribes of Judah and Benjamin when the tribes of the Northern Kingdom were exiled by the Assyrians.

Chapter 17 in the Hebrew is an outright description of the historical situation which the Targum follows closely. Chapter 19 is a poetic lament over the royal house of Judah. The imagery requires elaboration, which the Targum supplies. The lion whelps symbolize two kings of Judah. While the Targum mentions no names of the kings, even as the hebrew does not, there is no doubt that the king taken into captivity to Egypt is Jehoahaz. The king taken captive to Babylon, however, could either be Jehoiachin or Zedekiah. If the latter, the poetic imagery is historically correct, since Ḥamutal was the mother of both Jehoahaz and Zedekiah. But if the captive to Babylon is Jehoiachin, who was not a brother of Jehoahaz, the Targum is historically more accurate in its interpretation of the lioness as the congregation of Israel, (19:2, 10), and it must be assumed that it is in this light that the Targum understands the text, i.e. Jehoiachin is the king taken to Babylon referred to in the Hebrew text, 19:9.

Chapter 16 contains some historical discourse on the heathen past of the city of Jerusalem, and how Israel continued heathen practice.[39] A striking twist of Targumic exegesis is its rendering of 16:45. The Hebrew text speaks in poetic allegory: "You are the daughter of your mother, who despised her husband and her children. You are the sister of your sister(s), who despised their husbands and children. Your mother was a Hittite and your father was an Amorite." The Targum: "Why have you been the daughter of the land of Canaan, acting according to the practices of the people whose father was cursed together with his children?[40] And a sister of Sodom and Gomorrah, whose people were consumed, parents and children? Your mother Sarah lived among the Hittites but did not act according to their practices; and your father Abraham lived among the Amorites, but did not walk in their counsel."

Ezekiel enumerates the countries that assailed Israel and have descended into historical oblivion, 32:17 ff. The "land of life" or "of the living" is taken by the Targum as the land of Israel, 32:23, 24, 25, 26, 27, 32. The same equation is also found in 26:20.

There is one historical allusion in the Targum to the Gog passages that identifies Rome with Gog and the eschatological battle which will mark the final denouement of history. In 39:16 the Targum interpolates: "There, too, shall be thrown the slain of Rome, the city of boisterous crowds."

In 7:7, 10, there is an obscure expression *haṣefirah*, which seems to defy the commentaries. Kimḥi relates the word to the Aramaic *ṣafra'*, hence "the morning has come," i.e. the morning of the day of evil tidings, in keeping with the context of doom in chapter 7. Modern interpreters also regard it as some pronouncement of disaster, although admitting the uncertainty of its meaning.[41] The Targum translates

---

[39]Cf. Eichrodt, *Ezekiel*, p. 204.
[40]A reference to Gen. 9:25.
[41]Cf. *AB*, p. 148.

it "the Kingdom has been revealed to you."[42] We cannot rule out the possibility that the Targum had in mind an eschatological approach, sounding a note of comfort even in the midst of the darkness of doom, and I have so rendered it.

There is comfort, too, for those Jews living in the Diaspora. The Targum asserts that for them the Synagogue is divinely ordained, although it remains secondary to the Temple, 11:16.[43]

The Targum's Theology

In its theological posture, the Ezekiel Targum is basically Pharisaic-Rabbinic. The doctrines which it espouses are by and large a reflection of ideas which we encounter in the other Rabbinic sources, and in the main are similar to, or identical with, those expressed in the other official Targumim. Primarily it follows the school of R. Akiba, as does its halakah.[44] Occasionally, our Targum articulates a religious idea which is different from the usual norm, but this is true of Targumic interpretation generally,[45] and it does not necessarily follow that the idea is contrary to, or a negation of Rabbinic ideology.

Stressing the Merkabah as it does, Tg. Ezek. perceives God as the transcendent deity, whose abode is in the mysterious celestial realms, beyond the reach of the military forces of world empires; who is untouched by the destructive power of Babylon and Rome, and who will restore His Shekinah to Jerusalem and the Sanctuary of the future on Mt. Zion[46] The existence of God, as the One, exclusive deity in the universe, is assumed by the Targum, and one of the gravest sins is idolatry, dereliction from the worship of Him, which evokes the most severe punishment (14:7, 8; 18:30 a.e.).[47] By MT's "approaching day" Tg. understands the day of divine retribution (7:12). Tg. interprets the harlotry in chs. 16 and 23 as idolatry, and almost invariably wherever MT has sexual references.[48]

Almost equally repugnant to the Targum is the apotheosis of the human being, the deification or self-deification of mortal man. This is vividly portrayed in the prophecy against the king of Tyre, 28:2 ff. And while the Hebrew poetically says that the king resided in the Garden of Eden (v. 13), and Rabbinic legend understood it thus, Tg. interprets rationally, that he lived in luxury *as though he were* in the Garden of Eden.

God is so transcendent that Tg. considers it unseemly that man might rebel against Him or act treacherously towards Him, and so interposes the *Memra* as the one who is offended (2:3; 28:8, 13, 21, 27). And where MT reads that God has been forgotten,

[42]We might be tempted to translate the phrase, "The kingdom has been exiled," in line with the context of doom, but then 'alak becomes syntactically impossible.

[43]Cf. *b. Meg.* 29a.

[44]Cf. *S–A*, pp. 1 ff., 129.

[45]S.H. Levey, *The Messiah*, p. 143-4.

[46]This is the burden of chs. 40-48, both in the Hebrew and in the Tg. See especially 43:7, and note 6 thereto.

[47]Cf. *S–A*, p. 154 f.

[48]Cf. Tg. Jer. 2:20; 3:17; 5:7; 23:14. Cf. Y. Komlosh, *Ha-Mikra B' or Ha-Targum*, p. 400.

Tg. maintains that it is the *worship* of God that has been forgotten (22:12; 23:35). The blasphemous outburst of the populace that "the Lord does not see," is rendered "nothing is revealed before the Lord," 9:9, and the verb, "to blaspheme," itself is rendered, "caused anger before Me," 20:27.

In addition to His omnipresence, God is also omnipotent, expressed as *Šaddai* in 1:24 and 10:5, and elsewhere by His might or power (14:9, 13; 16:27; 25:7, 13, 16). He is likewise omniscient (20:32).

God is invisible, even to the prophet. MT may say that Ezekiel saw visions of the Lord, but Tg. says that he saw by means of his prophetic vision, the *glory of the Shekinah* of the Lord (1:1). But even that glory was so brilliant and so blinding that the eye could not bear to look at it (1:27).

God does communicate His will, but only to His prophets. And the communication is not direct, but through the instrumentality of the *Dibbur* the emanated power of the word, which takes precedence to the sound produced by the heavenly creatures (1:25), who are the agents of God, their Master (1:14). The *Dibbur* and prophecy, as well as the angelic function, all emanate from the Merkabah; but false prophecy is a crime, and the student who refuses to study Torah is as guilty as the false prophet (14:9, 10).

Man's approach to God is through prayer (21:5). Prayer and good deeds are attributes of the man who might be capable of interceding for the people and the community (22:30). Ezekiel himself is singled out to bear the sins of Israel, and for vicarious suffering as a means of atonement, his punishment being twice what it should be (4:4, 5). This double indemnity departs from the Rabbinic doctrine of measure for measure,[49] and contradicts Tg. Ezek. 21:32. But individual responsibility is one of the cornerstones of Ezekiel's concept of God's justice, and Tg. is undeviating in going along with this idea (ch. 18), and with Ezekiel's qualifications for righteousness, and conversely for the wicked, as found in the chapter. It agrees with Ezekiel, that no one, not even Noah, Daniel, or Job, righteous as they were, could save anyone other than themselves (14:14, 20). The righteous by observing the Torah, will be rewarded with eternal life (20:11, 13, 21), but the wicked will be punished with fiery destruction (1:8), and in Hell (26:20; 31:14, 16; 32:18 ff.)

God calls for repentance (14:6; 18:30), and repentance is open to the wicked who wish to return to righteousness and thereby they will be saved (18:21; 32:11 ff.). Repentance means return to the Torah (34:9).

Punishment also takes the form of exile and banishment, with all the attendant miseries, and it is the consequence to a nation which has not repented of its sins (12:11; 21:18; 22:15; 24:6; 36:15 ff.; 39:28). Repentance restores Israel to its own land (39:28). Tg. provides an unusual theological perception in one instance, 21:8, 9, where MT creates a problem of theodicy, explicitly stating that God will destroy the righteous and the wicked alike. Tg. negates this harsh view of God's justice, and introduces a compassionate view of exile: "I will exile the innocent from you, in order to destroy your wicked ones," who will remain behind.

---

[49]*b. Sanh.* 90a. Cf. Y. Komlosh, *Ha-Mikra*, p. 159, 366.

The resurrection of the dead was a cardinal doctrine of the Pharisaic-Rabbinic Tradition,[50] and is an indispensable dogma of faith in historical Christianity.[51] The *locus classicus* of the resurrection in the Hebrew Scriptures is 37:1-14, the vision of the valley of dry bones. Tg. follows MT faithfully and adds nothing to the Hebrew, except the adjective "human,"modifying the word "bones," in 37:1, at the beginning of the passage, but not elsewhere. Tg. makes sure that there is no mistake about their identity. Otherwise, it follows MT down through the allegorical explanation. Some Rabbinic opinion has it that Ezekiel resurrected the dead in the valley, but R. Johanan adduces from 37:13 that God Himself will effect the resurrection without any mediating agent.[52] There is no reference to a second death in Tg. Ezek., unlike Tg. Is. and Tg. Jer.[53]

The Rabbinic principle of *zekut 'abot*, "the merit of the fathers," finds a favorable response in Tg. The idea that the ancestral faithfulness to the covenant is sufficient for God to redeem their descendants is expressed in 16:6, which combines this idea with the observance of circumcision and the sacrifice of the Paschal lamb as the rationale for Israel's deliverance from Egyptian bondage.

Tg.'s perception of the restored Temple in the main follows MT. The dimensions of the Temple are the same as those in the Hebrew (chs. 40-42), as are its architecture, the allocation of space, the altar, the provision for the residence of the priests (who must be of Zadokite lineage) and the Levites who are assigned to the music and the lesser functions in the Temple (chs. 43, 44). The Sanctuary is the abode of the *Shekinah*, and the glory of the Lord, radiating an aura of holiness, permeates the sacred premises (ch. 43). The Temple is a replica of the Merkabah (43:3), and reverberates with the sound of those who bless the Lord's name (43:2), for it will be cleansed of all idolatry (vv. 7-10). Distinctively Targumic is its rendering of MT's peace offerings as "holy sacrifices" or "sacred slaughter"(43:27). The regulations concerning the Temple, and the sacrifices; the position of the prince, and the division of the land, all are faithfully followed by Tg. as in MT (chs. 44-48). There are mystic, eschatological overtones in the future name of Jerusalem (48:35).

The halakic-aggadic principle that prophecy was impossible outside the land of Israel[54] presents a problem in 1:3. The Targum resolves the issue by its opening gambit, that the word of prophecy from before the Lord was with Ezekiel, first in the land of Israel, and then again in the land of the Chaldeans by the river Chebar. This is a reflection of the Rabbinic concept that once a man began his prophecy in the Holy Land, he qualified for a continuation of prophecy outside of the land.[55]

Other halakic issues are discernible in our Targum, some explicit and some by implication. Tg. is always careful to specify that the bloodshed mentioned in MT is innocent blood (22:6, 9, 12; 23:45; 24:6-9; 36:18), because not all bloodshed is legally a crime.[56] Tg. 24:7 explicitly states that murder must be premeditated and not inadver-

[50]Josephus, *Bellum Judaicum*, 2, 8, 14; *m. Sanh.* 10:1 ff. *t. Sanh.* 13:1 ff. *b. Sanh.* 90b-92a.
[51]Acts 24:15; I Cor. 15:3, 4. Cf. M. McNamara, *Palestinian Judaism*, p. 180 ff.
[52]See ch. 37, n. 7, 8.
[53]See ch. 37, n. 1; Cf. *S-A*, p. 183.
[54]*Sifre, Šoftim*, 175. *Mekilta, Pisha* I. Lauterbach, I, p. 4.
[55]*Mekilta, loc. cit.* Cf. Judah Halevi, *Kuzari*, 1:95; 2:8-14.
[56]Cf. *m. Sanh.* 9:2.

tent to incur punishment. Two versions of Tg. 43:17 differ as to whether the altar had steps leading up to it, which might be a violation of Ex. 20:23. *m. Tamid* refers to the ascent as a ramp rather than steps (1:4; 3:1; 4:3). While MT has the slaughtering of the sacrifices *on* the tables in 40:41, Tg. renders *between* the tables, which were used for rinsing the entrails.[57] Tg. makes the difficult MT 40:43 to conform with the Mishnah, that the pillars in the slaughter chamber in the Temple had protruding hooks on which to hang the sacrifices.[58] In 44:18, where MT reads that priests are not to gird themselves with anything that causes perspiration, Tg. interprets that they should not gird their loins but their hearts. While this conforms with the halakah,[59] it is stated in such a way that the thrust could be ethical as well as legal. Permissible marriage for the priesthood is treated in Tg. 44:22, which presents some confusion in the matter. Laws concerning mourning are found in Tg. 24:17, 23 and 27:30.

Anthropomorphism and Anthropopathism

In recent years, scholars have questioned the notion that the Targumim are invariably anti-anthropomorphic and anti-anthropopathic. Among these are Harry M. Orlinsky[60] and Michael L. Klein.[61] Tg. Ezek. unquestionably *tends* to eliminate those elements in the biblical text which are blatantly human and could be misunderstood as investing the God of Israel with mortal attributes. Thus the biblical face of God is never translated literally (7:22; 15:7; 39:23, 24, 29. cf. Is. 54:8; Jer. 21:10). The same is true of the eye of God (8:18; 9:10; 20:17); loins (1:27; 8:2). The hand of God is *usually* rendered by Tg. Ezek. as "the spirit of prophecy" (1:3; 3:14; *passim*), or "the striking power of God's might" (6:14; 14:9; 25:7; *passim*); or simply "might" (39:21); or to swear an oath (20:5; 44:12).

However, there is evidence in Tg. Ezek. to support the view of Orlinsky, Klein, *et al.* Tg.'s translation of 20:33, 34 is literal, as anthropomorphic and anthropopathic as the poetic imagery in the Hebrew: "As I live, says the Lord God, With a mighty hand and with a raised up arm, and with outpoured anger will I be king over you." Our Tg. never conceals God's anger and His wrath (5:13, 15; 7:3, 8; 13:13; 20:8, 21; 22:20; 25:14; 43:8): Ezekiel's theme of destruction and dispersion was all too familiar at Yavneh. But God does feel pity as well (5:11). A striking example of the Tg.'s inconsistency in its translation of biblical anthropopathism is several renderings of divine jealousy. In 16:42, Tg. translates the word literally. In 23:25, 36:5, and 38:19 it is translated "punishment." In 16:38 it is rendered "wrath." In 36:6 it is translated "anger." We can attribute the differences to the Targumist's style, but whatever the reason, the inconsistency stares us in the face.

[57] Cf. *m. Šeq.* 6:4.

[58] Cf. *m. Tam.* 3:5, *Mid,* 3:5, *Pes.* 5:9.

[59] *b. Zeb.* 18b, 19a.

[60] H.M. Orlinsky, "On anthropomorphisms and anthropopathisms in the Septuagint and Targum," in *The Septuagint Translation of the Hebrew Terms in Relation to God in the Book of Jeremiah*, B.M. Zlotowitz, N.Y. 1981, p. xxiii.

[61] M.L. Klein, "The Translation of Anthropomorphisms and Anthropopathisms in the Targumim," *Congress Volume*, Vienna, 1980, pp. 162 ff. *S–A* also cites Leo R. Wolkow, D. Schreibman, and H. Fox, p. xii.

Divine Surrogates

Even more startling is the manner in which Tg. Ezek. employs *rugza'*, specifically, divine anger or wrath. Perhaps taking its cue from 7:3, "and I will send My anger against you," Tg. conceives of God's anger as a surrogate for God Himself in manifesting divine displeasure and in dispensing divine punishment. Where MT has God saying that God "is at," or "against" someone. Tg. renders the passage, "I am sending My anger against you" (5:8; 21;8; 29:3, 10; 30:22; 35:3; 38:3; 39:1). In this respect, it is a buffer, safeguarding God's transcendence, and an agent of God, carrying out his will, to punish only, however.

The *Dibbur* is the divine word, limited to speech, articulation, proclamation. It occurs only twice in Tg. Ezek., both instances in 1:25. It is the *Dibbur* which inspires the prophets and reveals the divine will to them. It evokes absolute reverence from the celestial creatures, who fall silent in its presence, when the spirit of prophecy is about to become audible.

The *Shekinah* is the representation of God's manifest being in the universe, of His omnipresence, whether in heaven above the cherubim (1:14) or on earth among people (43:9). It is used a number of times in our Targum, primarily to circumvent the biblical texts which might be construed as limiting God to physical space or place, and it sometimes serves as a circumlocution to avoid anthropomorphism. 7:22 is an excellent example where we find both usages in one and the same verse. MT reads: "And I will turn My face from them, and they shall profane My treasured place." Tg.: "And I will make my *Shekinah* depart from them, because they have profaned the land of the abode of My *Shekinah*." When there is a reference in the Hebrew to the land of Israel as the Lord's land, Tg. translates it as the land of the abode of His *Shekinah* (36:5, 20; 38:16), thus eliminating the ascription of territoriality to the deity. The same principle applies with reference to the Temple. Thus, in 43:7, where MT reads: "this is the place of My throne and the place of the soles of My feet, where I will dwell in the midst of the people of Israel forever." Tg. renders: "this is the place of the abode of My throne of glory, and this is the place of the abode where My *Shekinah* dwells, for I will make My *Shekinah* dwell there, in the midst of the Children of Israel forever." The New Jerusalem, likewise is where the Lord makes His *Shekinah* rest (48:35). In Tg. Ezek. the *Shekinah* is the surrogate of the transcendent deity, and while it dwells *among* God's creatures, it is not immanent *in* God's creation, nor are there any instances in which it rests upon or appears to an individual, which is how it is conceived in other Rabbinic sources.[62]

The *Memra* is the most versatile literary device in our Tg.'s theological exegesis, similar to Philo's *logos*. Like the *Shekinah*, it is a surrogate of God, but it is more than a manifestation of God's presence. It is everything that God is supposed to be, and its manifold activity encompasses the entire spectrum of divine endeavor, safeguarding divine dignity, shielding the deity from unseemly expressions and mundane matters. In the vision of the Merkabah (ch. 1), in which we find the *Shekinah*, the *Dibbur*, and the Glory, the *Memra* is also found, as the divine buffer which people

---

[62]Cf. E.E. Urbach, *The Sages, Their Concepts and Beliefs*, Jerusalem, 1975, pp. 37-65; L. Blau, "Shekinah" in *JE*, XI, 258 ff.

disobey (1:8. Also 2:3; 3:7). They also rebel against it, bringing punishment (2:3; 20;8, 13, 21; *passim*). In 3:17 the *Memra* delivers the word to the prophet as teacher. The *Memra* is the substitute for God's eye (5:11; 7:4, 9; 8;18; 9:10; *passim*), and God issues decrees by it (5:13, 15, 17; 6:10; *passim*). The *Memra* reproaches (13:22). It is the oracular power (14:3, 4, 7). It anoints and establishes the Davidic dynasty (17:22). God swears by it (20:5; 44:12; 47:14), and responds to inquiries by it (20:3). The Sabbath is a sign between it and Israel (20:20). Israel is perfidious towards it (20:27, 38; 39:23, 26). The *Memra* comes to help Israel at the ingathering of the Exile (34:30). Only a wall of the Temple separates the corpses of the kings from the *Memra* (43:8). The watch in the Temple is the watch of the *Memra* (44:8, 16). The *Memra* loathes (23:18), and does not spare, i.e., it punishes mercilessly (5:11; 7:4, 9; *passim*)

The employment of the *Memra* in Tg. Ezek. is in line with its usage in the other Targumim, and is beyond question one of the most original contributions to biblical exegesis.[63] Of course, the ubiquitous *min qadam* is encountered everywhere.

A distinctive feature of Tg. Ezek., which occurs in no other Tg., is its rendering of MT's "the uncircumcised." Where the word is used in 28:10; 31:18; 32:19, 21, 24, 25, 27, 28, 29, 30, 32, Tg. interprets as *hayyabaya'*, "the sinners," or "the guilty ones." However, in 44:7, 9, where MT reads "uncircumcised of heart and uncircumcised of flesh" Tg. translates as "wicked of heart and uncircumcised of flesh." I cannot provide a positive explanation of the interpretive rendering in chs. 28, 31, and 32. I can only conjecture that the Tg. felt the king of Tyre and the Pharaoh of Egypt were uncircumcised, and hence it would be no punishment for them to be associated with the uncircumcised in their deaths. So, stylistically and substantively, it places them with the sinners or the guilty.

Impact and Influence of Targum Ezekiel

The Targum of Ezekiel experienced some precarious times because it was associated with the Book of Ezekiel, which was nearly withdrawn from the religious life of the Jewish community. Yet, its emphasis on Merkabah Mysticism, which emerged as a viable instrumentality of Jewish survival, gave it a legitimate place in the hearts and minds of the Jewish people. The Throne of God in the celestial realms became the focal point of the Hekalot literature of Babylonian Jewry in late Talmudic and Gaonic eras, and found its way into the theurgic poetry and the liturgical hymnology of the Synagogue. The emotion-packed, cosmic majesty in the glorification of God, the earth-shaking awe and splendor articulated in these hymns, have the familiar ring of Targumic Merkabah, of the song of the angelic beings and the celestial creatures in praise of their Creator. The hymnology of the Sephardic liturgy for the High Holy Days as well as sundry prayers in the Jewish prayer book generally, have an infusion of passages from the Ezekiel Targum or language and mystical idiom reflected in or borrowed from our Targum.[64] One of the early Jewish holiday prayer books, the

[63]Cf. K. Kohler, "Memra," in *JE*, VIII, 464,5: M. McNamara, *Targum and Testament*, pp. 98 ff.; Churgin, pp. 21 ff.; R. Hayward, *Divine Name and Presence: The Memra*, Totowa, N.J. 1981.

[64]Cf. G.G. Scholem, *Major Trends in Jewish Mysticism*, pp. 57 ff. and cf. Tg. Ezek. 3:12 and note 6 thereto.

Mahzor Witry (11c.), includes Tg. Ezek. on ch. 37, the haftarah for the Sabbath during Passover. In this Targumic passage there is inserted a Midrash which identifies the dry bones as those of Ephraimites who sinned by leaving Egypt prematurely, without waiting for the precise time ordained for the divine redemption; a legend based on *b. Sanh.* 92a, and found in Tg. Ps.-J on Ex. 13:17.[65]

The Targum of Ezekiel gained recognition as an integral part of the Targum on the Prophets, and, like the others in this genre, was transmitted and recorded for posterity, first in manuscript form, and eventually included in the Rabbinic Bibles alongside the Hebrew text of Scripture. It is an indispensable vehicle of biblical interpertation which had to be reckoned with by Bible scholars, commentators, translators and teachers. Perhaps Tg. Ezek. was even more important than the others because the MT of this book is so unreliable in so many instances. There are a number of extant manuscripts, and versions of the work are to be found in the several polyglots and in the Rabbinic Bibles which have been produced since the advent of printing. The major opus representing the incredibly gigantic effort of collecting, collating, critical edition and presentation of the enormous mass of material, is that of Alexander Sperber, *The Bible in Aramaic*, Leiden, 1962, volume III. The basic text of the Sperber volume is Ms. Or. 2211 of the British Museum, and it is essentially this text which I followed. Deviations are indicated in the Apparatus, as are literal meanings of the Aramaic from which I departed as a matter of stylistic preference. I have also found it necessary to depart from the line of strict consistency by rendering the same Aramaic word or phrase differently in the English translation, depending upon context and my own feeling as to what the Targum had in mind.

A study of Sperber's work makes it abundantly clear how very important Tg. Ezek. was looked upon in Jewish lexicography and Scriptural study. It is cited in the *'Aruk* of Nathan b. Jehiel of Rome, the first extant lexicon of the Talmud and Midrashim, completed in the year 1101, and expanded into the twelve volume *Arukh Completum* of Alexander Kohut. Rashi, Rabbi Solomon b. Isaac [*Yiṣhaqi*], who lived in France (1040-1105), the greatest and most popular Rabbinic commentator on the Bible and Talmud, refers to Tg. Ezek. often. And Rabbi David Kimḥi, *Redak*, one of the most prominent of Jewish exegetes and Hebrew grammarians (1160-1235) rarely comments on a verse without quoting the Targum. Variant readings are frequent in these commentaries, which are now included in all Rabbinic Bibles. Maimonides, too, refers to Tg. Ezek., in his philosophical treatise, *Guide for the Perplexed* (III).

Modern scholars have also seen the vital relevance of the Ezekiel Targum to their biblical, rabbinic and historical research. Yadin cites it in his three-volume work on *The Temple Scroll*. The traditional Jewish *ArtScroll* translation of Ezekiel quite often uses the Targum instead of the MT in its rendering; the Christian *Revised Standard Version* at times substitutes the Targum for MT, especially where the Aramaic is in agreement with the Greek, Latin, and Syriac as against the Hebrew text (Ezek. 6:6, 9; 12:5; 37:26; and elsewhere); so, too, the new *JPS* (41:7). Aberbach,

---

[65]Cf. Churgin, p. 136.

Churgin, Grossfeld, Komlosh, Smolar and others acknowledge its importance. And Fr. Martin McNamara and his Editorial Board, in accepting my radical perceptions and interpretations of our Targum's exegesis, have recognized that the Targum of Ezekiel presents a fascinating interpretation in the finest tradition of biblical exegesis.

LOS ANGELES, CALIFORNIA
HOSHA'NA RABBAH, 5745

S.H.L.

TRANSLATION

CHAPTER 1

1. It was in the thirtieth year, *from the time that Hilkiah the High Priest found the Book of Torah in the Temple, in the court under the entrance; during the night, after the beginning of moonlight:*[a] *in the days of Josiah son of Amon king of the tribe of the House of Judah;*[1] on the fifth day of the month *of Tammuz.*[2] *The prophet said:* "I was among the exiles on the river Chebar,[b] the heavens opened and I beheld, *in the prophetic vision that rested upon me,* a vision *of the glory of the Shekinah* of the Lord." 2. On the fifth of the month, it being the fifth year of the exile of King Joiakin, 3. The word of *prophecy from before the* Lord was with Ezekiel son of Buzi[c] the priest, *in the land of Israel, and again once more He spoke with him* in the *country of the* land of the Chaldeans on the river Chebar; and there *the spirit of prophecy from before the Lord rested* upon him.[3] 4. And I saw, and behold, a whirlwind came from the north, a large cloud, and a flaming fire, surrounded by splendor; and *from the midst of the cloud, and from the midst of the whirlwind,* something similar to *hashmal*[4] from the midst of the fire. 5. And from the midst of it, the likeness of four creatures; their appearance — they had the likeness of a man. 6. Each had four faces *and each and every one of the faces had four faces, sixteen faces to each creature, the number of faces of the four creatures being sixty four.* Each had four wings *and each and every one of the faces had four wings, sixteen wings to every single face, sixty four wings to every single creature; the number of wings of the four creatures being two hundred and fifty six.*[5] 7. Their feet were straight feet[6] and the soles of their feet were like round soles,[7] *and when they moved they would shake the earth,* and they shone like burnished bronze. 8. Hands like the hands of a man were fashioned for them from beneath their wings on their four sides, *with which to take out burning coals of fire from among the cherubim underneath the expanse which was over their heads, placing them into the hands of the seraphim to sprinkle on the place of the wicked, to destroy the sinners who transgress His word.*[d8] And their faces and their wings were the same on the four of them. 9. Their wings were directed towards one another. They did not turn as they went — each creature went straight ahead. 10. And the likeness of their faces — the face of a man and the face of a lion were fashioned on the right side of the four of them; the face of an ox was fashioned on the left side of the four of them; and the face of an eagle on the four of them.[9] 11.

Apparatus, Chapter 1

[a] RB and K. The clause is missing in the other versions.

[b] K cites some versions: "Euphrates."

[c] K cites a Tg. Yerušalmi: "son of Jeremiah, the prophet." So does A.

[d] CR adds a marginal note; "The right hand extended to receive the sinners who have returned in repent-ance, to declare them innocent on the Day of Judgment, to enable them to possess eternal life; and the left hand extended to take out burning coals of fire etc...."

[e] My reconstruction of RB and the second version of K. (See footnote 11). SP and BM: "in the face of the eye to see."

Their faces and their wings were spread out above; each had two directed towards the other; and two covering their bodies.[10] 12. Each creature went straight ahead; they went to whatever place they wished to go; they did not turn as they went. 13. As to the likeness of the creatures, their appearance was like burning coals of fire; like the appearance of flaming fiery torches between the creatures; and there was brightness to the fire, and from the fire there went forth lightning. 14. And the creatures, *when they are sent to do the will of their Master who makes His Shekinah dwell on high above them, are like the eye seeing a bird on the wing,*[e11] they turn and *circle the*

Notes, Chapter 1

[1] *Tg.* supplies a more definitive date than does MT, calculating from the time of the Deuteronomic reformation. *Tg's* dating is significant, and theologically important, in that it associates Ezekiel's prophecy with the restoration of Yahwistic worship as a national policy. The historical fact that subsequent generations deserted pure Yahwism and engaged in pagan practice provided a prophetic rationale for the destruction of the Temple and the fall of Jerusalem, and the desperate need for national repentance and religious regeneration. This fits admirably with Ezekiel's prophecy, and provides a link between Deuteronomy and Merkabah of Ezekiel, and, by implication, the Merkabah mysticism of the school of Rabban Johanan b. Zakkai. Merkabah at Yavneh in the first century C.E., like Merkabah at the river Chebar in the sixth century B.C.E., is the key to Jewish revival and survival in the face of the two great catastrophes in ancient Israel. Cf. *Seder 'Olam* 25 and *Yal. Šim.* to Ezek. 1:1 (#336). Kimhi provides us with a slightly different calculation, dating from the time of the Jubilee, quoting his father's interpretation.

[2] *Tg.* reckons Nisan as the first month, hence the fourth month would be Tammuz, as the tenth month, with Tishri as the first month, see *Tg.* Ps.J. Gen. 8:5.

[3] MT: "the hand of the Lord was upon him there." *Tg's* rendering eliminates the poetic anthropomorphism of the Hebrew and correctly interprets the phrase as a reference to prophecy. The expression is peculiar to Ezekiel, occuring in 3:14, 22; 8:1; 33:22; 37:1; 40:1; but cf. *Tg.* Jer. 1:9. Cf. *AB*, p. 41 f.

[4] *Tg.* does not translate Mt's *hašmal*, but simply renders it in Aramaized form. For a critical view cf. *IB*, p. 70; *AB*, p. 43.

[5] By a strange mathematical formula, the *Tg.* arrives at a figure of 64 wings to each of the four creatures, a total of 256 for the four of them. The significance of this calculation is not immediately apparent nor definitively certain. We could speculate that perhaps it relates to the singing of the heavenly beings in praise of their Creator, since the song of the cherubim is produced by their wings (Ezek. 1:24; 3:13; 10:5; cf. *b. Hag.* 13b); hence 256 by *gematria* would be *rnu*, "they sang." Significantly, no other early Rabbinic source mentions 256 wings for each cherub, but Rashi picks up the theme from the *Tg.* On this issue, Kimhi, who usually refers to the *Tg.* freely, maintains complete silence.

[6] *Tg.'s* rendering *kewanan* may indicate a double entendre. While on the one hand the verb means "straight," it also has the meaning of "positioned correctly" or "properly directed." This would convey the idea that their feet were together, which, according to the Halakah, is the correct position of the feet during the *'amidah,* the prayer recited while standing. Hertz, *Authorized Daily Prayer Book,* p. 130. Cf. *b. Ber.* 10b, where this v. in Ezek. is cited as proof-text for this ritual ordinance.

[7] *Tg.* reads *'agul* instead of MT's *'egel*, perhaps an interpretive difference designed to eliminate the calf as a symbol of Israel's dereliction from Yahweh at Sinai, in the incident of the golden calf. This is also the intent of Resh Lakish in explaining why the ox in Ezek, 1:10 becomes a cherub in 10:14. "Said Resh Lakish, Ezekiel sought God's mercy for Israel, so that the accuser (the ox, i.e., the golden calf) became the defender (the cherub, since the Merkabah itself intercedes for Israel). *b. R. H.* 26a; *b. Hag.* 13b. Elsewhere, the Rabbis accept the MT, which has the soles of the living creatures looking like those of a calf, and apply the verse to the Sadducean priest who was dispatched on the Day of Atonement by an angel who struck him down, leaving the imprint of the hoof of a calf. *b. Yom.* 19b.

[8] *Tg.* follows Q., reading the plural, "hands," and interpreting the verse as applying to the punishment of the wicked. The Sages preferred the Ket. "His hand," with reference to God, who, in His capacity as the Merciful, extends His hand to accept the *ba'ale tesubah,* the repentant sinners, to protect them from punishment, *b. Pes.* 119a.

[9] The partial correspondence of the celestial Merkabah and the reconstructed Temple in Jerusalem is discernible in the reference to the faces. Cf. 41:18 *infra.* There are various interpretations of the four faces in the Merkabah. Cf. *Yal. Šim.* #337; *b. Hag.* 13b. LXX translates *šor* as *mosxou,* "calf." Cf. Rev. 4:17. In Christian interpretation, the four faces are said to represent the four Evangelists. Cf. *ICC*, p. 14.

[10] MT: "their legs." In v. 12, *Tg.* interprets *ruah* as "will."

[11] My translation is based on a plausible reading that does no violence to the text: *ke'agapa' 'eyna' lemiheze.* The creatures vanish like a bird. The phrase, as it stands, is difficult. A suggested reading of O.H. Schorr, *Hehaluṣ,* 13

world; and the creatures return together, quickly, like a flash of lightning. 15. And I beheld the creatures, and behold, one wheel was placed[f] just *below the heavenly heights,*[12] beside the creatures, on its four sides. 16. The appearance of the wheels and the way they were made were like a precious stone,[13] the four of them having one likeness; and their appearance and their operation was as though it were a wheel within a wheel. 17. When they went, they would go on their four sides, they did not turn as they went. 18. Their backs *were set opposite the expanse of the sky,* and they were tall and awesome, their backs being full of eyes round about all four of them.[14] 19. When the creatures went, the wheels went correspondingly, and when the creatures rose to just below the heavenly heights the wheels also rose. 20. Wherever they wished to go, there they would go, according to their will;[15] and the wheels rose correspondingly, for a spirit like that of the creatures was in the wheels. 21. When they would move, they would move; and when they stood still, they would stand; and when they rose to just below the heavenly heights, the wheels would rise correspondingly; for a spirit like that of the creatures was in the wheels.[16] 22. The likeness above the heads of the creatures was a firmament, like a mighty ice field, inclined towards their heads from above. 23. And underneath the firmament their wings were extended one towards the other; each had two covering them: each had two covering their bodies. 24. And I heard the sound of their wings, like the sound of many waters, like a sound from *before Shaddai;* as they went, *the sound of their words were as though they were thanking and blessing their Master, the everliving King of the worlds;* like the sound of the hosts *of the angels on high;* when they stood still, their wings became silent.[g][17] 25. *And at such time when it was His will to make the Dibbur audible to His servants the prophets of Israel,* there was a voice which was heard from above the firmament[h] which was above their heads. When they stood still, their wings became silent *before the Dibbur.*[18] 26. And above the firmament which was over their heads there was like the appearance of a precious stone, the likeness of a throne; and above the likeness of the throne there was the likeness of the appearance of *Adam,*[i][19] above it from on high. 27. I saw something like the *ḥashmal,* like the appearance of fire from the midst of it round about, an appearnace *of glory which the eye is unable to see, and such that is is impossible to look at it and upward;* an appearance *of glory which the eye is unable to see, and such that it is impossible to look at it and downward;*[20] I saw what appeared to be fire; and it was surrounded by splendor. 28. Like the appearance of the rainbow[21] that is in the cloud on a rainy day, so was the appearance of splendor round about. It was the likeness of the glory of the Lord. And when I saw it, I fell upon my face, and I heard a voice which was speaking.

Apparatus, Chapter 1 continued

[f] K: "different," "awesome."
[g] RB add: "from before the *Dibbur.*"
[h] RB add: "between the cherubim."

[i] SP, AP, and K. RB: "the appearance of a man."
   MM: "like the face of Jacob, our father."

CHAPTER 2

1. And He said to me, "Son of Adam,[1] stand up on your feet, and I will speak with you." 2. And the spirit entered into me when He spoke with me, and it stood me on my feet, and I heard that which was spoken to me.[2] 3. And He said to me, "Son of Adam, I am sending you to the Children of Israel, to rebellious peoples, who have rebelled against *My Memra;* they and their forefathers have rebelled against *My Memra* to this very day. 4. And they, their children, are *called* impudent of face and hard-hearted. I am sending you to them, and you shall say to them, 'Thus says the

Notes, Chapter 1 continued

(1888), p. 94, divides the phrase so that it reads the Greek, *auge phaneix,* "a shining appearance." However, this forces the phonetics. The idea of the disappearing flight of the creatures is borne out by the second part of the verse, and by *Gen. R.* 50.1, "The Rabbis say, It was like a shooting star to the eye," which is how it is rendered by S. Cf. *AB,* p. 46.

[12]In keeping with the Merkabah tradition, *Tg.* interprets *ba'ares* as meaning beneath or below the heavenly heights, retaining the celestial imagery. Rabbinic interpretation of this verse equates it with the angel Sandalfon, the brother of Metatron, whose height extends form earth to the heavenly creatures, *b. Ḥag.* 13b.

[13]For the Hebrew *tarśiś.* Elsewhere, according to context, *Tg.* renders the word by *yama',* "the sea" (27:12, 25; 38:13).

[14]*Tg.* renders both *wegabbehen* and *wegabbotam.* as "and their backs." So does LXX!

[15]*Tg.* renders the first *ruah* as "will"(cf. v. 12, *supra*), but in the second case it retains the biblical word as well as its meaning, "spirit." Kimhi's interpretation follows that of the *Tg.,* understanding *ruah* as the spirit of the wheels. Rashi takes it as the will of God.

[16]*Tg.* depicts the movement of the wheels as corresponding to that of the creatures, and continues to ignore the earth, stressing the celestial realm of the Merkabah.

[17]*Tg.* expands the text in terms of the Merkabah as referring to the chant of the angelic hosts in praise of God.

[18]This is a continuation of the Merkabah motif of the *Tg.* from v. 24. Significantly, it relates the Merkabah to prophecy. It also introduces the *Dibbur,* the revelatory word.

[19]Kimhi astutely observes: "Targum Jonathan did not translate the phrase *demut kemar'eh 'adam,"* supporting the versions that read Adam as a proper noun, and validating my rendering of *bar 'adam* as Son of Adam, or Adamite. Cf. *Gen. R.* 68:12 which maintains that Jacob's features were engraved on God's throne.

[20]Mt: "the appearance of his loins." This anthropomorphic verse came in for special prohibition by the Rabbis, *b. Ḥag.* 16a. Cf. *Num. R.* 14:3.

[21]The incidence of the rainbow and Merkabah mysticism is demonstrated in an anecdote of R. Joḥanan b. Zakkai and his disciples, *b. Ḥag.* 14b. Since the rainbow is equated with the glory of God, the view is expressed that it is irreverent to gaze at it. *b. Ḥag.* 16a; *Num. R.* 14:3.

Notes, Chapter 2

[1]See Introduction for my rendering of the Aramaic expression *bar 'adam* as "son of Adam," an expression of laudation and commendation, rather than a derogatory designation.

[2]The Masoretic *'et middabber 'elai* is difficult. The Hithp. form of the verb *dabar* is rare. See BDB, p. 181f. *Tg.* understand it as a passive, "was spoken." So, too, JPS (N), *ad loc.* But cf. *AB,* p. 62.

Lord God."[3] 5. And they, *if only* they would heed *the instruction,* and *if only* they would refrain *from sinning*[4] — for they are a rebellious people — then they would know that a prophet has been among them. 6. But you, Son of Adam, do not be afraid of them, nor fear their words, *even if they rebel and argue against you;*[5] for you dwell in the midst of *a people whose deeds are comparable to* scorpions; do not fear their words nor fall apart[a] because of them — for they are a rebellious *people.* 7. And you shall proclaim[b] My words of prophecy to them, that they might heed *the instruction* and refrain *from sinning;* for they are a rebellious *people.* 8. And you, Son of Adam, hear that which I am speaking with you: do not be rebellious like the rebellious people; *incline your soul and pay heed to that which I give you.*"[6] 9. And I saw, and behold, the *form* of a hand extended to the side, towards me, and behold, in it was a scroll of a book.[c] 10. And he spread it before me, and behold, it was inscribed on the face of it and on the reverse side of it, *that which was from the beginning and that which is destined to be in the end:*[7] in it was written that *if the House of Israel will transgress against the Torah the nations will have dominion over them, but if they observe the Torah, He will remove*[d] lamentation, weariness and groaning from them.[8]

CHAPTER 3

1. Then he said to me, "Son of Adam, *heed that which has been given unto you, obey that which is written*[1] in this scroll, and go *prophesy* against the House of Israel." 2. So I *inclined my soul,* and *He made me wise concerning what had been written* in this scroll. 3. And He said to me, "Son of Adam, *you will satisfy your soul* and fill your stomach,[2] *if you heed what is written* in this scroll which I give you." So I *heeded* it, and *its words were* in my mouth as sweet honey. 4. And He said to me, "Son of Adam, come, go to the Children of Israel, and *proclaim*[a] My words of *prophecy* to them. 5. For you are not sent *to prophesy* to a people of obscure[b] speech and difficult language,[3] but rather to the House of Israel, 6. not to many peoples of obscure speech and difficult[c] language whose words you cannot understand; if I had sent you to them, they would have listened to you. 7. But the House of Israel do not want to listen to you because they are unwilling to obey *My Memra,* since the whole House of Israel are hard-faced and hard-hearted. 8. Behold I have made[d] your face as

Apparatus, Chapter 2

[a] Lit. "be broken up."
[b] Lit. "prophesy."

[c] SP. RB: "scribe."
[d] Lit. "put an end to."

Apparatus, Chapter 3

[a] Lit. "prophesy."
[b] Lit. "profound."
[c] SP. RB: "hard."

[d] Lit. "given."
[e] Or "wind."

hard as theirs, and your brow as hard as their brow. 9. As the flint is harder than stone, so I have made your brow harder than their brows. Do not fear them, and *do not go to pieces before them;* for, they are a rebellious *people.*" 10. And he said to me, "Son of Adam, all the words which I shall speak to you, take into your heart and listen with your ears. 11. And come, go unto the exiles, unto the sons of your people, and prophesy to them, and say to them, 'Thus says the Lord God, O that they would heed *the instruction!* O that they would refrain *from sinning!*'"[4] 12. Then the spirit[e] lifted me up, and I heard behind me a great quaking sound, *for they[5] were offering praise and saying,* 'Blessed be the glory of the Lord from the place *of the abode of*

Notes, Chapter 2 continued

[3] *Tg.* transliterates *'adonai yhwh* as pronounced in the tradition, *'adonai 'elohim* (written *ywy 'elohim*), understanding it as a proper noun, the compound name of God. This is in line with the consistent rendering of these two words by all the Targumim, both official and otherwise. Cf. *Tg.* Onq. and Ps.J. Gen 2:4, *passim,* and *Tg.* Isa. 25:8, passim. Where MT employs the word *'elohim* as an ordinary noun, Targum translates by the Aramaic *'elaha'.* Cf. *Tg.* Ezek. 8:4, *passim.* LXX: *kurios,* elsewhere, *kurios 'o theos.* Cf. *ICC,* p. 32f; *AB,* p. 64f.

[4] An exegetical complement, expanding on MT, which simply says "whether they obey or cease." *Tg.* expands on the text by adding, "*if only* they obey *the instruction,* and *if only* they refrain *from sinning.*" the two clauses being taken in apposition, not opposition, to each other. This is an extraordinary reading of the Hebrew, a unique interpretation found nowhere except in the *Tg.* Both Rashi and Kimhi understand MT to mean whether they listen or whether they do not listen, Kimhi quoting the *Tg.*'s opinion as differing from his own. The implication of the targumic interpretation is that eventually the prophet's admonition will be heeded by the people, rebellious though they may have been, and they will ultimately repent, thus justifying and fulfilling his divine commission. This will happen because he speaks in the name of the Lord God. The test of the true prophet is the effective materialization of his prophecy, in keeping with Dt. 18:18 ff., and *Tg.* here reflects Scripture with respect to this, In the case of Ezekiel, it will be all the more remarkable, since the people of his generation were decidedly rebellious. For *'im* as a particle of wishing, see BDB, p. 50 (3). LXX, interestingly: "whether they hear or fear."

[5] MT: "though they are briers and thorns with you." But note the poetic puns.

[6] *Tg.* takes MT's "eat" figuratively, meaning to imbibe emotionally, to listen and pay attention to, to absorb the message.

[7] The writing on the front and the back of the scroll is interpreted as an allegory, referring to the history that was and the history that will be. It is also taken allegorically by Rashi, who cites *Tg.* verbatim, to that effect.

[8] *Tg.* converts the prophecy of doom into an avenue of redemption, the way of Torah.

Notes, Chapter 3

[1] MT: "eat this scroll."

Tg. sees the Hebrew as poetic imagery. The idea of eating the scroll is not taken literally, but understood to mean the spiritual intake of the message which the scroll contains, so as to be able to exude it in the form of prophecy. It is possible that *Tg.* regards the scroll as the Torah, with all its spiritual and ethical ramifications. This would reflect a Rabbinic opinion, which similarly emphasized the spiritual element in the concept of Torah as food for the faithful. "'The Lord said to Moses, Write down these words' (Ex. 34:27). This is what is written, It is well for me to have suffered, in order that I might learn Your statutes (Ps. 119:71); it was for Moses' own benefit that he fasted for one hundred and twenty days while he was receiving the Torah. And from where did Moses obtain sustenance? From the radiance of the Shekinah, as it is said, You sustain all of them (Neh. 9:6). Another opinion, from where did Moses obtain sustenance? From the Torah itself, as it says, *ben 'adam,* eat that which you find ... So I opened my mouth, and He fed me this scroll ... So I ate it, and it was in my mouth as sweet as honey (Ezek. 3:1-3). How so? For the Torah is sweet, as it says, Sweeter than honey and honeycomb (Ps. 19:11)" *Ex. R.* 47:7.

[2] Even though *Tg.* translates this phrase literally from the Hebrew, the Targumic interpretation remains unchanged, and expresses the thought that consuming the essential message of the scroll leads to a total permeation of the prophet's entire being, both soul and body, so that he is completely sated, hungering for nothing else.

[3] *Tg.* correctly interprets MT as referring to linguistic communication. Cf. *Tg.* Onq. Ex. 4:10, where *kebad peh* and *kebad lašon* are translated by *yaqir mamlal* and *'amiq lišan,* the same basic vocabulary and usage which we find here. Cf. also *Tg.* Onq. Ex. 6:12, 30, rendering of *'aral sefatayim.* Cf. *AB,* p. 68 f.

[4] See *supra Tg.* Ezek. 2:5 and note 3 thereto.

[5] Refers to the creatures in v. 13. *Tg.* clarifies MT by expanding upon it.

His Shekinah;[6] 13.   the sound of the wings of the creatures touching each other, and the sound of wheels beside them — a great quaking sound. 14. And the spirit[e] lifted me up and took me away, and I went along, bitterly, but by the strength of my spirit, and a *prophecy from before the Lord* overwhelmed me. 15. And I came to the exiles, to Tel Aviv, who were dwelling by the river Chebar, and I went down among them, where they were dwelling, and sat silently[7] among them for seven days. 16. And it was at the end of seven days that the word of *prophecy from before* the Lord came to me, saying, 17. "Son of Adam, I have appointed you a *teacher*[8] to the House of Israel. When you hear a word from *My Memra*, you must warn them *not to sin against Me.*[f] 18. When I say to the wicked, 'You shall surely die,' and you have not warned him — and you say nothing to warn the wicked from his evil way, so that he might live, he, being wicked, shall die in his sinfulness; but I will demand his blood from your hand. 19. But you, if you warn the wicked and he does not turn from his sinfulness and from his evil way, he shall die because of his sinfulness but you will have saved your life.[9] 20. And when the righteous turns from his righteousness and acts falsely, and I put a stumbling block before him, he shall die; he shall die because you have not warned him of his sinfulness, and the meritorious deeds which he has done shall not be remembered; then I will demand his blood from your hand. 21. But if you have warned the righteous, in order that the righteous should not sin, and he does not sin; because he has been warned he shall surely live; and you will have saved your life." 22. *The spirit of prophecy from before* the Lord rested upon me there, and He said to me, "Arise, go out to the valley, and I will speak with you there." 23. So I arose and went out to the valley, and behold, the glory of the lord was present[g] there like the glory which I beheld on the river Chebar, and I bowed down upon my face. 24. But, the spirit entered into me and stood me on my feet, and He spoke to me and said to me, "Go in and hide yourself within your house. 25. And as for you, Son of Adam, behold *I impose My word*[h] upon you, *as restraining as prisoners' chains,*[10] so that you cannot go out among them. 26. And I will make your tongue cleave to your palate and you shall be silent; you shall not be a man who reproves them; for they are a rebellious house. 27. But when I speak with you, *incline your soul* and say to them, Thus says the Lord God, Let him who will listen heed the *instruction* and let him who will refrain, let him refrain *from sinning;* for, they are a rebellious people."

CHAPTER 4

1. "And you, Son of Adam, take a stone for yourself and place it before you, and engrave upon it a city, Jerusalem. 2. And lay siege to it; build a siege-wall against it;[1]

Apparatus, Chapter 3 continued

[f] Lit. "before Me."
[g] Lit. "rested."

[h] RB: "of my mouth."

Apparatus, Chapter 4

[a] Lit. "given."

pile up a mound against it; and pitch camps against it; and appoint *military guards* around it. 3. And take for yourself an iron griddle, and place it as an iron wall between you and the city; and direct your face towards it, and it shall be in the siege, and you shall lay siege to it. It is a sign for the House of Israel.[2] 4. Then lie upon your left side, and place upon it the sins of the House of Israel; according to the number of days that you lie upon it, you shall bear their guilt. 5. I have imposed upon[a] you *two*[3] *for one for* their sins; according to the number of days, three hundred and ninety

Notes, Chapter 3 continued

[6]The Hebrew, "Blessed be the glory of the Lord from His place." is an important expression in Jewish liturgy. It is prominent in the *kedušah* (Sanctification) of the daily and Sabbath *šaharit,* and *musaf* of the Sabbath and the festivals; the *kedušah* of the *minhah* services; and the benedictions before the morning *šema'.* (See J.H. Hertz, *The Authorized Daily Prayer Book,* N.Y., 1959, pp. 113, 135, 277, 435, 455, 529, 577, *passim.*) Both the Hebrew verse in its entirety, and its *Tg.* are recited in *uva l'sion go'el* a prayer which precedes the *'alenu* in the daily *šaharit* (Hertz, p. 203), and as part of the *minhah* for Sabbath and festivals (Hertz, p. 571).

Tg. supplies the answer to an implicit question not elaborated in MT. The question is, where is "His place" since in the days of Ezekiel the First Temple was no more, and in the days when this *Tg.* was redacted at Yavneh under R. Johanan b. Zakkai, the Second Temple was no longer in existence. *Tg.* explains "His place" as "the abode of His Shekinah," which in Merkabah terminology would mean God's celestial palace, the chariot or the throne in the heavenly heights from which His glory emanates.

Tg. follows the Rabbinic Tradition that this hymn of praise is recited or chanted by the angelic beings, according to *b. Hul.* 91b-92a, the Ophanim. In the liturgy, as well, the context indicates that the angels chant not only this verse from Ezekiel but also *qadoš qadoš qadoš* the thrice-holy of Isaiah 6:3.

While *Tg.* relates *mimeqomo* of MT with Merkabah and the angelic beings, one Rabbinic opinion maintains that no one, not even the angels, knows where God's place is, *b. Hag.* 13b. In a theological frame of reference, Maimonides contends that the very term *maqom* connotes a spiritual—intellectual degree of perfection, not a physical or geographic locale. With reference to God, Ezek. 3:12, it signifies the highest degree of perfection, of incomparable rank. (Maimonides, *Moreh Nebukim,* tr. by Samuel Ibn Tibbon, Jerusalem, 5720, I:8, p. 25). For a critical emendation of the Hebrew, see *IB,* p. 81; *AB,* p. 70.

[7]*Tg.* understands the difficult MT, *mašmim,* which basically means "desolate," as, in a state of silence, lack of communication. Of all the English versions, the New English Bible comes closest to the *Tg.* with its translation "dumbfounded."

[8]MT: "watchman." *Tg.* equates the prophet with the teacher, the custodian of Torah, who safeguards the moral and spiritual values of the people. *Tg.* reads back into biblical history the Rabbinic ideal of learning and teaching. Cf. *b. Šab.* 119b, which has the same equation: "Do my prophets no harm (1 Chron. 16:22) refers to scholars." MT: "you must warn them against me," rendered by *Tg.* "warn them not to sin against me," a moral interpretation.

[9]The idea of forewarning the sinner or one who is about to commit a crime is incorporated into the Halakah, which requires both the testimony of two witnesses and *hatra'ah,* warning. *m. Sanh.* 5:1; *t. Sanh.* 11:1—5: *b. Sanh.* 40b, 41a; *y. Sanh.* 22a, b. Although the Halakah deduces this from Num. 15:32, Lev. 20:17, Ex. 21:14, and Dt. 22:24, the process itself must have been inferred from Ezekiel. The severe responsibility of the witnesses in capital cases, also probably generated by Ezekiel, is magnificently detailed in *m. Sanh.* 4:5.

[10]MT: "behold, they have put ropes upon you, and they have bound you with them."

Notes, Chapter 4

[1]*Tg.* translates the Hebrew *dayeq* by *karqom,* which can mean a total siege encircling a city, or any aspect of a siege. See Jastrow, I, p. 669. *Tg.* Onq. Dt. 20:20 uses the pl. form of the word to translate *maṣor. m. Git.* 3:4 uses the term for a besieging army surrounding a city. In *y. Ket.* 26d, R. Ba explains the word as "bells, chains, irons, geese, chickens, and military apparatus surrounding a city."

[2]R. Eleazar cites this to prove that since the destruction of the Temple an iron wall separates Israel from their Father in Heaven. *b. Ber,* 32b.

[3]The Hebrew *šene,* "years of" is taken as a number, "two." The Aramaic expression *'al had treyn,* "two for one," is exactly how the *Tg.* translates *kiflayim* "double," in Is. 40:2. The 390 days corresponds to Israel's 390 years of sinfulness, arrived at by various commentators through a variety of calculations, all of whom strain to arrive at this precise figure. The reasoning behind *Tg.*'s assertion that 390 is double the number of years of Israel's sinning, is not entirely clear. Even Kimhi, who is usually the main protagonist of the *Tg.,* confesses, "It is astonishing that which Targum Jonathan renders, I have given you two for one for their sins." We might conjecture that the *Tg.* finds Israel's sinning 390 years too staggering, hence mitigates by reducing it in half. Or, it might conceivably be that our *Tg.*

days you shall bear the sins of the House of Israel. 6. And when you have completed these, you shall lie down a second time, on your right side, and you shall bear the sins of the House of Judah for forty days; one day for every year, one day for every year have I imposed them upon you. 7. And you shall direct your face towards the siege of Jerusalem and *you shall strengthen your arm,* and you shall prophesy concerning it. 8. And behold, I *decree My word upon you,* as binding as cords so that you cannot turn from one side of you to the other until you have completed the days of your siege. 9. And you, take for yourself wheat, barley, beans,^{*b*} lentils, millet and spelt, and put them into one vessel and make them into food for yourself; you shall eat it during the number of days that you lie on your side — three hundred and ninety days. 10. And the food which you eat shall be by weight, twenty *plates full*[4] each day; you shall eat it at the same fixed time of the day.[5] 11. And water you shall drink by measure,[6] one sixth of a *hin;* you shall drink it at the same fixed time of the day.[5] 12. And you shall eat it as a cake of barley bread and you shall bake it on human excrement in front of their eyes." 13. And the Lord said, "Like this the Children of Israel shall eat their food: unclean, among the nations where I will exile them." 14. Then I said, "O Lord God, *hear my prayer!* Behold, my soul is not unclean; since my childhood until now I have not eaten what died a natural death or was torn by beast, nor have I eaten the unfit flesh of a sacrifice."[7] 15. So he said to me, "See I give you cow's dung instead of human excrement, on which to prepare your food." 16. Then he said to me, "Son of Adam, behold, I am breaking the food supply in Jerusalem; and they shall eat food by weight and in fear, and they shall drink water *in despair*[8] and in desolation; 17. so that they may lack food and water; and a man and his brother shall be dismayed, and they shall waste away because of their sins.

CHAPTER 5

1. "And you, Son of Adam, take a sharp sword for yourself, as a barber's razor; take it and pass it over your head and your beard; then take scales for weighing and divide them.^{*a*} 2. One-third you shall burn in the fire within the city when the days of siege have been completed. And take one-third and destroy it with the sword, round about it;^{*b*} and one-third you shall scatter *in every direction;* for, thus they shall be scattered; and I will incite after them *those who slay by* the sword. 3. And from there take a small number of them, and tie them up in your skirts. 4. And of these, again you shall take some and throw them into the midst of the fire, and burn them in the fire, for from it^{*c*} the fire shall go forth upon the whole House of Israel."[1] 5. Thus says the Lord God: "This is Jerusalem. I have placed her in the midst of the nations, with

Apparatus, Chapter 4 continued

^{*b*} RB. SP omits this.

Apparatus, Chapter 5

^{*a*} I.e. the hairs.
^{*b*} I.e. the city.
^{*c*} CR. Other versions omit "from it."

^{*d*} Most versions, following MT. MM: "but you have acted in accordance with the customs of the nations which are around you."

countries all around her. 6. And she altered My laws so as to sin by them, more than the other nations, and My statutes, more than the other countries which surround her; for, they have loathed My laws and have not walked in My statutes. 7. Therefore, thus says the Lord God: Because you have sinned more than the nations which surround you, have not walked in My statutes, nor observed My laws, nor even acted in accordance with the customs of the nations which are around you,[d] 8. therefore, thus says the Lord God; As for Me, behold I am *sending My anger* against you, and I will inflict *just punishment*[2] in your midst, in the sight of the nations. 9. I will do to you what I have never done, and the like of which I will never do again, on account of all your abominations. 10. Therefore, parents shall eat *the flesh of* their children in your midst, and children shall eat *the flesh of* their parents; and I will inflict *just punishment* upon you; and I will scatter all the rest of your people in all directions. 11. Therefore, as I live, says the Lord God, surely because you have defiled My sanctuary with all your detestable things and with all your abominations, as for Me, I will *cut off*[3] *the might of your arms*, for *My Memra*[4] will not spare you, nor will I

Notes, Chapter 4 continued

relates the Ezekiel passage to Is. 40:2, hence the rationale for his "two for one" interpretation, an interpretation unique and not found anywhere else in biblical exegesis. (For a critical view of the numbers, see *A B*, p. 105 f.) This concept is contrary to the principle of "measure for measure," *b. Sanh.* 90a, and to *Tg.* Ezek. 21:32!

Rashi explains that the left side, facing east, is to the north, thus symbolizing the Northern Kingdom: the right side is to the south, symbolizing the tribe of Judah. The 40 years of sin for Judah, was from the time of the destruction of the Northern Kingdom until the Babylonian exile. Rashi also understands Ezekiel's symbolic action as representing forgiveness and vicarious atonement. Kimhi understands it as an ordeal of punishment and suffering. Rashi probably follows the statement of R. Abbahu: "The Holy One, blessed be He, brings affliction on Ezekiel in order to wipe away the iniquities of Israel," *b. Sanh.* 39a, although he makes no references to it.

[4]*Tg.* renders Mt's *šeqel* by *pils*, a familiar term for "dish." Greek *phollis*. Cf. *S-A*, p. 96.

[5]The phraseology both in the Hebrew and its equivalent in the Aramaic, is an idiom meaning once in every 24 hour period.

[6]*mekilta'*, here used simply as a measure of capacity. Elsewhere in *Tg.* Ezek. (45:11, 13, 24; 46:5, 7, 11, 14), the word is consistently used for the Hebrew *'ephah*, specifically, unlike *Tg.* Onq. on Ex. 16:36; Lev. 5:11; 28:5, which renders *'ephah* by "three seah." But cf. *Tg.* Onq. Lev. 19:36 where the pl. *mekilan* is used, the same as *Tg.* Ezek. 45:10. Cf. *S-A*, p. 96.

[7]*besar merahaq*, targumic rendering of the Hebrew *piggul*, the flesh of a sacrificial animal which has been eaten on the third day. Cf. *Tg.* Onq. Lev. 7:18, 19:7. All the meats mentioned here are halakically forbidden.

[8]MT: "by measure."

Notes, Chapter 5

[1]So Kimhi interprets. MT: "From the fire which I commanded you to burn, a fire shall go forth against the whole House of Israel."

[2]*pur'anut dinin*, lit., "punishment of laws" or "legal punishment," which is used by *Tg.* Ezek. for MT's *mišpatim* and *šefatim*, the judgments which Yahweh will impose upon Israel for its sins. For stylistic reasons I have rendered the phrase "just punishment." This applies to the nouns which depict God's judgment. However, for the verbal forms *Tg.* uses the phrase *'itpera' min*, "exact payment from," "demand an accounting," "exact punishment from." See *infra* Ezek. 7:3, 8, 27, *passim*. "To judge between" the verb *din [dun]* is used. Cf. 34:17, 20, 22. "To reprove," the Hebraism *ykh*, 20:4, 22:2, 23:36.

[3]MT: *'egra'*, "I will diminish (you)." *Tg.* reads: *'egda'* "I will cut off," adding the exegetic complement. See Kittel, *ad loc.* for similar variant.

[4]MT: "My eye."

One of the obvious exegetical features of the *Tg.* in this chapter is the theological thrust making the Memra the agent of God for the evil decrees against Israel, instead of the Lord himself, which the Hebrew maintains. This feature is found in this verse and in verses 15 and 17. Of course, the ultimate responsibility lies with God, who, even in the *Tg.*, is the author of the decree. We must assume that the *Tg.* is reluctant to attribute such a horrible catastrophe as befell Israel directly to the transcendent deity, hence the convenient use of the Memra. In v. 11 it is the Memra which will not spare Israel, and the Lord who withholds His compassion, which mitigates the brutality somewhat. Cf. *Tg.* on v. 13, which implies that God's forgiveness follows the imposition of punishment. Note also that God's anger is another surrogate for the deity as the instrument of punishment. *Supra*, v. 8.

have pity. 12. One-third of you shall die by pestilence and be destroyed by famine in the midst of you; one-third I will scatter in every direction; and *those who slay by* the sword I will incite after them. 13. Then My anger shall be consummated, and I will lay to rest My fury towards them, and bring it to an end; and they shall know that I the Lord *have decreed it by My Memra*[5] and I have fulfilled it, when My anger at them has been consummated. 14. And I will make you a desolation and a reproach among the nations that surround you, in the sight of everyone who passes by. 15. You[6] shall be a reproach and a boasting against you, a waste and a desolation, to the nations that surround you, when I impose *just punishment* upon you, in wrath and fury and fierce anger. I, the Lord, *have decreed it by My Memra*. 16. When I let loose against you devastating famine,[7] severe afflictions which lead to destruction, which I will send to destroy you; and I will increase the famine upon you and I will break off your food supply. 17. And I will send against you famine and the wild beast and they shall leave you childless; and pestilence and killing shall pass through you; and I will bring upon you *those who slay by* the sword; I the Lord *have decreed it by My Memra.*"[8]

CHAPTER 6

1. The word of *prophecy from before* the Lord was with me, saying, 2. "Son of Adam, *hear the prophecy* against the mountains of Israel and prophesy against them. 3. And say, 'O mountains of Israel, hear the word of the Lord God. Thus says the Lord God to the mountains and the hills, to the mountain passes[1] and the valleys, behold, I bring upon you *those who slay by* the sword and I will destroy your high places. 4. And your heathen altars shall be demolished, and your obscene sun-statues shall be broken, and I will cast your slain before your *decaying* idols.[2] 5. And I will place the corpses of the Children of Israel before their *decaying* idols,[3] and I will scatter your bones around your heathen altars. 6. In all your habitations, cities shall be destroyed and the high places shall be demolished; so that your heathen altars shall be destroyed and desolate,[4] and your idols broken and be no more; your obscene sun-statues shall be cut down and your works shall be wiped out. 7. And the slain shall be thrown among you; and you shall know that I am the Lord. 8. But I will leave a remnant of you among the nations, when some of you are saved from the sword, and when you are scattered among the countries. 9. And those of you who escape shall remember *My worship,* among the nations to which they have been led captive; how I broke[5] their *foolish* heart[6] which had deserted *My worship,* and the sight of their eyes which had strayed after idols; and they shall feel remorse,[a] and they shall recognize the evil which they had done by all their abominations. 10. And

Apparatus, Chapter 6

[a] Lit. "sob," "regret."   [b] Or, "for nothing," "without cause."

Apparatus, Chapter 7

[a] Lit. "arrived."   [b] Lit. "directions."

they shall know that I am the Lord, that not in vain[b] have I decreed *by My Memra* to do this evil to them." 11. Thus says the Lord God: "Clap with your hand and stamp with your foot,[7] and say, Alas! over all the evil abominations of the House of Israel, who shall be removed by the sword, by famine, and by pestilence. 12. He who is far off shall die by pestilence; and he who is near shall be slain by the sword; and he who survives and enters the besieged cities shall die by famine; thus My anger at them shall be consummated. 13. And you shall know that I am the Lord, when their slain shall be in the midst of their *decaying* idols around their heathen altars, on every high hill; on all mountaintops; under every leafy tree, and every spreading terebinth, the place where they offered *sacrifices for the worship of* all their heathen idols.[8] 14. And I will raise up against them My *destructive might*,[9] and I will make the land a desolation and a waste, from the wilderness of Diblah, in all their habitations. And they shall know that I am the Lord."

CHAPTER 7

1. The word *of prophecy from before* the Lord was with me, saying: 2. "You, Son of Adam, thus says the Lord God to the land of Israel, The end *has come!*[a] The *retribution of the end which was to come*,[1] has come[a] upon the four corners[b] of the

Notes, Chapter 5 continued

[5]MT: "in My jealousy." an anti-anthropopathism by *Tg.*

[6]*Tg.* reads *wehayit* (2fs) instead of MT's *wehaytah* (3fs). In this respect it is in agreement with LXX and S.

[7]*Tg.* takes "arrows" in the Hebrew text as poetic allegory, and ignores its literal meaning. However, it does retain the imagery by use of the verb "to let loose."

[8]For an excellent critical treatment of the symbolic acts in chapters 4 and 5, see *AB*, pp. 117-128.

Notes, Chapter 6

[1]*pasidaya*, which could mean "rivulets," or "channels," or "mountains where ore is mined." The basic meaning is "to cut through," and in view of the context which deals with the high places of pagan ritual, I have rendered the word "mountain passes." See Jastrow, II, p. 1204 and Levy, II, p. 281, sub *pasid*.

[2]Cf. *Tg.* Onq. Lev. 26:30.

[3]V. 5a is omitted in LXX.

[4]*Tg.* reads *w'yeshmu* instead of *w'ye'eshmu* of MT. So, too, Symmachus, V, and S. LXX omits this word altogether. See *AB*, p. 133.

[5]*Tg.* like V and S, reads an active form, rather than the passive MT.

[6]MT: "whoring heart."

[7]Tapping with the feet is regarded as one of the signs or rituals of mourning. Cf. *b. M.K.* 27b

[8]MT: "for a pleasing odor." In rendering the Hebrew *reah nihoah. Tg.* distinguishes between an offering to idols and an offering to Yahweh. The former is translated, "a sacrifice for the worship of idols" as found here and in Ezek. 16:19, 20:28. Where it is a legitimate offering to Yahweh, *Tg.* translates the phrase "a sacrifice favorably accepted" or "accepted with pleasure." Cf. *Tg.* Ezek. 20:41; *Tg.* Onq. and Ps.-J. Gen. 8:21; Ex. 29:18, 25; Lev. 1:9, 13, 17; *passim.*

[9]MT: "My hand."

Notes, Chapter 7

[1]*pur'anut qissa' lemete.* In theological terminology, the word *qissa'* usually means the eschatological denouement of history to which the Messiah is integral. Cf. *Tg.* Ps.-J. on Gen. 49:1 and Frg. *Tg.* to the same verse. Levy, *The Messiah*, p. 5, Ps.-J. Gen. 49:1: "Then Jacob called his sons and said to them: 'Purify yourselves of uncleanness, and I will tell you the hidden secrets, the concealed date of the End, the reward of the righteous and the punishment of

land. 3. Now, *the retribution of the end which was to come,* has come[a] upon you and I will send My anger against you, and *exact payment from you* in accordance with your ways; and I will visit[c] upon you all your abominations. 4. *My Memra*[2] will not spare you, nor will I have pity, but I will visit[c] upon you the sinfulness of your ways, and *the punishment* for your abominations shall be in the midst of you; and you shall know that I am the Lord. 5. Thus says the Lord God, evil *after*[3] evil, behold it comes. 6. The end has come.[a] The retribution *of the end which was to come upon you,* behold, it comes. 7. *The Kingdom has been revealed*[4] to you O inhabitant of the land! The time of misfortune has arrived, the day of tumutuous confusion is near, and there is no *escaping to* the mountain *strongholds.*[5] 8. Now, soon, I will pour out My wrath upon you, and My anger shall be spent in you, and I will *exact payment from you* in accordance with your ways, and I will visit upon you all your abominations. 9. *My Memra* will not spare you and I will have no pity. I will requite[c] you according to the sins of your ways, and *the punishment for* your abominations shall be in the midst of you; and you shall know that I the Lord have brought this blow upon you. 10. Behold, the day of retribution![d] Behold, it is coming! *The Kingdom has been revealed!* The *ruler's* rod[6] has blossomed! Wickedness[e] has sprung up. 11. *Violent men* have arisen to support[f] the wicked; nothing shall remain of them, nor of their *noisy crowds,* nor of *their children,* nor of *their children's children.*[7] 12. The time has arrived *for the repayment of debts;*[8] the day *of punishment for sins*[8] draws near; let not the buyer rejoice, nor the seller be sad,[9] for there is anger from *before* Me upon all their *noisy* crowds. 13. For the seller shall not return to what he has sold;[9] for while they are still alive they shall be carried away bodily;[g10] for the *prophets prophesy* to all their *noisy* crowds,[h] but they do not repent; and every man willingly commits his sins; *but until they stand in repentance* they shall have no strength. 14. *They go forth* at the blast of the trumpet, and they prepare themselves *with weapons,* but there is none who goes to war, for there is anger from before Me against all their *noisy* crowds. 15. The sword is outside, and pestilence and famine are within: he who is in the field shall be slain by the sword, and he who is in the city, famine and pestilence shall make an end of him. 16. And the survivors among them who may escape, will be on the mountains like doves of the valleys, all of them moaning, everyone over his own sins. 17. All hands shall be weakened, and all knees

Apparatus, Chapter 7 continued

[c] Lit. "give."
[d] RB add "have arrived."
[e] SP. RB reads "the wicked."
[f] SP. K reads "to stir up."

[g] Lit. "in their bodies," MM. SP: "they shall move slowly."
 RB: "they shall be dominated."
[h] RB and AP add "to return in repentance."

shall be poured out like water. 18. And they shall bind themselves with sackcloth, and degradation shall cover them; shame shall be on all their faces and baldness on all their heads. 19. They shall throw their silver into the streets, and their gold shall become a contemptible thing. Their silver and their gold will be unable to save them on the day of the Lord's anger; they shall not be satisfied nor fill their stomachs with

Notes, Chapter 7 Continued

the wicked, and what the pleasure of Paradise will be.' The twelve sons of Israel gathered together around the golden bed on which he lay. As soon as the date of the End when the King Messiah would arrive was revealed to him, it was immediately concealed from him ..." It is interesting that *Tg*. Neof. omits the Messianic reference.

In the Rabbinic sources sometimes the phrase *qes mešiha'*, "the Messianic End," is used. *b. Meg*. 3a.

In our Targumic text, the reference is a limited non-Messianic eschatology, in keeping with the non-Messianic character of *Tg. Ezek*.

A mystic interpretation is found in the Zohar (210b) depicting two Ends, right and left, good and evil, the latter dominating the destruction, the former, triumph, and reconstruction of Temple and mankind.

[2]The Memra serves as a substitution for the poetic anthropomorphism *'ayyin* in MT.

[3]*Tg*. reads *'ahar* for MT's *'ahat* "one." S reads *tahat*, "in place of" or "for." Kimhi, while trying to make sense out of MT, recognizes that the *Tg*. has a different reading: "It seems that Targum Jonathan had read it *'ahar ra'ah* since he translates it, evil after evil."

[4]The mighty Kingdom of God, reflecting the prophetic depiction of "the day" or "Day of Yahweh," one aspect of which is retributive justice. The meaning of *hasefirah* in MT is obscure and uncertain. LXX omits this part of the verse entirely. Rashi understands it as "dawn," (of the day of evil) as does Mezudat David, from the Aramaic *s'far* or *safra'*. Kimhi also inclines in this direction, although he does acknowledge *Tg*.'s rendering and explains its exegetical rationale thus: "And Targum Jonathan, who translates it, 'the Kingdom has been revealed,' interprets *hasefirah* as in Is. 28:5 *welisfirat tif'arah* (beautiful diadem), which is a crown, and it is the symbol of royalty." In fact, *Tg*. Is. 28:5 interprets the passage Messianically! See Levey, *The Messiah*, p. 58. Here and v. 10 *infra*, the "Kingdom" is intimately connected with "The Day" of Yahweh, day of retribution. Cf. BDB, p. 862, sub *sefar* III.

[5]This may be an allusion to the historical incident of Masada, built by Herod as a fortress, and used by him as a refuge for his family, and by the Jews fighting Rome under Titus and again under Hadrian. The Targumist must have been an eyewitness to some of these circumstances. Note the phonetic play of the Aramaic *bimesady* in relation to the name *masada*.

[6]*šultana*, in addition to "rulership" or "dominion" or "the ruling power," also has the meaning of "the ruler's rod," (Jastrow, II, p. 1534) which conforms with MT's *mateh*. In this instance it may refer to Nebuchadnezzar as the rod or agent of God's retributive wrath. Cf. Is. 10:5, 24. Both Rashi and Kimhi take it so.

Vv. 10 and 11 are both difficult, uncertain, obscure in the Hebrew, the text of which is corrupt. The versions, the commentaries, and the translators all strain to make some sense of them. *Tg*.'s interpretive rendering is as good as any, indicating that God has reached the limit of His patience, has revealed Himself as the arbiter and guide of history, that He has summoned Babylon as the instrumentality of His retribution against Israel, and that it is because of the widespread corruption and the moral breakdown of society, that God is bringing disaster upon her. She will not recover for generations to come. This concept of the *Tg*. fits in admirably with the prophetic tone of chapter 7.

[7]MT: "nor their people, nor their tumult." The exegetical thrust of the *Tg*. in referring to their children and their children's children derives from MT's *mehemehem*, as though it were "from them, from them," the first *mehem* referring to their children and the second *mehem* referring to their children's children. This is how Kimhi explains it. *Tg*. makes no reference whatsoever to *lo' noha bahem* of MT, which may mean "there is no wailing among them." Some MSS. of S, and the V do read *noah* with a *het*! The implication is that there is not even one righteous man among them, as Noah was in his generation.

[8]By means of the exegetic complement, *Tg*. expands on MT, which says simply that the time has come and the day draws near, explaining that these refer to the imminence of divine retribution.

[9]The reference to buyer and seller, and return to what he has sold, may refer to the land, and its return to its original owner during the year of the jubilee. Lev. 25:23; Num. 36:7. The idea expressed here in Ezek. is that the people will go into exile to Babylon, where the biblical land-laws will not apply. The emotional response to a transaction expressed in this v. is thought to be a universal experience. "It is characteristically human that when a man sells a precious object to his fellow, the seller grieves and the buyer rejoices ..." *b. Ber*. 5a.

[10]According to the version in MM, which makes the most sense, in that it is a reference to exile.

it, because it shall be[11] a sinful[i] stumbling-block. 20. And his beautiful ornament[12] I have given him for glory, but they worshipped[j] therein the images of their abominations, their detestable things; therefore I have made it for them into *something contemptible.*[13] 21. And I will turn it over to the hand of the wicked to plunder, and to the sinners of the land as a spoil, and they shall profane it. 22. *And I will make My Shekinah depart from them,*[14] because they have profaned *the land of the abode of My Shekinah,* and wicked ones[15] shall enter it and profane it. 23. Make a chain, for the land has become full of those who *deserve to be executed,*[16] and the city has become full of robbers. 24. And I will bring in the worst of the nations, and they shall take possession of their houses. And I will put an end to the haughtiness[k] of the wicked, and their holy places shall be profaned. 25. *Destruction* has come, and they shall seek peace, but there is none. 26. Misfortune[m] upon misfortune shall come, there shall be report upon report; and they shall seek *instruction* from the *scribe,*[17] and the decision[18] shall cease from the priest, and counsel from the *sage.*[19] 27. The king shall mourn, and the prince shall clothe himself in despair, and the hands of the people of the land[20] shall be terrified. I will do with them according to their ways, and *exact payment from* them in accordance with their practices and they shall know that I am the Lord."

CHAPTER 8

1. It was in the sixth year in the sixth month, on the fifth day of the month that the prophet said: I was sitting in my house and the elders of the House of Judah were sitting before me; and *the spirit of prophecy from before* the Lord God rested upon me there. 2. I saw, and behold, a likeness, like the appearance of fire, *a manifestation[a] of glory which the eye could not perceive[b] and at which it was impossible to look.* Downward[l] there was a fiery appearance, *a manifestation[a] of glory which the eye could not perceive[b] and at which it was impossible to look.* And upward[1] there was like a *manifestation[a] of splendor like that of hashmal.*[2] 3. He stretched out the form of a hand, and he seized me by *the hair* of my head. And a spirit[c] lifted me up between earth and heaven, and brought me into Jerusalem, by a *prophetic* vision from *before* the Lord *which rested upon me;* by the entrance of the inner gate which faces[d] north, where was the seat of the statue[3] of jealousy which *provokes anger.*[4] 4. And behold, the glory of the God of Israel was there, like the vision which I had seen

Apparatus, Chapter 7 continued

[i] Lit. "of sins."
[j] Or "made."

[k] MM reads "to those of the house."
[.m] Lit. "breach."

Apparatus, Chapter 8

[a] Lit. "an appearance."
[b] Lit. "see."
[c] Or "wind."
[d] Lit. "opens to."

[e] Lit. "by way of."
[f] Lit. "bad, wicked."
[g] RB and A. SP: "mountain." MM: "smoke."
[h] CR. SP and RB: "do you see."

in the valley. 5. And He said to me, "Son of Adam, lift up your eyes, towards*e* the north." So I lifted up my eyes towards*e* the north; and behold, north of the altar gate there was this statue of jealousy in the entrance. 6. And He said to me, "Son of Adam, do you see what they are doing, the great abominations which the House of Israel are committing here, driving Me far from My Sanctuary? But you shall further see still greater abominations." 7. Then He brought me into the gate of the courtyard, and I saw, and behold, there was a hole in the wall. 8. And He said to me, "Son of Adam, now dig in the wall." So I dug in the wall and behold, there was a door. 9. And He said to me, "Go in, and see the awful*f* abominations which they are practicing here." 10. So I went in and saw and behold, every form of creeping things and detestable beasts, and all the idols which the House of Israel *was worshipping,* carved upon the wall all around. 11. And seventy men of the elders of the House of Israel were standing in front of them and Jaazaniah the son of Shaphan[5] was standing among them. Each man had his incense pan in his hand, and a rising pillar*g* of the cloud of incense went up. 12. And He said to me, "Son of Adam, have you seen*h* what the elders of the House of Israel are doing in the dark, each man in the

Notes, Chapter 7 continued

[11]It is strange that *Tg.* would read the imperfect rather than MT's perfect tense. Perhaps he feels silver and gold, i.e., their love of material possessions, will lead to their ultimate downfall. *Ex. R.* 31:4 expresses the thought that they were punished for violating the biblical prohibition against usury.

[12]This is a reference to the Temple, according the the *Tg.* supported by the translation in v. 22 of the Hebrew *ṣefuni* (My treasured place) as "the abode of My Shekinah." Rashi and Kimḥi follow the *Tg.*

[13]For the Hebrew *niddah,* the usual term for a menstruous woman.

[14]MT:"I shall turn My face away from them." Note the circumlocution to avoid the anthropomorphism.

[15]In this context, this could be a reference to the Roman profanation of the Temple in 70 C.E. "The wicked" is a common Rabbinic appellation for Rome and Romans. Cf. *b. Ber.* 61b.

[16]MT:"the judgment of blood." *Tg: hayyabe qatul,* which is the Aramaic equivalent of *hayyabe mitah,* those who have committed capital offenses and have incurred the death penalty. The chain is a symbol of their punishment, being led away into captivity, where execution might await them.

[17]MT:"vision from the prophet." *Tg.'s* "instruction from the scribe" may hint at the Yavnian redaction of *Tg.* Ezek. There are no prophets, but there are scribes; the Temple is no more, so the priests are no longer the decision-makers; and the "elders" understood as the sages, are at a loss as to how to meet the crisis. This passage seems to be a striking revelation of the predicament of the Jewish people following the catastrophe of 70 C.E. Cf. *m. Sotah* 9:15.

[18]MT:"and Torah," which the *Tg.* would usually translate *'orayta'* indicating that *Tg.* no longer considered the priesthood as the repository of Torah. Our word means "decision" or "instruction."

[19]MT: "the elders." *Tg.* implies Rabbinic identification.

[20]A literal rendering of the Hebrew, meaning the common people as distinguished from the nobility. See BDB, p. 766., sub *'am* 5. In Rabbinic Hebrew the term means "the ignorant" or "the illiterate."

Notes, Chapter 8

[1]In keeping with *Tg.'s* tendency to avoid anthropomorphism, *Tg.* omits the Hebrew *matnaw* "His loins."

[2]MT: *"the hasmal."* *Tg.* leaves the Hebrew untranslated. See note 4 on 1:4, *supra.*

[3]MT: "the site of the image of jealousy." *Tg.: selem,* for the unusual Hebrew *semel* which unmistakeably is a statue of idolatrous worship. See Dt. 4:16, and *Tg.* Ps.-J. *ad loc.* Also Dan. 2:31.

[4]*Tg.: demargzin.* Presumably, the statue provokes the anger, not the jealousy, of Yahweh, different from MT. The identity of the statue is not disclosed. Some would identify it with the idol that Manasseh had set up in the Temple, 2 K. 21:7. See *ICC,* p. 92 and *AB,* p. 168. Any statue or idol would provoke Yahweh for blasphemy, *Tg.* Onq. Lev. 24:11. Afel of *rgz* is also the technical term for blasphemy, *Tg.* Onq. Lev. 24:11. Jastrow II, p. 1447.

[5]Shaphan was the scribe who brought the scroll of the Torah to King Josiah (2K 22:10), and possibly Jaazaniah was his son. Ezekiel may have mentioned him by name to indicate that even those who belonged to Jeremiah's inner circle had defected to idolatry. Or, it may be a case of mistaken identity. (Cassuto, *Sefer Yehezkel,* p. 30).

chamber of his bedroom.[6] For they are saying, *'Our deeds are not revealed before the Lord,*[7] the Lord has abandoned[8v]*the inhabitants*[9] *of* the land.'" 13. And He said to me, "You shall see still greater abominations which they practice." 14. So He brought me into the entrance to the gate of the Holy Temple of the Lord, which faces north; and behold, women sitting there lamenting the Tammuz.[10] 15. Then he said to me, "Have you seen, O Son of Adam? Again, you shall see greater abominations than these." 16. Then He brought me into the inner court of the Temple of the Lord and behold, at the door of the Sanctuary of the Lord, between the vestibule and the altar,[11] there were about twenty-five men, their backs to the Sanctuary of the Lord, and their faces to the east, and behold, they joined together,[f12] bowing in worship to the sun, eastward. 17. Then He said to me, "Have you seen, O Son of Adam? Is it too small a thing for the House of Judah to do, to commit the abominations which they are doing here, that they must fill the land with violent *men,* and provoke Me to further anger? Behold, *they are bringing disgrace right in front of them.*[13] 18. Therefore, I also will act in anger. *My Memra* will not spare, nor will I have pity. They shall pray to me in a loud voice, but I will not hear *their prayers."*

CHAPTER 9

1. Then he called out, and I heard a loud voice, saying, "Come near, you who are appointed over the city each with his weapon of destruction in his hand." 2. And behold, six men[a1] coming from the direction of the upper gate which faces north, each with his weapon of dispersion in his hand; and one man among them clothed in garments with a scribe's tablet at his loins. And they came in, and stood by the side of the bronze altar. 3. Now the glory of the God of Israel ascended by[b] the cherub upon which it had been resting *in the abode of the Holy of Holies,* and it rested above, by the threshold of the house;[c] and He called to the man who was clothed in garments, with the scribe's tablet at his loins. 4. And the Lord said to him, "Pass through the midst of the city, in the midst of Jerusalem, and draw a mark[2] on the foreheads of the men who moan and who grieve over all the abominations which are committed in the midst of her." 5. And to the others He said, and I heard it, "Pass through the city after him, and slay; your eye shall not spare, and you shall have no pity. 6. Old men, young men, and virgins, little children and women you shall slay utterly,[d] but you must not come near anyone upon whom the mark is drawn. And you shall start from My Holy Temple." So they began with the old men who were in front of the House. 7. Then he said to them, "Defile the House, and fill the courts with the slain. Go forth." So they went forth and slew in the city. 8. And it was, while they were slaying,

Apparatus, Chapter 8 continued

[i]SP. RB and AP: "acting destructively."

Apparatus, Chapter 9

[a] CR: "six angels of destruction having the appearance of six men."

[b]K: "like."

[c] AA and CR: "the Temple."

[d]Lit. "to destruction."

that I remained, and I fell upon my face and cried out and said, "*Hear my petition, O Lord God. Are You going to destroy the entire remnant of Israel, in pouring out Your fury upon Jerusalem?*" 9. Then He said to me, "The sins of the House of Israel and Judah have become exceedingly great therein, so that the land has become full of *those who deserve to be executed,* and the city has become filled with perversion of justice, for they said, 'The Lord has abandoned the *inhabitants of* the land, and *there*

Notes, Chapter 8 continued

[6] *Tg.* reads *miškabto* "his sleeping quarters" for MT's *maskito.* "his idolatrous symbols." See BDB, p. 967, sub *maskit. Lam. R.* Pet. 22, takes this v. as the first step in a progression of idolatry in Jerusalem. "What caused Jerusalem to be destroyed? Because they left no place in it where they did not worship idols. At the outset, they worshipped it in secret, as it is written, He said to me, Have you seen, O son of man, what the elders of the House of Israel are doing in the dark? (Ezek. 8:12). And when there was no protest against them, they then practiced their idolatry behind the door ... then on the rooftops ... then in the gardens ... then on the mountain tops ... then in the open fields ... then at the cross-roads ... in the streets ... in the towns ... and finally inside the Holy of Holies, as it is said, This statue of jealousy was in the entrance, Ezek. 8:5."

b. Yoma 76b-77a interprets one idolatrous practice mentioned in this chapter as an unseemly insult to Yahweh. In bowing down to worship the sun, they had their backs towards the Temple, uncovered themselves and performed an unseemly bodily function while in that position.

[7] MT: "the Lord does not see us." Theologically, *Tg.* cannot render MT's phrase literally, even though it is the sinners who are speaking. This would imply an insufficiency in God which *Tg.* would hesitate to utter. Exegetically, *Tg.* avoids the anthropomorphism, the sinners maintaining that God is unconcerned about their sinful deeds.

[8] *Tg.: raheq,* lit., "moved far away from," conveying the idea of rejection. Official *Tg.* consistently uses this verb for the Heberw *'azb,* when the subject is Yahweh. Cf. *Tg.* on Dt. 31:17; Is. 41:17; 49:14, *passim.* But when the subject is Israel, forsaking Yahweh, official *Tg.* invariably uses the verb *šbq,* followed by "worship of Me." Cf. Dt. 28:20, 31:16; Josh. 24:20; Judg. 2:12; Is. 1:4; Jer. 2:13; *passim.* However, *Tg.* Ket. uses *šbq* even when the subject is God. Cf. Ps. 22:2, 38:22, 71:11; Lam. 5:20; *passim.*

[9] *Tg.*'s interpretation provides the theological thrust that God has not abandoned the land, which remains forever His, but He has only abandoned its sinful inhabitants.

[10] *Tg.*'s rendering follows the Hebrew precisely: the verb is in the Pa'el, followed by the sign of accusative case, *yat,* then *tamuza'* with the definitive ending, hence my translation "lamenting the Tammuz." There seems little doubt that the reference is to the god who is annually reborn in the springtime and dies with the heat of the summer, the spouse of Ishtar, worshipped in the Sumerian, Assyro-Babylonian, and near eastern cults as far back as the third millenium B.C.E. Jerome, Origen, and Cyril of Alexandria identify him with the Phoenician Adonis and the agricultural fertility cult of Byblos. The Egyptian equivalent is Osiris. V translates it as Adonis. For a critical analysis, see *ICC* pp. 96 ff.; *AB,* p. 171; *IB,* p. 107.

The older Rabbinic sources are silent on the god Tammuz, perhaps because of the embarrassment of having a memorial to a pagan god in the form of a month in the Jewish calendar, assumed, of course, from the Babylonians. There are no comments of this verse, nor on Tammuz the deity in the Talmud or Midrashim. Rashi and Kimḥi, *ad loc.,* as well as Maimonides (*Moreh* 3:29), have a number of fanciful explanations.

[11] One of the most sacred areas. Cf. Joel 2:17; *m. Kel.* 1:9.

[12] MT: *mištaḥawitem,* an impossible grammatical form. Rashi and Kimḥi explain that it is a word compounded from two roots, *šhh,* "bowing down in worship to the sun," thereby *šht,* "destroying the Temple." *m. Suk.* 5:4 maintains that the priests of the Second Temple would pronounce this verse as referring to a former practice, and adding, "but our eyes are in the direction of Yah(weh)." For a critical discussion of sun-worship in relation to this passage, see *AB,* p. 172; *IB,* p. 109.

[13] MT: "Behold, they extend the branch to their nose." Probably an idolatrous practice. See *IB,* p. 109.

Notes, Chapter 9

[1] The six men are identified in *Lam. R.* 2:3 as angels. CR incorporates this idea in the body of its version: "six angels of destruction in the form of six men." *b. Yoma* 77a identifies the scribe as Gabriel, who functioned as inquisitor, executioner, and high priest. *b. Šab.* 55a regards the six men as representing six powers of destruction, including *mekalleh,* "complete annihilation."

[2] The tradition assumed that the mark on the forehead was the last letter of the Hebrew alphabet, *taw,* based on MT's *taw* "sign" or "mark." "The Holy One blessed be He said to Gabriel, 'Go, mark a *taw* in ink on the foreheads of the righteous, so that the angels of destruction can have no dominion over them; and on the foreheads of the wicked, a *taw* in blood, so that the angels of destruction should have dominion over them ...' And why the letter *taw* in

is nothing that is revealed[e] before the Lord.' 10. And as for Me, also, *My Memra*[3] will not spare, nor will I have pity; I will visit[4] upon their heads *the punishment for their ways."* 11. And behold, the man clothed in garments with the tablet at his loins, replied, saying, "I have done[5] as You have commanded me."

CHAPTER 10

1. And I looked, and behold, in the firmament which was over the head of the cherubim there was something like a precious stone that appeared to be in the form of a throne, visible above them. 2. Then He said to the man who was clothed in garments, saying, "Go in among the wheels[1] under the cherub, and fill your hand full of burning embers from between the cherubim and sprinkle them over the city." So he went in, while I was watching. 3. Now the cherubim were standing to the south of the House, when the man entered, and a *dense*[a] cloud filled the inner court. 4. And the glory of the Lord went up by the cherub upon which it had been resting, and rested above, in front of the threshold of the House.[b] And the House was filled with a *dense* cloud, and the court was filled with the splendor of the glory of the Lord. 5. And the sound of the wings of the cherubim was heard as far as the outer court like a sound[c] from before *Shaddai*[2] in speech.[3] 6. And it was, when He commanded the man who was clothed in the garments, saying, "Take fire from between the wheels, between the cherubim," that he went in and stood beside the wheel. 7. Then the cherub extended his hand from among the cherubim to the fire which was between the cherubim, and he took some and put it into the hands of the one who was clothed in the garments, who took it and went out. 8. And there appeared among[d] the cherubim the form of a man's hand, under their wings. 9. I saw, and behold, there were four wheels by the side of the cherubim, one wheel beside one cherub, and another wheel beside another cherub; and the appearance of the wheels was like that of a precious[4] stone. 10. And as for their appearance, all four of them had the same form, as if it were a wheel within a wheel. 11. When they went, they would go upon their four sides, not turning as they went; for they would go towards the place where the first one faced, following behind it; they did not turn as they went. 12. And the entire body of all four of the wheels, and their backs, and their arms and their wings, the wheels were full of eyes round about. 13. As for the wheels,[5] it[6] was called "Galgal";[c7] *I heard it.* 14. Each had four faces: the face of the one was the face of a cherub;[8] the face of the second was the face of a man; the third was the face of a lion; and the fourth was the face of an eagle. 15. Then the cherubim raised themselves up.

Apparatus, Chapter 9 continued

[e] RB. SP: "this is not revealed."

Apparatus, Chapter 10

[a] Or "dark," "misty."
[b] A: "Temple."
[c] Or "voice."
[d] Lit. "to."

[e] RB. SP, MM, and CR: "gilgal.'"
[f] AP. SP and RB: "like the spirit."
[g] First RB reads "their faces."

These were the creatures which I had seen by the river Chebar. 16. And when the cherubim went, the wheels went alongside of them; and when the cherubim raised their wings to rise from *below to the heights of heaven,*[9] the wheels also would not turn from beside them. 17. When they stood still, they too, would stand still; and when they rose, they too, would rise with them, for the spirit[f] of the creatures was in them. 18. Then the glory of the Lord which had been resting above, by the threshold of the House, removed itself, and *rested*[10] above the cherubim. 19. And the cherubim raised their wings[g] and rose from *below to the heights of heaven,* and I saw when they went out; and the wheels were beside them; and it[11] stood at the entrance to the east-gate of the Holy Temple of the Lord, and the glory of the God of Israel was upon them, from above. 20. They were the creatures which I had seen below *the glory of* the God of Israel by the river Chebar; and I knew that they were cherubim. 21. Each had four faces, and each had four wings, and the likeness of the hands of a man was underneath their wings. 22. As for the likeness of their faces, they were the faces whose appearance I had seen by the river Chebar; and as for them, each creature was going in a forward direction.

Notes, Chapter 9 continued

particular? Rab said, *'taw* for *tihyeh* (you shall live), and *taw* for *tamut,* (you shall die).' Samuel said, *'taw* for *tamah,* ended is the merit of the Fathers.' Resh Lakish said, *'taw* is the last letter of the seal of the Holy One blessed be He,' for R. Hanina said, 'the seal of the Holy One blessed be He is *'emet,* Truth.'" *b. Sab.* 55a.

[3]Avoiding the anthropomorphism, *Tg.* renders "My Memra" for "My eye" of MT.

[4]Following the MT, which has the prophetic perfect.

[5]Significantly, *Tg.* follows Ket. rather than Q., "all that" implying that God's attribute of Mercy prevailed, and the righteous and the innocent were not slain.

Notes, Chapter 10

[1]The Hebrew for the first time introduces the term *galgal,* which in v. 13 is identified with *'ofan. Tg.* had invariably translated *'ofan* as *galgal.*

[2]Targum retains the Hebrew *šaddai* as is, but omits *'el* of MT. In 1:24 *supra, 'el* does not occur in the Hebrew, nor in *Tg. Tg.* Onq. where *'el šaddai* occurs in the Hebrew, Gen. 17:1, 28:3, 35:11, 43:14, 48:3; Ex. 6:3, renders the term by transliterating MT. LXX here has *theou šaddai* but omits *šaddai* and the entire phrase in 1:24. For a critical analysis, see *ICC* p. 114 f. Throughout the Book of Job this designation of deity is used without *'el.* In general it carries the meaning of absolute power and might, and this is the implication of its use in Ezekiel, to indicate the massive sound of the cherubim. V makes this abundantly clear by its rendering *omnipotens.*

[3]The pronominal suffix of MT is omitted in *Tg.* The reasoning behind this is not entirely clear. It is perhaps theological, the implication being that *šaddai* denotes reverberating, over-powering action, rather than words, in which case *bemilula'* would modify *weqal,* and not *šaddai.*

[4]MT: *taršiš,* some kind of marine gem.

[5]*Tg.* here uses an Aramaised form of the Heb. *'ofanim,* which it usually rendered *galgelaya'.*

[6]*Tg.* has the singular, instead of MT's plural, perhaps because *galgal* is singular.

[7]In keeping with the Masoretic vocalization of the Hebrew. Other *Tg.* versions read *gilgal.* It is fascinating that LXX also takes this word as a proper noun, vocalized *gelgel,* transliterated, not translated.

[8]As opposed to Ezek. 1:10 *supra,* MT has "cherub" in place of "ox" and the juxtaposition is altered as well, with the face of the cherub first, whereas in 1:10 the ox was third. The substitution of the cherub for the ox did not go unnoticed by the Tradition. Resh Lakish explains that Ezekiel pleaded with God for mercy, since the ox which is associated with the sin of the golden calf, would be a symbol of accusation against Israel. This would make no sense, because the chariot was presumed to have intercessory power, and should therefore come to the defense of Israel. Hence God changed the ox to a cherub. But if the cherub looks like a man, there would be two faces of a man in the chariot, which would be incongruous. No, the face of the cherub is that of a little boy, whereas the other is the face of a grown up man. *b. Hag.* 13b. LXX omits v. 14 entirely.

[9]MT: "from the earth."

[10]MT: "stood."

[11]Targum follows MT in reading the singular, "it stood," the subject being the glory of the Lord, in v. 18. LXX and S: "they stood." Cf. *IB,* p. 117; *y. 'Erub.* 22c, for the seven names of the eastern gate.

CHAPTER 11

1. Then the spirit lifted me up and brought me into the east gate of the Holy Temple of the Lord which faces east. And behold, at the door of the gate there were twenty-five men; and I saw among them Jaazaniah the son of Azzur and Pelatiah the son of Benaiah, princes of the people. 2. And He said to me, "Son of Adam, these are the men who are planning to do violence, and who are giving evil counsel in this city, 3. who say, 'Is it not soon enough to build houses?[1] We consider it to be[a] like a caldron, and we *are thought of* within it as meat *which is boiled within a caldron.'*4. Therefore, prophesy against them, prophesy, O Son of Adam." 5. Then the spirit of *prophecy from before* the Lord rested upon me, and He said to me, "Say, Thus says the Lord: So you have said, O House of Israel, but *what you are planning and* what comes to your mind *are revealed before Me.* 6. You have increased your slain in this city; and you have filled its streets with the slain. 7. Therefore, thus says the Lord God: Your slain, whom you have placed in the midst of it, they are like meat, and it is like a caldron; and I shall *exile* you from the midst of it. 8. You have feared *those who slay by* the sword; and *those who slay by* the sword will I bring upon you, says the Lord God. 9. And I will *exile* you from the midst of it, and I will turn you over to the hand of strangers; and I will inflict upon you *just punishment.* 10. You shall be slain by the sword; I will *exact payment from* you at the border of the land of Israel; and you shall know that I am the Lord. 11. It shall not be as a caldron for you; but you shall be in the midst of it like meat *which is boiled in a caldron;*[2] I will *exact payment from* you at the border of the land of Israel. 12. Then you shall know that I am the Lord, in whose statutes you have not walked, and My laws you have not observed; but you have done according to the practices of the nations who surround you." 13. Now it came to pass while I was prophesying that Pelatiah the son of Benaiah died; and I bowed down upon my face and cried out in a loud voice, and I said: "*Hear my prayer,* O Lord God. Are you going to effect the complete annihilation of the remnant of Israel?" 14. Then the word of *prophecy from before* the Lord was with me saying 15. "Son of Adam, your brother, your brother, your near kinsman,[b3] and all the House of Israel, all of them, are those to whom the inhabitants of Jerusalem are saying: 'Remove yourselves from *the worship of* the Lord, for the land

Apparatus, Chapter 11

[a] Lit. "it is considered by us."
[b] Or "close relative." AP: "kinsmen" (pl.)
[c] All versions except SP, who reads "you" instead of

"I".
[d] Lit. "wonderful," or "reverent."
[e] SP. RB, AP, and MM: "their."

has been given to us to possess it.' 16. Therefore, say: 'Thus says the Lord God: Because I[c4] scattered them in the countries, therefore I have *given them synagogues, second only to* My Holy Temple,[5] *because they are few in number*[6] in the countries to which they *have been exiled.'* 17. Therefore, say, 'Thus says the Lord God: I will bring you in[7] from among the nations, and I will gather you from the countires in which you have been scattered, and I will give you the land of Israel.' 18. And they shall come in there, and they shall remove from it all of its idols and its abominations. 19. And I will give[8] them a *faithful*[d] heart and will put a *faithful*[d] spirit into your[e9] insides, and I will *break the evil* heart, *which is as hard* as stone, from their

Notes, Chapter 11

[1] *Tg.* translates the Hebrew literally, and the meaning seems to be rather certain. Reading it as a question makes the most sense in terms of the syntax of the verse. It can be understood only against the background of the historical situation immediately after the first captivity of the Jews in 597 B.C.E. The surviving nobility in Jerusalem considered themselves to be inviolable, that Babylon would have no further power over them, and that Ezekiel's dire predictions would not materialize, so they might just as well start to rebuild the city. The simile of the caldron and the meat would imply that they do not feel ready to be removed, or exiled, that they have a sense of security and well-being. Also that they are the meat, the choicest elements in the body-politic of the nation.

Rashi and Kimhi do not read it as a question, but they understand the meaning and the implication as my explanation above. Both interpret the verse thus: the prophecy of doom is not about to be fulfilled, therefore proceed with building houses. We will not be removed until our time has come, as the meat is not removed from the caldron until it is completely boiled.

[2] The meaning of the passage is that Jerusalem will not serve as protection for those who had remained within it, but the time has come for them to be exiled, as meat fully cooked, is ready to be taken out of the pot.

[3] *Tg.* renders the singular where MT has plurals, possibly intended as a collective singular. AP is the only version that reads the pl. *anše,* but *ahk* in the singular. The reference is to the exiles in Babylon. Cf. *AB,* p. 189; LXX: "the men of your captivity," reading *galuteka.* So, too, in S.Cf. *IB,* p. 121.

[4] Sperber's version reflects the thought that the responsibility for the Exile lay with the residue of Jewish leaders in Jerusalem, and not with God.

[5] According to MT, God is the Sanctuary of Israel in Exile, but Targumic interpretation sees the synagogue as the sanctuary, surrogate of the Temple which has been destroyed. If *Tg.* Ezek. was redacted at Yavneh, this would apply to the Second Temple as well as the first. Critically speaking this passage in the *Tg.* may throw some light on the controversy as to where the synagogue originated. It tends to support the contention of W. Bacher ("Synagogue," *J E,* XI, 619) that it probably originated in Babylon during the Exile, and was brought to Palestine by those who returned from the Captivity. (Cf. L. Finkelstein, *The Pharisees,* vol. II, pp. 652 ff. G.F. Moore, *Judaism,* vol. I, pp. 281ff. But cf. S. Zeitlin, "The Origin of the Synagogue" *Proc. Am. Acad. Jew. Res.,* 1931, pp. 72ff.

Theologically, implied in the *Tg.'s* comment is the corrolary idea that as the synagogue is the surrogate of the Temple, prayer and the ethical life of Torah are the surrogate of the sacrificial cult.

This thought is conveyed in *'Ab. d' R. Nat.* A, ch. 4: "On one occasion, R. Johanan b. Zakkai was leaving Jerusalem and R. Joshua was following him. When he saw the Temple in ruins, R. Joshua said, Woe unto us that this is destroyed, the place where they would atone for the iniquities of Israel. R. Johanan said to him, My son, let it not grieve you; we have an atonement which is just like it, namely, deeds of loving-kindness, as it is said, (Hos. 6:6), For I desire loving-kindness and not animal sacrifice." Cf. the parallel account in *'Ab.d' R. Nat.,* B, ch. 8.

Ezek. 11:16 is cited in the Talmud, *b. Meg.* 29a. "R. Isaac says, This refers to the synagogues and the houses (or academies) of learning which are in Babylon." According to R. Eliezer Ha-Kappar, the synagogues and the houses of learning which are in Babylon will in the future be transplanted in the land of Israel, reflecting a Messianic era of restoration in which the synagogue and the house of learning play a dominant role, along with a reconstructed Temple.

[6] MT: "yet have I been a small sanctuary for them."
Tg. understands the Hebrew *me'at* as referring to the people, not the sanctuary.

[7] Lit., "draw you near," *we'aqreb,* in contrast to the verb *'arheq,* which *Tg.* uses to express expulsion, driving off far away.

[8] Note the use of the verb *natan* instead of the customary *yehab.*

[9] *Tg.* follows MT, which changes persons from 3mp to 2mp and back to 3mp. Other *Tg.* versions read 3mp throughout, as do LXX and S. See Kittel *ad loc.*

flesh, and I will give them a heart *which is faithful*[d] *to Me, to do My will,*[10] 20. in order that they may walk in My statutes and keep My laws and observe them; and they shall be My people and I will be their God. 21. Their heart has gone astray after their idol-worship and their abominations; I have visited punishment on their heads for their ways, says the Lord God." 22. Then the cherubim raised their wings, with the wheels at their sides, and the glory of the God of Israel was over them from above. 23. And the glory of the Lord went up from the midst of the city and *rested* on the Mount *of Olives,*[11] which is east of the city. 24. And the spirit lifted me up and brought me to the country of the land of the Chaldeans, to the exiles, in a vision *by the prophetic spirit which had rested upon me from before* the Lord. Then the vision which I had seen departed from me. 25. Then I *prophesied* to the exiles all the words of the Lord which he had showed me.

CHAPTER 12

1. The word of *prophecy from before* the Lord was with me, saying, 2. "Son of Adam, you are dwelling in the midst of a rebellious *people,* who have eyes to see, but do not see, and who have ears to hear, but do not hear, because they are a rebellious *people.*[1] 3. So you, Son of Adam, make[a] for yourself exile-equipment[2] and go into exile during the daytime before their very eyes. And you shall go into exile from your place to another place, before their very eyes — perhaps they will see[b] that they are a rebellious people. 4. And you shall take out your equipment, as exile-equipment, during the day before their very eyes; and you shall go out in the evening before their very eyes, like those going into exile. 5. Before their very eyes, you shall take it on your shoulder; you shall go out in the dark; you shall cover your face so that you cannot see the ground; for I have given you as a sign to the House of Israel." 7. So I did thus as I had been commanded. I brought out my equipment, as exile-equipment, during the day, then, in the evening I broke through the wall for myself, by hand; I went out in the dark; I carried it on my shoulder before their very eyes. 8. The word of *prophecy from before* the Lord was with me in the morning saying: 9. "Son of Adam, if, indeed, the House of Israel, the rebellious *people,* say to you, 'What are you doing?' 10. Say to them 'Thus says the Lord God, the burden of this prophecy concerns the prince, in Jerusalem, and the entire House of Israel who are among them.' 11. Say, 'I am your sign. As I have done, so shall it be done to them: they shall go into exile, into captivity.' 12. And the prince who is among them, shall carry it on

Apparatus, Chapter 12

[a] SP, as MT. RB and CR: "prepare."
[b] SP. RB and AP: "perhaps they shall be struck with fear." (understanding the verb in MT from *yare'* not *ra'ah*.)

[c] SP. Other versions omit "with his eyes."
[d] K: "Because he sinned, they shall put out his eyes so that he cannot see the land."

his shoulder; he shall go out in the dark; they shall break through the wall by which to bring him out; he shall cover his face; *because he sinned* with his eyes,^{c} he shall not see the land.^{d3} 13. And I will spread My net over him, and he shall be caught in My snare; and I will *exile* him to Babylon, to the country of the land of the Chaldeans, but he shall not see it; and there he shall die. 14. And all who are around him, his helpers and all of his troops, I will scatter in all directions; and *those who slay by* the sword I will incite after them. 15. Then they shall know that I am the Lord, when I *exile* them among the nations and scatter them in the countries. 16. But a remnant of them — a limited number of men — I will spare from the sword and from famine, and from pestilence, in order that they may recount all their abominations among the nations to which they have been *exiled;* and they shall know that I am the Lord." 17. And the word of *prophecy from before* the Lord was with me, saying, 18. "Son of Adam, your *food* you shall eat in trembling, and your water you shall drink in *despair* and *desolation.* 19. And you shall say to the people of the land, Thus says the Lord God to the inhabitants of Jerusalem upon the land of Israel: They shall eat their *food* in trembling and they shall drink their water in *desolation,* because the land shall be made desolate of everything within it by reason of the violence of all who inhabit it. 20. And the cities which were inhabited shall be laid waste, and the land shall become a desolation, and you shall know that I am the Lord." 21. The word of *prophecy from before* the Lord was with me, saying: 22. "Son of Adam, what is this proverb which you have in the land of Israel, saying: 'The days are extended and every prophecy ended?' 23. Therefore, say to them, 'Thus says the Lord God, I have made void this proverb, and they shall no longer use it as a proverb in Israel.' Rather, *prophesy* to them, The days draw near, and so, too, the word of every prophecy. 24. For, there shall no longer be any false prophecy or lying divination in

Notes, Chapter 11 continued

^{10}MT: "I will give them one heart, and put a new spirit within you. I will remove the stony heart from their flesh, and give them a heart of flesh." The theological implications of the Targumic interpretation of this verse are Judaically bold and quintessential to the Jewish faith. It is not a "new" or "different" heart and a "new" spirit which the *Tg.* sees here, but a faithful heart and spirit. *Tg.*'s interpretation may be based on the Masoretic *'ehad,* "one," associated with the cornerstone of the Jewish religion and the central theme of Jewish prayer, the *Šema',* "Hear O Israel, the Lord our God, the Lord is *'ehad,*" (Dt. 6:4).

^{11}According to the Tradition, the Shekinah, upon leaving the Sanctuary made a journey of ten stops, one of which was the Mount of Olives. This verse serves as proof-text. *Lam. R.* Pet. 25.

Notes, Chapter 12

^{1}MT: "house."

^{2}What were these? "R. Ammi in the name of Rab said, ... these are a light, a dish, and a mat." *b. Ned.* 40b.-41a. "R. Hiyya b. Abba said, A skin container, a mat, and a dish, and each serves a double purpose. The skin container he uses as a kneading trough and as a pillow. The dish he uses to eat and to drink. The mat is both for sitting on it and sleeping on it. R. Simeon b. Halafta said, This refers to a basket with four handles which can hold everything." *Lam. R.* 1:22.

^{3}The reference is to Zedekiah, who was blinded by Nebuchadnezzar (2K 25:7). The version of SP reflects the Rabbinic view enunciated in *m. Sot.* 1:7: "In the same measure in which one measures, so do they mete out to him." The Talmud expands upon this Mishnah, and the following one, which mentions Samson, who sinned with his eyes and therefore was blinded (Judg. 16:21); and Absalom, who gloried in his hair, and therefore was hanged by his hair (2 Sam. 18:9). How Zedekiah sinned with his eyes is not specified, but probably implied, that he followed his eyes in idolatrous practice. "The Rabbis taught: five were created with features that were superhuman, and all of them were smitten in those features; Samson in his strength, ... Saul in his neck ... Absalom in his hair ... Zedekiah in his eyes ... Asa in his feet." *b. Sot.* 10a. Cf. *AB,* p. 213.

the midst of the House of Israel. 25. For I the Lord will speak what I will speak, the word, and it shall be fulfilled; it shall never again be voided; for in your days, O rebellious *people,* I will speak the word, and I will fulfill it, says the Lord God." 26. The word of *prophecy from before* the Lord was with me, saying: 27. "Son of Adam, behold the House of Israel are saying, '*The teaching which he teaches*[4] is for many days hence, and he is prophesying for a time far off.' 28. Therefore, say to them, Thus says the Lord God, Never again shall any of My words be nullified; whatever word I speak shall be fulfilled, says the Lord God."

CHAPTER 13

1. The word of *prophecy from before* the Lord was with me, saying: 2. "Son of Adam, prophesy against the *false* prophets of Israel who are prophesing[a] and say to those who prophesy according to their own wishful thinking,[b] 'Hear the word of the Lord.' 3. Thus says the Lord God, Woe to the *false* prophets who are foolish, who follow the *fantasy[c] of their own minds,*[1] but who have seen nothing. 4. Like foxes in the ruins, have your *false* prophets been, O Israel.[2] 5. You *have not stood up for yourselves in the gates,* and *you have not performed good deeds for yourselves, to petition* for the House of Israel, to stand up *and pray for mercy on their behalf,* at the time when those who make war *came against them,* in the day of the Lord's *anger.*[3] 6. They prophesy falsehood, and they teach lies. They say, 'Says the Lord,' but the Lord has not sent them. Yet they *impudently insist* that their word will be fulfilled. 7. *Have you not prophesied false prophecies* and uttered a divination of lies by saying, 'Says the Lord,' when it was not spoken before Me?"[d] 8. Therefore, thus says the Lord God; "Because *you have prophesied* falsehood, and *you have taught* lies, on that account, behold I am *sending My anger*[4] against you, says the Lord God. 9. And *the striking power of My might*[5] shall be against the *false prophets who prophesy falsehood and who teach* lies; they shall not be among those who enjoy the *secret good which is hidden away* for My people; and in the inscription *for eternal life which is inscribed for the righteous* of the House of Israel, they shall not be inscribed;[6] and they shall not re-enter the land of Israel; and you shall know that I am the Lord God. 10. Because *they have prophesied falsehood* and because[7] they have led My people astray, saying, 'Peace,' when there is no peace, *they are like* one who builds a *flimsy* wall and plasters it with *plain* mud *not mixed with straw.*[8] 11. Say to him who builds a *flimsy* wall and plasters it with *plain* mud *not mixed with*

Apparatus, Chapter 13

[a] RB et al. SP and K: "foolish," "insane."
[b] Lit. "desire" or "will of their own minds."
[c] Lit. "imagination," "impure thoughts."

[d] RB, CR, and MM: "before the Lord."
[e] A. SP: "armpits."

straw, 'It shall fall.' Now, there shall be an overpowering deluge of rain, and hailstones shall come down, and a powerful windstorm shall split it; 12. and behold, when the wall falls, will it not be said, 'Where is the plaster with which you plastered it?' 13. Therefore, thus says the Lord God: I will bring *a king who is as mighty as* a powerful windstorm, in My fury, and *nations as murderous as* an overpowering deluge of rain shall come because of My anger, and *kingdoms which are as hard as* hailstones, in anger, to destroy it. 14. And I will break down the *the city in which you prophesied false prophecies,*[9] and will cast it to the ground, so that its foundation will be uncovered; it shall fall, and you shall be destroyed within it; and you shall know that I am the Lord. 15. Then My anger shall be accomplished on the *city* and on *the false prophets who prophesied false prophecies within it,*[10] and *it shall be said of you,* There is no *city* and *there are no false prophets,*[11] 16. the *false* prophets of Israel who were prophesying concerning Jerusalem and who were *leading her astray* with a doctrine of peace, when there was no peace," says the Lord God. 17. "And you, Son of Adam, *hear the prophecy*[T2] against the daughters of your people who are prophesying according to their own wishful thinking,[b] and prophesy against them. 18. And you shall say, Thus says the Lord God: Woe to them, to those women who sew black patches on all elbows[e] and make embroidered shawls to cover the heads of those of every stature, *for the destruction of lives.*[13] Are you able to destroy *or preserve* the lives of My people *when you cannot even* save your own lives? 19. You have defiled *My favor* for My people, for handfuls of barley and dishes of bread;[14] causing the

Notes, Chapter 12 continued

[4]MT: "the vision which he sees." Cf. *Tg.* on 7:26 *supra.*

Notes, Chapter 13

[1]MT: "who follow their own spirit."

[2]Like foxes, they seek only their own escape, not that of the people. *Ruth R.* Pet. 5.

[3]MT: "the Day of Yahweh." The *Tg.* here understands and correctly interprets the prophetic Day of Yahweh as a day of the Lord's wrath. Targumic exegesis on the entire verse is remarkable, transforming the military allusions allegorically, into expressions of prayer, pleas for justice, and living the righteous, ethical life; all this as it applies to the false prophets, who have not done these things as the true prophets would do. Rashi's comment follows along the same line.

[4]Note the *Tg.*'s use of anger as the agent of God.

[5]MT: "My hand." *Tg.* avoids the anthropomorphism.

[6]The theological thrust of *Tg.*'s exposition in expanding on the biblical text is impressive. The eschatological element of retribution against the wicked reflects the Pharisaic-Rabbinic basic religious belief. See G.F. Moore, *Judaism* vol. II, pp. 318 ff. Kimhi's comment reflects the *Tg.*

[7]Targumic exegesis interprets the double use of the word *ya'an* as implying two separate ideas, and renders the verse accordingly by expanding on the text. This is a consistent Targumic pattern. Cf. *Tg.* Ezek. 16:6-8, 23; 36:3, *infra.*

[8]MT: "and when he builds a wall, they daub it with whitewash."

[9]MT: "the wall that you have daubed with whitewash."

[10]MT: "on the wall and on those who daubed it with whitewash."

[11]MT: "and I will say to you, The wall is no more, nor are they who daubed it."

[12]MT: "set your face."

[13]MT: "to entrap souls."

[14]The Talmud cites this passage as evidence that women practiced witchcraft for a paltry fee. b. *'Erub.* 64b. The Midrash lays down the principle that true prophets of the Lord do not accept compensation for their prophecy. *Num. R.,* 10:5.

death those who do not deserve to die, *do you not put them to death?* And preserving the lives of those who do not deserve to live, *do you not keep keep them alive,* by your lying to My people, who listen to lies? 20. Therefore, thus says the Lord God: Behold I am *sending My anger* against the black patches by which you lead astray, *saying, with these we bewitch souls to destruction;*[15] I will remove them from your arms, and I will save the souls *which you bewitch, even their souls which were to be destroyed.* 21. And I will remove your embroidered shawls, and I will save My people from your hands; and no longer shall they be turned over to your hand to be finished off; and you shall know that I am the Lord. 22. Because you have made faint[f] the heart of the righteous leading him to become false, when he did not deserve reproach *before My Memra:* and you have strengthened the hands of the wicked, so as not to turn from his evil way to save his life; 23. therefore, you shall not prophesy falsehood, nor teach false doctrine any more, but I will save My people from your hand; and you shall know that I am the Lord."

CHAPTER 14

1. *The prophet said:* Men came to me, of the elders of Israel, and they sat before me. 2. And the word of *prophecy from before* the Lord was with me, saying: 3. "Son of Adam, these men have taken *the worship of* their idols into their hearts, and the stumbling block of their sins they have placed in front of them. Shall there be oracular inquiry of *My Memra* for them? 4. Therefore, *prophesy* to them, and say to them, Thus says the Lord God: Any man of the House of Israel who shall take into his heart *the worship of* his idols, and who shall place the stumbling block of his sins in front of him, yet shall come to the prophet, I the Lord will respond to him by *My Memra;* for he comes *in search of instruction from before Me, even though he is confounded* by his many idolatries; 5. in order *to bring the House of Israel near, to offer repentance in their hearts,*[1] for all of them have defected[2] from *My worship and have become unclean* by their idol *worship.* 6. Therefore, say to the House of Israel, Thus says the Lord God: return *to My worship,* and remove from yourselves *the worship of* your idols and put far away from your faces all *the sins* of your idolatrous abominations. 7. For anyone of the House of Israel or of the *proselytes who have embraced the Jewish faith,* who shall *deviate from My worship,* and shall take his idol *worship* into his heart, and shall place the stumbling block of his sins in front of his face; yet if he shall come to the prophet to inquire for himself of *My Memra,* I the Lord will respond to him, by *My Memra.* 8. I will *direct[a] My anger*[3] at that man and

Apparatus, Chapter 13 continued

[f] Or, "denounced."

Apparatus, Chapter 14

[a] Lit. "give."   [b] Lit. "false."

I will make him for a sign and by-words, and I will destroy him from the midst of My people Israel.[4] And you shall know that I am the Lord. 9. And if the prophet shall err speaking a word, I the Lord have misled that prophet and I will *raise the striking power of My might*[5] against him, and I will destroy him from the midst of My people Israel. 10. And they shall bear their guilt. The guilt of *the one who comes to learn but doesn't learn*,[6] shall be as the guilt of the *false* prophet, 11. so that the House of Israel shall no longer stray from following *My worship,* and they shall no longer be defiled with all their *rebellions;* but they shall be a people *before* Me, and I will be God for them, says the Lord God." 12. The word of *prophecy from before* the Lord was with me, saying: 13. "Son of Adam, if a land shall sin before Me by being faithless,[b] and I *raise the striking power of My might*[5] against it and break off within it the support of *food,* and send famine into it and destroy man and cattle therein, 14. and even if these three men were in it — Noah, Daniel, and Job[7] — they, by their merit, could save only their own lives, says the Lord God. 15. If I cause wild beasts to pass through the land, and they leave it in a state of bereavement, and it shall become a desolation, devoid of passers-by because of the wild beasts: 16. even if these three men were in it, as I live, says the Lord God, no sons or daughters would be saved, but these alone would be saved, and the land would become a desolation. 17. Or, if I will bring upon that land *those who slay by* the sword, and I say, *Those who slay by* the sword shall pass through the land, and I will destroy man and cattle therein: 18. and

Notes, Chapter 13 continued

[15] MT is extremely difficult. As it stands, it reads: "with which you trap the soul to make them fly." *Tg.* interprets this to mean to fly into perdition, or Gehenna, hence "to destruction." This accounts for *Tg.*'s rendering. This is also how Rashi understands it. For a critical analysis, cf. *AB*, p. 239 f.; *IB*, p. 132 f.; *ICC*, p. 145 ff.

Notes, Chapter 14

[1] MT: "to take hold of," "to catch."

[2] MT: "turned away," *Tg.* translates *disto,* "they have defected" or "deviated" in the religious sense, have become renegades. BDB maintains that in the *Tg.*, the root *sta'* means to apostatize, p. 962 sub *sut.* Cf. *The Complete Bible, An American Translation,* Ezek. 14:11.

[3] MT: "I will set My face."

[4] While the Hebrew insists that God himself will respond to the idolater, by-passing the prophet, even a true prophet, but especially one who is suspect, in *Tg.* it is the Memra which tends to this matter. From the standpoint of the Halakah, one cannot be a pagan and a Jew at one and the same time. He is either a total Jew, religiously speaking, or no professing Jew at all. The context of this chapter indicates that it is forbidden to the Jew even to harbor a thought of idolatry, thereby impinging upon his absolute faithfulness to the Lord God. See Maimonides, *Mishneh Torah, Sefer Hamada', Hilkot 'Avodat Kokabim,* Chapter 2, which gives a summation of the Tradition on this theme. Idolatry is so heinous a sin that when one professes it, it is tantamount to denying the entire Torah; but when one rejects it, it is tantamount to professing the entire Torah. See especially, Maimonides, *loc. cit.,* 2:3, 4.

[5] MT: "I will stretch out My hand."

[6] MT: "the one who inquires."

[7] Noah, Daniel, and Job are cited as paragons of righteousness by Ezekiel, probably because they were not only known to the Jews, but were equally prominent among the Babylonians, although the names vary. The great flood, in which Noah plays the dominant role in the Hebrew sources, was a popular epic in Sumer and Akkad. Daniel is a hero of the Ras Shamra inscriptions as a righteous man; even in our Ezek. text *dan'el* the *Ket.* is without the *yod,* although the *Q.* is *Daniel,* with *hireq.* Job, even according to Jewish sources, is regarded as a Gentile prophet, *b. B.B.* 15b, and by some as having lived during the Babylonian Exile (15a). In any case, they would be familiar to the contemporaries of Ezekiel in Babylon. Jer. 15:1 mentions Moses and Samuel as the two giants of righteousness who would be unable to save the Jewish community from destruction, in a similar frame of reference as we have here in Ezekiel.

S.S.R. 2:15 regards the three men in this v. as having a modicum of intercessory power. For a critical appraisal, cf. *AB*, p. 257 f.

these three men were in the midst of it, as I live, says the Lord God, they shall not save sons and daughters but only they alone would be saved. 19. Or, if I will send pestilence upon that land and pour out My fury upon it *by slaying,*[8] destroying man and cattle from it, 20. and Noah, Daniel, and Job were in it, as I live, says the Lord God, they could save neither son nor daughter; they, by their merit,[c] would save only their own lives." 21. For thus says the Lord God, "All the more, when I send upon Jerusalem four terrible punishments, the sword, famine, wild beasts and pestilence;[9] to destroy man and cattle from her. 22. But behold, if there remain in her a remnant who escape, with sons and daughters who can be led out, and they come out to you; and you shall see their ways and their deeds, and shall be comforted for the evil which I have brought upon Jerusalem, for all that I have brought upon it. 23. They shall comfort you when you see their ways and their deeds, and you shall know that not for naught[d] have I done all that I have done in it," says the Lord God.

CHAPTER 15

1. The word of *prophecy form before* the Lord was with me, saying: 2. "Son of Adam, *what is different*[1] about the vine-bush from all other twig-trees that are among the trees of the forest? 3. Can they take of it wood, to use for work? Can they take of it a peg to hang any vessel on it? 4. Behold, it is delivered to the fire to be destroyed; when the fire has consumed both of its ends, and the middle of it is charred, will it be fit for use? 5. Behold, when it was whole it was not fit for use, how much less, when the fire has consumed it and it is charred, can it still be fit for use? 6. Therefore, thus says the Lord God: Like the vine-bush among the trees of the forest, which I have delivered to the fire to be destroyed, so have I delivered the inhabitants of Jerusalem. 7. I will *inflict My punishment upon them.*[2] *They have transgressed the words of Torah which were given from the midst of the fire;*[3] *therefore, nations who are as violent*[a] *as fire, will destroy them.*[4] So, you shall know that I am the Lord when *My anger is accomplished*[b] on them. 8. And I will make the land a desolation, because they have acted faithlessly,[c] says the Lord God."

Apparatus, Chapter 14 continued

[c] Or, "righteousness."

[d] Or, "without cause," "in vain."

Apparatus, Chapter 15

[a] Lit. "strong."
[b] Lit. "takes effect."

[c] Lit. "falsely."

Apparatus, Chapter 16

[a] R adds "preceding you."

CHAPTER 16

1. The word of *prophecy from before* the Lord was with me saying, 2. "Son of Adam, admonish[1] *the inhabitants*[2] *of* Jerusalem and show them their abominations. 3. And say, Thus says the Lord God to *the inhabitants of* Jerusalem: The place of your sojourn[3] and your birthplace are of the land of the Canaanites. *There I revealed Myself to Abraham your father between the pieces of the covenant–offering, and I made known to him that you would go down to Egypt; that with a raised-up arm I would redeem you and by the Merit of your Fathers*[a] *I would drive out the Amorites from before you, and destroy the Hittites.*[4] 4. *And also, when your forefathers went down to Egypt, they were sojourners in a land not their own. The Congregation of Israel was enslaved and oppressed. It was like a new-born child who is abandoned in*

Notes, Chapter 14 continued

[8]MT: "with blood."
[9]Cf. Rev. 9:13 ff.

Notes, Chapter 15

[1]Targum simplifies in its own words the unusual syntactical structure of MT, thus providing it with an uncomplicated meaning.
[2]MT: "I will set My face against them." *Tg.* avoids the anthropomorphism of God's face.
[3]Cf. Ex. 19:18.
[4]"Said R. Judah quoting Rab, Fire will consume anyone who departs from the words of the Torah, as it is said, I will set My face against them: they came forth out of the fire and the fire shall consume them (Ezek. 15:7) ... R. Jonathan said, Whoever separates himself from the words of the Torah will fall into Gehinnom (hell)." *b. B.B.* 79a. "The words of the Torah are compared to fire; both were given by God and both are eternal." *Sifre, Deut., Berakah*, 343. "When Scripture refers to the kingdoms of the nations metaphorically, it compares them to fire only, as it is written, ... fire shall consume them (Ezek. 15:7)." *S.S.R.* 2:37.

Notes, Chapter 16

[1]*'owkh*, a Hebraism from the root *ykh*, used here in the Afel, corresponding to the Hebrew Hiphil. See BDB, pp. 406-7; Jastrow, I, p. 577. *Tg.*'s influence: this ch. known as *tokahat yerušalaim. t. Meg.* 4:34.
[2]*Tg.* expands on MT by referring to the people rather than to the city itself, possibly because it feels that Jerusalem is sacred whereas its people are sinners. Cf. 15:6 *supra*.
[3]*Tg.* reads *megurayk* for the Masoretic *mekorotayk*, "your origin."
[4]MT: "your father was an Amorite and your mother a Hittite." *zekut 'abot*, Merit of the Fathers, here based on Gen 15:17-18, a popular theological concept among the Sages, who believe that God would show special favor to the Jews by virtue of the mutual affection and promises between Him and the patriarchs, based on Ex. 32:11; Lev. 6:42. *passim. b. Šab.* 30a; *Tanhuma, Wayyera,* 9; *Pes. Rab.* 10:9, 40:5, 44:9. *Pirqe d'R. Eliezer,* 48, *passim.* Cf. G.F. Moore, *Judaism,* vol. I, pp. 536 f.

the field;[5] whose umbilical cord was not cut, and who has not been washed with water to cleanse him, and who has not been rubbed with salt, nor wrapped in swaddling clothes. 5. The eye *of Pharaoh* had no pity on you, to do even one good thing for you, to sigh for you *because of your servitude,* to have compassion upon you; *but he decreed upon you a decree of extermination, to throw your male children into the Nile,*[6] *to destroy you,* at the time that you were in Egypt. 6. *And the memory of the covenant of your forefathers came in before Me, so I revealed Myself in order to redeem you,* for it was revealed before Me that you were oppressed by your servitude[7] and I said to you, By the blood *of the circumcision I will have pity on you;* and I said to you: By the blood of the *Passover lambs*[b] *will I redeem you.*[8] 7. I made you a myriad, as the plants of the field, *and you became numerous and strong, you became families and tribes; and because of the good deeds of your forefathers, the time had come for the redemption of your congregation, because you were enslaved and oppressed.* 8. So I revealed *Myself to Moses in the thorn-bush, because it was revealed before Me that* the time *of your redemption had come;* and I protected you *by My Memra, and I* removed your *sins;* and I swore *by My Memra to redeem you,* as I had sworn *to your forefathers,* says the Lord God, so that you might become *a people serving before Me.* 9. *So I redeemed you from the servitude of the Egyptians, and I removed their terrible tyranny from you, and led you into freedom.*[9] 10. Then I clothed you in embroidered garments, *from the precious things of your enemies;* and I put costly shoes on your feet. And *I consecrated priests from among you that they may serve before Me* in linen *headgear, and the high priest* in colorful *vestments.* 11. *I improved*[10] *you by the perfection of the words of the Torah, inscribed on two stone tablets, and given by the hands of Moses; and I sanctified you by the holiness of My great name.* 12. *I placed the ark of My covenant among you, with My cloud of glory covering you, and an angel, sent from before Me, leading the way ahead of you.* 13. *And I placed My tabernacle in your midst,* set with gold and silver and a curtain of linen and colored cloth and embroidery. And I fed you *with manna which was as good as* fine flour and honey and oil. *And you waxed rich and became very very powerful. I made you prosper and I gave you dominion over all kingdoms.*[11] 14. Then, *O Congregation of Israel,* your renown went forth among the nations because of your beauty, for My glory which I had bestowed upon you, was perfect, says the Lord God. 15. But you trusted in your beauty, and you went astray because of your renown and you joined, with all passers-by, *to worship idols; although it was not proper*[12] *for you to do so.* 16. You took some of your garments and made for yourself high places covered with embroidered veils *and you worshipped idols on them,*

Apparatus, Chapter 16 continued

[b]SP. All other versions have sing., "lamb."

which was not proper nor was it fitting. 17. And you took your precious vessels of My gold and My silver which I had given you, and you made for yourself male images and went astray with them. 18. And you took your embroidered garments and covered them, and My oil and My fragrant incense you placed before them. 19. And My *good things* which I had given you — the fine flour, the oil and the honey

Notes, Chapter 16 continued

[5]The Targumic exegesis, which understands this ch. as poetic allegory, is a remarkable exposition interpolated into MT, designed to counteract the prophetic denunciation of Israel as a worthless piece of brush by its very nature (Ezek. 15:5), and Jerusalem as an offshoot of the Amorites and Hittites in v. 3. Instead, it harks back to the biblical story of Abraham, and the promise of redemption from Egyptian slavery, the invocation of the Merit of the Fathers to drive out the Amorites and the Hittites to make way for Israel. The skill in tying together the MT after these intrusions, in using a word here and there in MT as a springboard for its Midrashic interpretation, is indicative of *Tg.*'s exegetical genius, an amazing feat of the use of Scripture, which continues throughout the chapter.

In the MT the denunciation of Jerusalem is so fierce and so frightening that R. Eliezer, a Shammaite and staunch nationalist, disciple of R. Johanan b. Zakkai at Yavneh, forbids this chapter to be read as Haftarah. *m. Meg.* 4:10. The Halakah is contrary to R. Eliezer: that the chapter may be read in the Hebrew, but only with the accompanying Targum! The Gemara records an incident in which a certain man did read this passage in the synagogue in the presence of R. Eliezer, who said to him, "as long as you are investigating the abominations of Jerusalem, go and investigate the abominations of your mother." They investigated this man and found him to be illegitimate. *b. Meg.* 25b. Cf. *t. Meg.* 4:34; *y. Meg.* 75c.

The Rabbinic exposition on this passage, dealing with the dispute with R. Eliezer and his point of view that this chapter may not be read as Haftarah, and the Halakah that it may be read but with the Targum, would indicate some support for my contention that *Tg.* Ezek. was redacted at Yavneh, where they probably included the historic passages to bolster the Jewish morale after the detruction of the Temple in 70 C.E. In actual synagogal practice, this chapter is not used in the worship service.

For a critical view of this passage, see *AB*, pp. 292 ff., where *Tg.* vv. 3-13 are cited (p. 302), and referred to for the "fantastic length" to which it went in its historical interpretation of the Scriptural text.

[6]*benahara'.* The word has the basic meaning of "the river," but in the context of Egypt it always means the Nile, *hay'or* always rendered thus in *Tg.*, Onq. Gen. 41:1, 2, 3, 17, 18; Ex. 1:22; *passim*. Rashi's comment on Gen. 41:1 is interesting: "None of the other rivers are called *y'orim* except the Nile, because the entire country consists of man-made irrigation ditches, and the Nile rises in the midst of it and supplies them with water." Nahmanides cites Rashi, but points out that Onqelos (sic) translates *ye'o rehem* (Ps. 78:44) as *'rytehon*, "their channels," to distinguish them from the natural rivers.

[7]MT: "thrashing in your blood."

[8]MT: "in your blood, live ... in your blood, live."

Targumic exegesis finds a hidden meaning in the repetition of the phrase "in your blood, live." The first time it is used, *Tg.* interprets as referring to the blood of the covenant, circumcision, which evokes God's mercy. The second refers to the blood of the Passover sacrifice, which evokes God's redemption of Israel from Egyptian bondage. Thus circumcision and the Passover are linked together into a bond of love and compassion, which makes God's involvement in the redemptive procsss inevitable. The pl. in SP's version could be an anti-Christian thrust against the designation of Jesus as *the* lamb of God (John 1:29, 36; Rev. 5:6, *passim,* especially 12:11), and against Paul's denigration of the rite of circumcision (Romans chs. 2-4). See *Mekilta, Pisha,* 5, Lauterbach, I. p. 33f; *Ex. R.* 17:3, and especially 19:5: "The blood of the Passover lamb blended with the blood of circumcision." Also *Num. R.* 14:12; *passim*. Critically speaking, the repetition is probably a scribal dittography. LXX omits the second part. V reads as MT.

[9]MT: "and I bathed you with water, and washed the blood from you, and anointed you with oil."

Rashi's comment is worthy of note: "The entire theme is nothing but allegory, and Targum Jonathan explains it all, and there is no need to add to what the Targum has to say." Then Rashi proceeds to quote the entire Targum from v. 3 through v. 12. Rashi on v. 9.

[10]The verb, *tqn* in the Pa'el, as in the Hebrew Pi'el, has the force of "making perfect" that which is imperfect. Cf. paragraph 2 of the *'Alenu* prayer, "to perfect the world under the Kingdom of the Almighty." See Hertz, *Daily Prayer Book,* pp. 210-11.

[11]MT (vv. 11-13): "And I decked you with ornaments, put bracelets on your arms and a necklace around your neck. And I put a ring on your nose, and earrings in your ears, and a beautiful crown on your head. You were adorned with gold and silver, and your garments were of linen, silk, and embroidery. You ate of fine flour, and honey, and oil. You became very, very beautiful, and you advanced to royalty."

[12]*kašar*, "ritually permissible." *Tg.* takes the difficult Hebrew *lo yehi* and reads it as a negative *lo' yehi* "it should not have been," and renders it, "it was not proper to do so." This was possibly on the basis of the negative in v. 16.

which I had fed you — and you set them before them as *ritual offerings.*[13] *Wasn't all this so,*[14] says the Lord God. 20. *How you have greatly increased the anger before Me, O Congregation of Israel, in that* you have led your sons and your daughters, *from whom were destined to come out a generation sacred before Me,* and these you slaughtered to them *as ritual sacrifices. Was your idolatry so insufficient in your eyes,* 21. that you had to slaughter the children by offering them, by passing them through[15] to them. 22. And with all the sins of your abominations and your *idolatries,* you[16] did not remember the former days when you were *homeless and abandoned,* when you were *oppressed in your servitude.*[17] 23. What will be your end, for all your wickedness? O prophet, say to her, Woe unto you *that you have sinned;*[c18] woe unto you[19] *that you have not repented,* says the Lord God. 24. You have built for yourself heathen altars, and made for yourself high places in every street. 25. At the head of every cross-road you built your high places, *and you profaned your holiness,* and you *associated yourself* with anyone who passed by, *to worship idols,* and you increased your *idols.* 26. And *you strayed* after the sons of Egypt, your neighbor, overgrown with flesh; increasing *your idols* to cause anger before Me.[20.] 27. Now behold, I *have raised the striking power of My might* against you, and have *withheld your good,* and have turned you over to the hand of your enemies — the Philistine *cities, who, if I had sent My prophets to them, would have submitted; but you have not turned from your ways in the counsel of sinners.* 28. And you *strayed* after the sons of Assyria *because you would not know the Torah,* and you went astray with them, and also *you knew not repentance.*[21] 29. And you increased you *idolatry* by associating yourself with the *merchant people,*[d22] *going according to the religions[e] of* the Chaldeans; and also in this, *you knew not the Torah.* 30. How strong was the wickedness of your heart, says the Lord God, in your doing all these things, *like* the deeds of a woman prostitute who thinks she is supreme, 31. By building your heathen altar at the head of every cross-road; your high places you have made in every street; yet you were not like the harlot who profits from her hire. 32. The *Congregation of Israel is like* a woman who *is beloved of* her husband, *yet is faithless to him; she forsakes her husband* and goes astray after strangers. 33. They give reward to every harlot, but you please all your lovers with your rewards, by bribing them to come to you from all around *with your idolatries.* 34. In your *idolatries,* you were different from other *countries, O Congregation of Israel;* and after you, there was none who strayed like you; in that you gave reward while no reward was given to you; so you were different. 35. Therefore, *because her deeds were like*[23] a harlot, *O Congregation of Israel,* hear the word of the Lord. 36. Thus says the Lord God: Because your shame was revealed, and your disgrace was made visible, in that you strayed after your lovers, and for all the sins of your *worship of* idolatrous abominations, and the sin of the blood of your children whom you *slaughtered* for them, 37. therefore, behold, I will gather all your lovers in whom you have delighted to go astray after them; and all those whom you loved, together with those whom you

Apparatus, Chapter 16 continued

[c] SP: "for all that you have sinned."
[d] R and RB. SP: "people of the land of Canaan."

[e] Or, "laws," "practices."
[f] RB. SP's *mitrin,* "rains," is a scribal error.

hated; and I will gather them unto you from round about, and I will uncover your *shame*[24] to them, and they shall see all your *disgrace.*[24] 38. And I will *exact punishment from* you, the *punishment* for adulteresses and for shedding blood; and I will turn you over *to be slain* in anger and *fury.*[25] 39. And I will turn you over into their hands, and they shall break through *your wall* and demolish your high places; and they shall strip from you your costly garments and remove from you your fine ornaments and they shall forsake you, *homeless and abandoned.*

40. And they shall bring up encampments of soldiers[f] against you and they shall pelt you *with stone of a sling,* and they shall cut you to pieces with their swords. 41. And they shall burn your houses with fire and they shall inflict *just punishment* upon you in the sight of many *countries;*[26] and I will put an end to your being *like* a harlot, and you shall no longer give out reward. 42. And I will discontinue My fury against you, and My jealousy shall depart from you. I will *end it,*[27] and My anger shall be no more. 43. Because you have not remembered the days of yore; but you have angered Me with all those things; even though I have visited upon your head punishment for your ways, says the Lord God, you have not taken for yourself counsel to repent for all your abominations. 44. Behold, everyone who uses proverbs, will apply this proverb to you, saying, Like *the deeds of* the mother so, too, the daughter. 45. *Why have you been* the daughter *of the land of Canaan, doing according to the deeds of a*

Notes, Chapter 16 continued

[13] MT: "for a pleasing odor." Cf. *Tg.* Ezek. 6:13 and n. 8 thereto, *supra.*

[14] The positive *wayyehi,* rendered as a negative question, which the Aramaic has a tendency to do. It is more forceful and more applicable, from the standpoint of exegesis.

[15] *bea'bara,* a literal rendering of the Masoretic *beha'abyr,* the meaning of which is, passing the children through the fire as a sacrifice to Molech. See Lev. 18:21; Dt. 18:10.

[16] *Tg.* prefers the Q. 2fs. Ket. reads ls. which Kimḥi interprets as referring to God: "I did not remind you during the days of your youth (when I was kind to you), that in the future you would sin, but I had compassion on you during the days of your youth." Rabbinic theology maintains that God is merciful even though He knows that the individual may in the future become unworthy. "Said R. Isaac: God judges a man only according to his deeds up to that time (and not what he may do later)." *b. R. H.* 16b.

[17] MT: "when you were naked and bare, were thrashing in your blood."

[18] SP adds "all," but the beautiful cadence of the Aramaic comes across better in RB, which omits "all."

[19] Here again we see the *Tg.* finding significance in the Masoretic repetition, "Woe, woe" and elaborating the meaning.

[20] MT (vv 25b, 26): "you made your beauty abominable by spreading your legs for anyone who passed by, increasing your harlotry; and you played the harlot with the Egyptians, your neighbors large of phallus, increasing your harlotry, thereby provoking Me to anger."

These vv. provide a remarkably excellent example of how the vivid sexual symbolism of MT is transformed by *Tg.* into manifestations of idolatry.

[21] MT (vv. 27, 8): "So, behold, I stretched out My hand against you, and diminished your allotment, and delivered you to the will of your enemies, the daughters of the Philistines, who were ashamed of your lewd conduct. So you played the harlot with the Assyrians, because you were insatiable: but even whoring with them, you remained unsatisfied." *Tg.* points to Torah and repentance as modes of true contentment.

[22] Rashi explains that "Canaan" means "merchant" in MT. For use in *Tg.*, see Jastrow, I, p. 650, sub *kna'ni.* In LXX: some MSS. omit "Canaan."

[23] Throughout these verses, *Tg.* modifies MT by interpreting the harlot as a simile, and harlotry as an allegorical reference to idolatry. So, too, the faithless wife in v. 32. Cf. *Mek. Bahodesh,* 8 (Lauterbach, II, p. 262f.).

[24] MT: "your nakedness."

[25] MT: "I will judge you according to the judgments pertaining to adulteresses and women who shed blood, and I will make you bloody in anger and jealousy."

[26] MT: "women."

[27] MT: "I will be quiet."

people whose parents with their children were banished? And *why have you been* the sister of *Sodom and Gomorrah, whose parents with their children were thrown out? Was not* your mother *Sarah living among* the Hittites, *and yet did not do according to their deeds?* And was not your father *Abraham, among* the Amorites, *and yet did not walk in their counsel?*[28] 46. Your older sister is Samaria *and its suburbs,* situated to the left (north) of you, and the sister younger than you, which is situated to your right (south) is Sodom and *its suburbs.* 47. If you had walked in their ways and performed according to their abominations your sin would have been minor; but rather you were more corrupt than they in all your ways. 48. As I live, says the Lord God, your sister Sodom and *its suburbs* had not done as you and *your suburbs* have done. 49. Behold this was the sin of your sister Sodom; they were arrogant; it and *its suburbs* had plenty of bread, tranquility and peace, but the hand of the poor and the needy it did not support.[29] 50. And it became haughty and committed abomination before Me, so that I drove them out, when this became apparent to Me. 51. Samaria was not guilty of half your sins but you committed more abominations than they; you made your sisters seem righteous by all the abomination which you have committed. 52. Also, you must suffer the humiliation which you sought for your sisters; because you were guilty of committing abominations worse than theirs, they have become more worthy than you.   You should be ashamed of yourself and suffer your humiliation, because you made your sisters seem righteous. 53. I will bring back their people to them: the people of Sodom and *its suburbs;* the people of Samaria and *its suburbs;* and I will bring back the exile of your people along with them; 54. so that you may suffer your humiliation and be ashamed for all that you have done, when you comfort them. 55. Then your sister Sodom and *its suburbs* shall return to their former state; and you and *your suburbs* shall return to your former state. 56. Was not your sister Sodom a *lesson* in your mouth, in the heyday of your greatness, 56. before your wickedness was revealed? Now, that the *villages* of Aram and all of its surroundings have been put to shame, the *villages* of the Philistines, who dispised you, from all sides. 58. You must accept the guilt of your sinful *counsel* and *the worship* of your abominations, says the Lord. 59. Thus says the Lord God, I will *punish you* according to what you have done in that you have despised the oath by *altering* the covenant. 60. Yet I, for My part, will remember My covenant with you of former days and I will establish an everlasting covenant with you. 61. And you shall remember your ways and be humbled, when you *wage war against countries that are mightier than you, together with those that are smaller than you, and I hand them over to you to surrender,*[30] *even though you did not observe the Torah.*[31] 62. Then shall I establish My covenant with you, and you shall know that I am the Lord. 63. In order that you may remember and be ashamed, and never again speak arrogantly,[g] because you will have been humbled, when I forgive you for all that you have done, says the Lord God."[32]

Apparatus, Chapter 16 continued

[g] Lit., "have arrogance in the words of your mouth."

CHAPTER 17

1. The word of *prophecy from before* the Lord was with me, saying: 2. "Son of Adam, compose a riddle and draw a parable concerning the house of Israel. 3. And say, Thus says the Lord God, A great eagle with large wings and long pinions, its plumage like embroidery, came to the Lebanon, and took a branch of the lofty cedar.[1] 4. He took its topmost twig and carried it to *a land which was not subject to servitude, like*[2] the land of Canaan *before the House of Israel had entered it,* and placed it in a city of merchants. 5. And he took of the seed of the land and placed it in a fertile field, that its shoot might take seed beside abundant waters; he made it a choice vine. 6. So it sprouted and became a mighty vine, short in height so that its branches would turn to it and its roots would be under it. And it became a vine and

Notes, Chapter 16 continued

[28] *Tg.* transforms the MT, so that the proverb in v. 44 loses its force, affirming that though the populace acts like its mother, Canaan, and sister, Sodom (and Gomorrah), it need not have been so. The Matriarch and the Patriarch were not infected by the paganism of the Hittites and Amorites among whom they sojourned. So, in reality, Israel was not the child of Sarah and Abraham, as it should have been, but its deeds followed the heathen of the land instead. But cf. *b. Sanh.* 44b, which takes MT literally.

[29] Cf. *Pirq. de R. El.* ch. 25. *b. Sanh.* 104b. *Num. R.* 9:24.

[30] MT: "when you take your big sisters with those who are smaller than you, and I give them to you as daughters." The Targumic interpolation refers to a future expansion of the boundaries of Judaea, so that it would include Samaria and Sodom and possibly other territory as well. The reference could conceivably reflect the historical situation during the period of Hasmonean consolidation of their military successes against the Seleucids, 165-104 B.C.E., and the establishment of the second Judaean state.

[31] MT: "but not because of your covenant."
Tg. equates Torah with covenant. The observance of Torah is the indispensable condition of living by the covenant. This reflects Yavnian reconstruction of Jewish life.

[32] It is good Rabbinic theology that if one is ashamed of his sins, he is on the road to repentance and God will forgive him. A statement by Rabbah b. Ḥinena the Elder, in the name of Rab, cites this v. in Ezek. as the proof-text for his observation: "Whoever commits one act of transgression, and is ashamed of it, God forgives him for all of his sins." *b. Ber.* 12b. The impact of this v. is so powerful that it prompts R. Joshua b. Levi to remark: "If the entire book of Ezekiel had not been written, but only the verse in which God says, That you may remember and be ashamed ... then I will forgive you for all that you have done, it would have been sufficient." *Mid. Teh.* 31:3.

Notes, Chapter 17

[1] The parable deals with the historical scene towards the end of the kingdom of Judah. The great eagle represents King Nebuchadrezzar (cf. Jer. 48:40; 49:22); the Lebanon is the land of Israel (Kimhi); the cedar is the Davidic dynasty (cf. Jer. 22:5-6); the topmost twig is King Jehoiachin; and the city of merchants is Babylon (cf. Ezek. 16:29). Ezekiel was an eyewitness to these events, including the captivity of Jehoiachin, in which he was one of the captives; the vassal-king, Zedekiah (depicted as the lowly seed in v. 5); the breaking of the vow of loyalty to Babylon and the conspiracy with Egypt, leading to the Exile of 586 B.C.E., all of which is related by allegorical symbolism in this chapter, and interpreted, in the second half of the chapter.

[2] By emendation, *kaf* instead of *bet,* following Kimhi's explanation of the *Tg. Tg.* retains MT's *kena'an,* but by exegetical complement explains it as an illustration of Babylonia's fierce independence, unconquered and not subject to any other nation, just as the land of Canaan was before the Hebrew conquest. LXX, V, and S all follow MT retaining *kena'an,* but obviously the reference is to Babylon, which the *Tg.* ingeniously explains.

produced twigs and sent forth branches. 7. But there was one[3] great eagle,[4] with large wings, and abundant plumage; and behold, this vine bent[5] its roots towards him, and sent out its branches towards him, to water it from the bed of its planting. 8. In a fertile field by abundant waters was it planted, to produce foliage and to bear fruit and to become a mighty vine. 9. Say, Thus says the Lord God, can it thrive?[a] Will he not break off its roots, and strip off its fruit, so that all of its sprouting leaves shall wither and become useless?[b] And not with *many armies*[6] or many people shall they come to pull it up from its roots. 10. But behold, even though it is planted, can it thrive? Will it not wither completely when the east wind comes near it? It will dry up on the bed where it is planted." 11. The word of *prophecy from before* the Lord was with me, saying, 12. "Say now to the rebellious people, Do you not know what these are? Say, Behold, the king of Babylon came to Jerusalem and seized its king and its princes and carried them off with him, to Babylon. 13. And he took of the seed of royalty and made a covenant with him, and brought him into it by an oath. The nobles of the land he carried off, 14. so that it should be a weak kingdom, that it should not become great, and so that he should keep his covenant to *be subservient to him.*[c7] 15. But he rebelled against him by sending his messengers to Egypt, to give him horses and a large force of people. Can he succeed? Should one who does these things be spared?[d] 16. As I live, says the Lord God, surely in the very place of the king who appointed him king, whose oath he disdained and whose covenant with him he violated, in the midst of Babylon he shall die. 17. Not with a great army and with a force of many people will Pharaoh fight a war alongside of him,[e] when mounds are thrown up and siege towers are erected, to destroy many *provinces.*[8] 18. He scorned an oath, thereby violating a covenant, yet behold, he extended his hand *to Pharaoh*. He did all these things. He shall not be spared. 19. Therefore, thus says the Lord God, As I live, it was My oath that he scorned, and it was My covenant that he violated, so I shall visit upon his head *the punishment of his way.* 20. I will spread My net over him and he shall be caught in My snare, and I will exile him to Babylon and there will I *exact payment* from him for his perfidy which he committed[f] towards Me. 21. And all the *valiant men*[9] *of all his armies* shall be slain by the sword, and those who remain shall be scattered in all directions; and you shall know that I the Lord, *have decreed it by My Memra."* 22. Thus says the Lord God, "I Myself will bring near *a child from the kingdom of the house of David*[10] which is likened to the lofty cedar, *and I will establish him from among his children's children; I will anoint and establish him by My Memra* on[g] a high and exalted mountain. 23. On the *holy* mountain of Israel will I *establish him, and he shall gather together armies and build fortresses and become a mighty king;* and *all the righteous shall rely upon him, and all the humble* shall dwell in the shade *of his kingdom.*[11] 24. And all *the kings of the nations* shall know that I the Lord *have humbled the kingdom which was mighty and*

Apparatus, Chapter 17

[a] Or "prosper."
[b] Or "superfluous."
[c] Lit. "to serve him."
[d] Or "saved."

[e] Lit. "with him."
[f] Lit. "his falsehood which he dealt falsely."
[g] All versions except SP, who reads: "like."

Apparatus, Chapter 18

[a] MM: "our fathers."

have made mighty the kingdom which was weak. I have humbled the kingdom of the nations which was mighty as a green tree, and *have made mighty the kingdom of the House of Israel, which had been as weak as* a dried-up tree. I the Lord, *have decreed it by My Memra and I* will fulfill it."[12]

CHAPTER 18

1. The word of *prophecy from before* the Lord was with me, saying: 2. "What is it with you that you quote this proverb concerning the land of Israel, saying, *'The[a] fathers have sinned and the children have been punished?'*[1] 3. As I live, says the Lord

Notes, Chapter 17 continued

[3]LXX, V, and S read *'aher,* "another." *Tg.* follows MT, *'ehad,* "one."

[4]This other great eagle was the king of Egypt, to whom Zedekiah turned for help. Jer. 37:7, 44:30.

[5]We have here an interesting linguistic situation. MT has *kafnah,* which BDB takes as an Aramaism, in the sense of hungering for. (p. 495 sub *kfn*). *Tg.* renders it *kft,* from *kuf,* "to bend," but *kfn* in Aramaic also has the meaning "to bend," as well as "to hunger." See Jastrow, I, p. 660 sub *kfn* I.

[6]MT: "a strong arm."

[7]*Tg.* reads *l'abdoh* for MT's *l'amdah,* "to stand."

[8]MT: "souls."

[9]*Tg.* reads *mibeharaw,* for MT's *miberahaw,* "his fugitives." So, too, S.

[10]This is a striking instance of the manner in which *Tg.* Ezek. avoids mentioning the usual Targumic title *mešiha',* by which the Messiah is designated, hence my contention that *Tg.* Ezek. is *exegetically* non-Messianic. There can be no doubt that in the Hebrew text the Davidic line is poetically symbolized by the lofty cedar, as in vv. 3 and 4 *supra.* Kimhi identifies the person poetically referred to in this v. as Zerubbabel, son of Shealtiel, son of Jehoiakin, of Davidic lineage, who assumed the post of governor of Judaea by the edict of the Persian rulers. Zerubbabel was regarded as a Messianic figure by the prophet Zechariah (4:7). Kimhi concludes, "There are some who interpret this passage as referring to the Messiah, and this appears to be the opinion of Targum Jonathan who translates etc. etc." Rashi sees this as a Messianic reference.

For a suggested explanation of this strange reluctance of *Tg.* Ezek. to designate the Messiah as such, see S.H. Levey, *The Messiah: An Aramaic Interpretation,* pp. 78 ff. A later, somewhat different analysis, and the one to which I still subscribe, is found in my article, "The Targum to Ezekiel," *HUCA* vol. 46, pp. 139 ff.

The earlier Rabbinic sources are strangely, almost mysteriously, silent concerning these verses as harbingers of a Messianic message. Of the earlier versions of the Bible only V finds this to be outrightly Messianic, and so interpreted by Jerome.

IB tends to regard the passage as eschatological, and questions its Messianic implications! p. 156.

[11]MT: "On the mountain height of Israel will I plant it, and it shall put forth branches and bear fruit, and become a noble cedar; and all birds of every wing shall dwell under it; they shall dwell in the shade of its branches."

[12]MT: "And all the trees of the field shall know that I the Lord have brought low the high tree, and have raised high the low tree; I have dried up the green tree, and made the dry tree to bloom. I, the Lord, have spoken, and I will do it."

Notes, Chapter 18

[1]MT: "the fathers have eaten sour grapes, and the children's teeth are set on edge." *Tg.* does not bother translating the proverb literally, but immediately gives its essence and meaning in the theological terms in which Ezekiel's contemporaries used and understood it. The substance of it is the self-exculpation on the part of the populace, attributing the blame for the catastrophe which has befallen them, not to their own shortcomings but to the sins of their ancestors. Jeremiah cites the same proverb (31:29 which *Tg.* Jer. renders exactly as *Tg.* Ezek.), which was obviously current in Jerusalem, but has also been exported to Babylon among the exiles, where Ezekiel had to cope with it. Both he and Jeremiah fiercely object to this primitive concept that guilt is transmitted from one generation to another, and both proceed to eliminate it as a moral and religious principle. The proverb itself was probably used by the populace as a fatalistic philosophy to avoid the admonitions of the prophets and their call to repentance.

God, you shall never again have this proverb quoted in Israel. 4. Behold, all souls are Mine. Before Me, as the soul of the father so is the soul of his son: the person who sins, he alone shall die. 5. If a man is righteous and does what is lawfully right and meritorious, 6. on the mountains *he has not worshipped idols,*[2] and has not lifted up his eyes to the idol worship of the House of Israel; and he has not defiled his neighbor's wife, and has not approached a menstruous woman; 7. who did not oppress anyone; who has returned the pledge on a debt; and has not committed robbery; and who has given of his bread to the hungry, and clothed the naked with his own garment; 8. who has not given money on interest, nor taken usury; who has withheld his hand from falsehood; who has practiced true justice between man and man; 9. who has walked in My statutes and has observed My laws by acting truthfully: he is righteous; he shall surely live, says the Lord God. 10. Now, he may have begotten a son who is wicked, who sheds blood, and does to his brother[3] any one of these things; 11. even though he himself has done none of these things. Rather, the son *worships idols* on the mountains, and defiles his neighbor's wife; 12 he has oppressed the poor and the needy; he has committed robbery; he has not returned the pledge; and he has lifted up his eyes to idolatry; he has committed an abomination. 13. He has given money on interest and has taken usury; shall he survive?[4] He shall not survive. He has committed all these abominations, he shall surely die; *he alone is to blame for his violent death.*[b][5] 14. And behold, he has begotten a son who saw all the sins which his father had committed; who saw,[6] but did not imitate them. 15. He has not *worshipped idols* on the mountains, and has not lifted up his eyes to the idolatrous worship of the House of Israel; who has not defiled his neighbor's wife; 16. who has not oppressed anyone; who has not taken a pledge; who has not committed robbery; who has given of his bread to the hungry; and who has covered the naked with his own clothes; 17. who has not withheld his hand from the poor; who has taken no interest or usury; he has obeyed My law; he has walked in My statutes; he shall not die for the sins of his father; he shall surely live. 18. His father, because he practiced oppression, robbed *one* of his brothers,[7] and who did not do what was proper in the midst of his people, behold, he has died for his sin. 19. And you say, 'Why is not the son punished for the sins of the father?' But the son has done what is truly just and meritorious, he has kept all My statutes and performed them: he shall surely live. 20. The person who sins, he shall die. The son shall not be punished for the sins of the father, and the father shall not be punished for the sins of the son; the merit of the righteous shall be fulfilled in him[c][8] and the sin of the wicked shall be upon him.[9] 21. But the wicked, if he repents[d] of all the sins which he had committed, and keeps all My statutes and does what is truly just and righteous, he shall surely live, he shall not die. 22. None of the sins which he had committed shall be remembered against him. For the righteousness which he has done he shall survive. 23. Do I desire at all the death of the wicked? says the Lord God. Is it not rather that when he turns from his way, he shall survive? 24. And when the righteous turns away from his righteousness and deals falsely, committing all the abominable

Apparatus, Chapter 18 continued

[b] Lit. "the guilt for his violent death shall be in him."
[c] According to all other versions. SP reads "in it."

[d] Or "turns from."
[e] Or "explained," "defined."

things which the wicked practices, shall he survive? All the righteousness which he had done shall not be remembered; for the falsehood which he has practiced and for the sins which he committed, he shall die. 25. Yet you have said, 'The *good* ways of the Lord *have not been declared[e] to us.'* Now, listen, O House of Israel. *Have not* My *good* ways *been declared[e] to you?*[10] Is it not your ways, surely yours, which are not right? 26. When the righteous man turns away from his righteousness and deals falsely and dies because of them, he shall die for the falsehood which he has committed. 27. And when the wicked man turns away from the sins which he has committed and does that which is truly just and righteous, he shall save his life. 28. He has seen and repented for all the sins which he had committed, he shall surely live, he shall not die.[11] 29. Yet the House of Israel have said, The *good* ways of the Lord *have not been*

Notes, Chapter 18 continued

A tangential theological problem is the question of original sin, which emerges from the idea that sin and guilt are transmitted biologically, which is the implication of the proverb with which Ezekiel deals, He had to cope with that proverb, but also with the primitive notion found in biblical legislation in Ex. 20:5., while Dt. 24:16 negates this. Ezekiel is probably the first to formulate a detailed response to the proverb. It became the Judaic perception of God as the arbiter of justice and mercy, and of the individual human being as a free agent who has the moral capacity to choose the direction of his life, for good or for evil, and who is solely responsible for his conduct. The Sages acknowledged this innovative contribution of Ezekiel. "R. Jose b. Hanina said: Four severe decrees did Moses our teacher decree upon Israel, but along came four prophets and nullified them ... Moses had said, The Lord visits the iniquity of the fathers upon the children and upon the children's children ... (Ex. 20:5). Along came Ezekiel and nullified it, by declaring, The soul that sins, it alone shall die." *b. Mak.* 24a.

This enlightened theological point of view has prevailed in Judaism to this very day, emphasized again and again in every generation. It is boldly stated in the Syriac Apocalypse of Baruch 54:19 (Charles, *Pseudepigrapha*, p. 477 f.) and R. Akiba in *m. 'Abot* 3:19. As it happens in the history of religions, supplanted ideas have a way of persisting and surfacing from time to time, in this instance the doctrine of original sin as expounded by Paul in Rom. 5:12 ff., but the doctrine is not acceptable to normative Judaism. For a critical discussion, including the variation of Hebrew tenses in Ezek. and Jer., see *AB*, p. 327 f.; *IB*, p. 158.

[2]MT: "if he does not eat upon the mountains." In vv. 6-8 MT has the verbs in the impf. tense, but *Tg.* translates them in the perfect.

[3]The scribal slip in MT, *'ah*, probably a partial dittography from the suceeding word *me'ahad*, is retained in the *Tg.* But see v. 18, *infra.*

[4]*Tg.'s* translation provides us with a subtle theological inuendo. Instead of the simple verb *hyy*, "to live," *Tg.* translates *ha'itqayam*, "will he be enabled to continue," implying that God is involved in the process of human survival. See v. 22 *infra.*

[5]*Tg.* reads *yamut* for *yumat*. Also, MT: "his blood shall be upon himself."

Tg.: hobat qatoleh the latter word having the force of "his being slain" or "executed." Indeed, the Halakah is that among the crimes which he committed, there are some which are punishable by one or another form of execution. *b. Sanh.* 81a. *Tg.* reads a variant, *mot yamut*. See SP IV B, p. 337.

[6]*Tg.* follows Q. Ket: *wayyira'* "he feared," *Tg.* suggesting that his righteous conduct was not motivated by fear. LXX and V follow the Ket.

[7]See v. 10 n. 3, *supra.*

[8]SP may imply the Rabbinic concept that righteousness is its own reward. Cf. *m. 'Abot* 4:2, the statement of Ben Azzai: "The reward of *mitzwah* is *mitzwah.*"

[9]The problem of theodicy is discussed in *b. Ber.* 7a.

[10]MT: "Yet you say, 'The way of the Lord is not right.' Hear, now, O House of Israel: Is My way not right?"

[11]The efficacy of repentance is a cardinal doctrine of Rabbinic theology. See K. Kohler, *Jewish Theology*, pp. 246 ff.; G.F. Moore, *Judaism*, vol. I, pp. 507 ff.

A magnificent pericope sums up the development of the Jewish view of sin and repentance, atonement and forgiveness. "They asked Wisdom, What is the punishment of the sinner? It said to them, Evil relentlessly pursues sinners (Prov. 12:21). They asked Prophecy, What is the punishment of the sinner? It said to them, The soul that sins shall die (Ezek. 18:4). They asked Torah, What is the punishment of the sinner? It said to them, Let him bring a guilt-offering and it shall make atonement for him (Lev. 1:4). They asked the Holy One, blessed be He, What is the punishment of the sinner? He said to them, Let him repent, and it shall make atonement for (it shall be forgiven) him (Ps. 25:8)." *y. Mak.* 31d, version of *Yal. Šim.* Ezekiel, #358.

declared^e to us. Have not My *good* ways *been declared^e to you,* O House of Israel? Is it not rather that your ways, yours, are not right? 30. Therefore, from each according to his ways will I *exact punishment from* you, O House of Israel, says the Lord God. Return *to My worship,* and remove *idol worship* from you, that it should not be a sinful stumbling block for you. 31. Put far from you all your sins by which you have sinned and make for yourselves a *faithful$^{f/12}$* heart and a *faithful$^{f/12}$* spirit. Why should you die, O House of Israel? 32. For I have no desire in the death of anyone who *deserves* to die, says the Lord God. Return *to My worship,* and you shall survive."^{13}

CHAPTER 19

1. And you, take up a lamentation over the princes of Israel. 2. And say, How *the Congregation of Israel,*^{1} *has been compared to* a lioness! Among the *kings* she crouched; among the *rulers* she reared her *sons.* 3. She raised up^a one of her *sons* and he became a *king;* and he learned to *kill mercilessly;*^{b} he *slew people.*^{2} 4. When the nations heard about him, he was seized in their snare, and they brought him in chains to the land of Egypt. 5. When she saw that *he had failed,*^{3} that her hope was lost, she *anointed* one of her other *sons* and made him *king.* 6. He went among the *kings,* a *king* was he, and he learned to *kill mercilessly;* he *slew people.* 7. He made *desolate* his *castles*^{4} and laid waste their cities. The land and everything in it were astounded by the noise of his roaring. 8. Then the nations from all the surrounding provinces gathered together against him; they spread their nets over him and he was caught in their snare. 9. And they put him in a yoke, in chains, and carried him off to the king of Babylon; they brought him into prison, so that his voice might no longer be heard on the mountains of Israel. 10. *The Congregation of Israel,*^{1} *when it observes the Torah,* is compared^5 to a vine planted by springs of water, whose branches are sturdy^c and whose boughs are thick; she is *planted near* abundant waters. 11. In her there were *mighty rulers, kings powerful enough to subdue the kingdom, and exalted* by its might *over the kingdoms,* excelling in *its military forces and its many valiant men.*^{6} 12. But she was uprooted by force from the land *of the abode of the Shekinah; she was exiled to another land; and a king who was as violent^d as* the east wind, *slew her people, and her mighty rulers were exiled; and the nations that were as fierce^d as* fire *destroyed them.*^{7} 13. And now she is *like* a vine which is planted in the wilderness, in a desolate and dry land. 14. *Nations, who are as fierce as* fire, *have come; because of her presumptuous sins, they have slain her people. She has no mighty rulers, kings who are heroic enough to subdue the kingdom."*^{8} The prophet has *uttered* a lamentation. It is *a prophecy,* but it shall become a lamentation.^{9}

Apparatus, Chapter 18 continued

^{f} Or "worshipful," "reverent."

Apparatus, Chapter 19

^{a} Or "anointed."
^{b} Lit. "to kill, killing."

^{c} Lit. "good," "pretty."
^{d} Lit. "strong."

CHAPTER 20

1. It was in the seventh year, in the fifth month, on the tenth day of the month, *says the prophet,* there came men from the elders of Israel, to *request instruction* from *before* the Lord; and they sat down before me. 2. And the word of *prophecy from before* the Lord was with me, saying: 3. "Son of Adam, *prophesy* to the elders of Israel and say to them, Thus says the Lord God, *Is it to request instruction from before* Me that you have come? As I live, I will not respond to you *by My Memra,* says the Lord God. 4. Would you admonish[1] them, O Son of Adam, Would you admonish them? Then let them know the abominations of their fathers! 5. And say to them, Thus says the Lord God: On the day that I chose Israel, and I swore *by My Memra* to the seed of the House of Jacob, and I revealed Myself *in order to redeem them* in the land of Egypt; and I swore to them *by My Memra,* to bring them out of the land of Egypt into the land which I *have given*[2] them, producing milk and honey;

Notes, Chapter 18 continued

[12]MT: "a new heart and a new spirit."
[13]SP IV B, p. 337 errs in suggesting variant *šubu.* Cf. v. 30, *supra.*

Notes, Chapter 19

[1]MT: "your mother." *Tg.* takes the mother to be the Congregation of Israel, which is linguistically f. gender. Actually, the reference is to the people of Israel, or to the nuclear group in Judah. Kimḥi understands "lioness" as a poetic symbol of the Davidic dynasty, observing that the *Tg.* takes MT's "lions" as kings, and "young lions" as rulers. Biblical critics differ in their interpretations of the mother metaphor. See *ICC,* p. 206; *IB,* p. 164; *AB,* p. 350. Since the context makes it clear that the cubs are Jehoahaz and Jehoiakin or Zedekiah, the mother may actually refer to Ḥamutal, wife of Josiah, 2K. 23:31.

[2]MT: "he ate men."
[3]MT: "she had waited in vain."
[4]*Tg.* reads *wayyera' 'arm'notaw,* instead of MT's *wayyeda' 'alm'notaw,* "he consorted with his widows." V follows MT. Most modern versions follow *Tg.,* translating the verb as "he ravaged." But cf. BDB, p. 74, sub *'armon.*
[5]MT: "in your blood," *bedam'ka,* is uncertain. *Tg.* seems to understand the word in the Aramaic sense, "likened" or "compared." Cf. *AB,* p. 353.
[6]MT: "It had branches strong enough for rulers' scepters. It grew tall, among the clouds, conspicuous by its stature, with its many branches."
[7]MT: "And it was uprooted in fury, and flung to the ground; the east wind dried up its fruit, which broke off and withered. Fire consumed its strong stem."
[8]MT: "And fire has gone forth from the stem of its branches, and has consumed its fruit. There is no strong stem in it, a scepter with which to rule."
[9]MT: "This is a lamentation, and it has become a lamentation." LXX and S; "it shall become a lamentation."

Notes, Chapter 20

[1]MT: "would you judge." *Tg.: hatokah,* a Hebraism from the root *ykh,* in the causative, "to argue with," "to reprove," "to rebuke," etc. *Tg.* uses this expression to convey the idea that passing judgment is for the purpose of repentance. Rashi and Kimḥi follow the *Tg.*
[2]MT: "I have searched out for them."

she is the most glorious of all countries. 7. And I said to them, Let every one remove the detestable things from before his eyes, and do not defile yourselves with the idol *worship* of the *Egyptians;* I am the Lord your God. 8. But they rebelled against *My Memra* and did not want to listen to *My prophets,*[3] not one of them removed their detestable things, which were before their eyes and they did not forsake the idol *worship* of the *Egyptians.* So I thought I would pour out My wrath upon them, that My anger against them should be accomplished in the midst of the land of Egypt. 9. But I acted for the sake of My name, that it might not be profaned in the eyes of the nations among whom they were; for I revealed Myself by redeeming them before their very eyes, by bringing them out of the land of Egypt. 10. So I brought them out of the land of Egypt and led them into the wilderness. 11. And I gave them My statutes, and I made known to them My laws, which if a man observed, he would live by them *in eternal life.*[4] 12. Also, my Sabbaths, I gave them, that they should be a sign between *My Memra* and them, to know that I am the Lord who sanctifies them. 13. But the House of Israel rebelled against *My Memra* in the wilderness. They did not walk in My statutes, they spurned My laws, which, if a man did observe, he would live by them *in eternal life;* and My Sabbaths they profaned exceedingly. So I thought I would pour out My wrath upon them in the wilderness to make an end of them. 14. But I acted for the sake of My name,[a] that it might not be profaned in the eyes of the nations, before whose eyes I had brought them out. 15. And also I swore to them *by My Memra*[b] in the wilderness that I would not bring them into the land which I had given,[c] producing milk and honey; she is the most glorious of all countries, 16. because they spurned My laws, and did not walk in My statutes, and profaned My Sabbaths, for their heart goes astray after their idol *worship.* 17. But *My Memra*[5] had pity on them in not destroying them, and I did not make an end of them in the wilderness. 18. I said to their children in the wilderness, Do not walk in the *religious decrees*[6] of your fathers, and do not abide by their laws,[7] nor defile yourselves with their idol *worship.* 19. I am the Lord your God: walk in My statutes, abide by My laws and perform them, 20. and sanctify My Sabbaths that they might be a sign between *My Memra* and you, to know that I am the Lord your God. 21. But the children rebelled against *My Memra,* they did not walk in My statutes, and by My laws they did not abide, to observe them, which if a man did observe, he would live by them *in eternal life.* My Sabbaths they profaned, and I thought I would pour out My wrath upon them and accomplish My anger against them in the wilderness. 22. But I withheld[d] My *destructive power*[8] and I acted for the sake of My name, that it might not be profaned in the eyes of the nations in whose sight I had brought them out. 23. Also, in the wilderness I swore to them *by My Memra,* to *exile* them among the nations and to scatter them among the countries, 24. because they did not observe My laws and they spurned My statutes, and profaned My Sabbaths, and their eyes followed after the idol *worship* of their forefathers. 25. So, too, *since*

[a] CR: "My Memra."
[b] Omitted in SP.
[c] MM adds "them." So do LXX and S.

[d] Lit. "turned away."
[e] RB. SP omits.

they had rebelled against My Memra, and did not wish to listen to My prophets, I removed them and delivered them into the hand of their enemies;[e] *they followed their stupid inclination and they obeyed*[9] *religious decrees which were not proper and laws by which they could not survive.*[10] 26. And I defiled them by their gifts, in their causing every first-born to pass through the fire; so that I might make them desolate, in order that they should know that I am the Lord. 27. Therefore, O Son of Adam, *prophesy* to the House of Israel, and say to them, Thus says the Lord God, In this, too, your fathers *caused anger before Me,* in that they were perfidious with *My Memra.* 28. When I brought them into the land which I had sworn *by My Memra* to give to them, and they saw every high hill and every tree thick with leaves, and they offered their sacrifices; and there they gave their anger-provoking offerings; and there they set their *sacrificial worship,*[11] and there they poured their libations. 29. Then I said to them, What is the high place to which you are coming, where *you*

Notes, Chapter 20 continued

[3]MT: "Me." The force of the rendering is that God Himself cannot be rebelled against, and He does not speak directly to the people themselves, but delivers His message through His prophets, who speak for Him.

[4]Rabbinic experience and perception of reality disclosed that living a righteous life and observing the commandments of the Torah did not guarantee security in this insecure world, nor reward in this life. Hence they projected the reward for righteous conduct to life in the hereafter. The classic example of this is the case of Elisha b. Abuyah, the apostate derogatorily referred to as Aḥer, teacher of R. Meir. One reason given for his dereliction from Judaism was that he observed a man ascend to a loft, send the mother bird away, and was killed by a serpent upon descending. In connectin with this *mitzvah,* the Torah says, that your days may be prolonged and that it may be well with you (Dt. 22:6), and the incident led him to doubt the Torah. *y. Hag.* 77b. The demonstration is even stronger in *b. Kid.* 39b. "R. Jacob said, There is no guarantee of a reward in this world for the performance of the commandments . . . There is not a single commandment written in the Torah, whose reward is specified along side of it, that is not contigent on the resurrection of the dead (i.e. the World to Come). With reference to Honor your father and mother, it is written, In order that your days may be prolonged and that it may be well with you (Dt. 5:16). With reference to sending off the mother bird, it is written, That it may be well with you and that you may live a long life (Dt. 22:6 f.). For instance, one's father said to him, Ascend the loft and bring me fledglings. So, he ascended the loft, sent off the mother and took the young. On his return he fell and died. Where is this one's well-being? And where is the prolongation of this one's life? Rather, That it may be well with you, means in a world which is completely good; and, In order that your days may be prolonged, means, in a world which is eternally long." *Tg.'s* adding "in eternal life" is without doubt a reflection on this theological point of view of the Sages. *Tg.* Onq. and Ps.-J. on Lev. 18:5 have an identical intepretation. Kimḥi follows *Tg.*

[5]MT: "My eye."

[6]*Tg.* uses the term *bigezerat* implying an evil connotation regarding heathenism.

[7]MT: "their ordinances." *Tg.* renders this by a Greek word with an Aramaic ending, *nimosehon,* from Gk. *nomos,* "law," thereby emphasizing the taint of paganism.

[8]MT: "but I held back My hand." *geburti,* a qualitative attribute of God, here eliminating the anthropomorphic *yadi,* "My hand." *hageburah* is used in the Rabbinic sources, which do not use the biblical names of God except when they quote the Scriptures directly, as one of the designations of God. Cf. Mark 14:62 and Synoptic parallels. See Jastrow, I, p. 205 sub *geburah.*

[9]I have translated the word *wa'badu,* "and they obeyed," in the sense of serving, according to version of RB, which has them in the power of their enemies, hence having to abide by foreign laws. If we accept the version of SP, which omits "enemies," God delivers them into the power of their stupid inclinations, so they go "and they make" the unworthy religious decrees and laws.

[10]MT: "I also gave them statutes which were not good and ordinances by which they could not live." *Tg.'s* rendering of this verse, makes God responsible for retaliating against them by delivering them to their enemies, whose unworthy laws they were compelled to obey; all because they would not obey God's laws. MT is theologically unacceptable to *Tg.*

[11]MT: "their pleasing odors." Cf. *Tg.* Ezek. 6:13 and n. 8 thereto, *supra.*

engage in ecstatic practices?[12] So its name is called "a high place" to this day. 30. Therefore, say to the House of Israel, Thus says the Lord God, Will you defile yourselves in the way of your fathers, and will you go astray after their idols?[13] 31. And in offering your gifts, causing your children to pass through the fire, you defile yourselves with all your idol worship to this day. And should I respond to you *by My Memra,* O House of Israel? As I live, says the Lord God, I will not respond to you *by My Memra.* 32. As to *what you are planning,* and what arises in your mind, *before Me it is revealed,*[14] that you say, Let us be like the nations, like the offspring of the countries, serving[15] wood and stone. 33. As I live, says the Lord God, With a mighty hand,[16] and with a raised up arm,[16] and with outpoured anger,[16] will I be king over you. 34. I will bring you out from among the nations, and I will gather you in from the countries in which you have been scattered, with a mighty hand,[16] and with a raised up arm,[16] and with outpoured anger.[16] 35. And I will bring you into the wilderness of the nations, and I will *demand an accounting*[17] from you there, face to face.[16] 36. As I *demanded an accounting*[17] from your fathers in the wilderness of the land of Egypt, so will I *demand an accounting* from you, says the Lord God. 37. And *I will lay upon you the decree of My justice,*[18] and I will bring you into the covenantal *tradition.*[19] 38. I will separate from you those who have rebelled against and who have dealt falsely with *My Memra.* I will bring them out of the land of their sojourn, but they shall not enter into the land of Israel; and you shall know that I am the Lord. 39. As for you, O House of Israel, thus says the Lord God, Every one of you go indulge in your idol *worship;* but after *you have repented,*[f][20] will you not choose to listen to *My Memra* and profane My holy name no longer with your gifts and your idols? 40. For on My holy mountain, on the *holy*[21] mountain of Israel, says the Lord God, there all the House of Israel, all of them, shall worship before Me, in the land *of the living.*[22] Their sacrifices shall be accepted there *readily,*[g] and there I will require your heave-offerings and the first of *your kneading-trough*[23] with all your sacred things. 41. *Your sacrifice as an acceptable offering*[24] shall be *readily* accepted, when I bring you out from among the nations and I gather you in from the countries in which you have been scattered, and I will be sanctified through you in the eyes of the nations. 42. And you shall know that I am Lord, when I bring you into the land of Israel, to the land which I have sworn *by My Memra* to give to your fathers. 43. There you shall remember your ways and your deeds by which you defiled yourselves, and you shall show regret when *you recognize* all the evils which you have committed. 44. And you shall know that I am the Lord when I deal with you for the sake of My name, not according to your evil ways and destructive deeds, O House of Israel, says the Lord God."

Apparatus, Chapter 20 continued

[f] All versions except SP, which reads: "and after you have sinned."

[g] Or, "quickly."

CHAPTER 21

1. The word of *prophecy from before* the Lord was with me, saying: 2. "Son of Adam, *hear a prophecy*[1] about that which is in the south direction, and *teach*[2] about the south, and prophesy against the forest field of the south.[3] 3. And say to the forest

Notes, Chapter 20 continued

[12]The phrase may also mean "to work yourselves into a frenzy."

[13]*Tg.* uses the cognate term as the Hebrew, *šiquṣehon,* "their abominable things." "Idols are so called because they are abominable." *Sifra, Kedoshim,* 1.

[14]*Tg.* ignores MT's "it shall never come about" and substitutes for it, "it is (or "they are," according to SP) revealed before Me." Perhaps *Tg.* felt that MT's thought is unrealistic, even untrue, to the historical evidence of the idolatrous cults that did exist in Israel.

[15]*lešamaša,* the usual Targumic rendering of Hebrew, *lešaret,* meaning "to minister to." It is possible that *Tg.* intends a double entendre, since the Aramaic *šamasa'* means a prostitute. Jastrow II, p. 1602.

[16]An instance in which the anthropomorphisms of the MT are rendered literally by *Tg.* This would lend support for H.M. Orlinsky's contention that it is only a gratuitous assumption that *Tg.* is invariably anti-anthropomorphic (see Introduction); and for Michael Klein's point of view that there is no consistency in Targumic rendering of anthropomorphisms and anthropopathisms in Scriptures. Klein limits his discussion to the Targumim on the Pentateuch, especially Neofiti. Here is an instance from *Tg.* Neb. M.L. Klein, "The Translation of Anthropomorphisms and Anthropopathisms in the Targumim" in *Congress Volume,* Vienna, 1980, pp. 162 ff.

[17]MT: "as I entered into judgment with."

[18] MT: "I will make you pass under the staff." *Tg.* interprets the poetic expression in MT, taking *haššabet,* as the divine scepter, symbol of God's power and justice. V: "My scepter." LXX: "My rod."

[19]MT has a *hapax legomenon, bemasoret,* which *Tg.* carries over by transliteration rather than translation, but likely with the Rabbinic meaning, transmission or tradition. Rashi takes it in this sense. Kimḥi derives it from *'asr,* "to bind," and so, too, BDB, p. 64. I have chosen to render the phrase "covenantal tradition." in keeping with Rashi's "into the covenant which I have transmitted to you." LXX: "by number," reading *bemispar.* Cf. *IB,* p. 174; *AB,* p. 372.

[20]According to all the extant versions of the Targum except SP, which reads "and after you have sinned." The problem arises from MT's *w'ahar* which stands by itself, simply, "and afterwards." But *Tg.* feels that something is missing and supplies the complement. Because of the preponderance of "and after you have repented," I believe that SP is a scribal error of one letter, *het* for *taw.* If this is so, then I am compelled to read the rest of *Tg.'s* verse as a question, which makes sense, *Tg.* understanding the Hebrew *'im,* as a negative, as it is in case of a vow. The Rabbis see the biblical v. as prooftext (1) that if one must sin, let it be in secret, so as not to profane God's name publicly, *b. Kid.* 40a; and (2) that idolatry is less of a sin than profaning God's name in public, *Mid. Teh.,* 27:5

[21]MT: "high."

[22]This is a distinctive designation by the *Tg.* of the land of Israel, as distinguished from the countries of the Dispersion.

[23]MT: "your choice offerings.' *Tg.* understands this as *hallah.*

[24]MT: "as a pleasing odor." *Tg.* is anti-anthropomorphic. God does not smell the sweet odor, literally. The expression is merely a poetic indication of acceptability to God. Cf. *Tg.* Ezek. 6:13 and note 8 thereto, *supra.*

Notes, Chapter 21

[1]MT: "set your face," which *Tg.* understands as being attentive, hence "hear the prophecy."

[2]MT: *wehatef,* the hiph. of *ntf,* "to cause to drip," hence to discourse, BDB, p. 643. This is the probable rationale for *Tg.'s* rendering "teach," since the discourse of the teacher must be dripping or fluent.

[3]The biblical poetry refers to three different places, all south of Babylon, so *Tg.* renders all three by "south." The allegorical imagery is explained in v. 7 ff.

of the south, Hear the word of the Lord. Thus says the Lord God, Behold I am kindling a fire in you and it shall *kill* every green tree and every dry tree within you; its destructive flame shall not be extinguished, and all faces from south to north shall be scarred[a] by it. 4. And all *children of* flesh shall see that I the Lord have kindled it; it shall not be extinguished." 5. Then I said, "*Hear my petition,* O Lord God. Behold, they are saying of me, 'Is he not a spinner of riddles?'"[b4] 6. Now, the word of *prophecy from before* the Lord was with me, saying: 7. "Son of Adam, *hear the prophecy* against Jerusalem, and *teach* against the sanctuaries, and prophesy against the land of Israel. 8. And say to the land of Israel, Thus says the Lord, Behold I *send My anger* against you, and I will draw My sword from its sheath, and I will *exile your righteous from you, in order to destroy your wicked.*[5] 9. Because *I will exile your righteous from you in order to destroy* your wicked, therefore My sword shall come out of its sheath against all flesh[6] from south to north. 10. And all *children of* flesh shall know that I the Lord have drawn My sword from its sheath, it shall never again return. 11. And you, Son of Adam, sigh! with trembling loins and bitterly, you shall sigh before their eyes. 12. And it shall be, when they say to you, 'Why do you sigh?' you shall say, 'Because of the tidings at the coming of which every heart shall melt and all hands shall hang limp, and every spirit shall grow faint, and all knees shall pour out like water. Behold it is coming and it shall be fulfilled,'" says the Lord God. 13. The word of *prophecy from before* the Lord was with me, saying: 14. "Son of Adam, prophesy and say, Thus says the Lord God. Say, The sword *of the king of Babylon shall slay,* and the sword *of the Ammonites* shall be sharpened and *shall destroy.*[7] 15. In order to slay relentlessly[c] has it been drawn, in order to *inflict punishment*[8] has it been burnished. *Because* the tribe *of the House of Judah and Benjamin* rejoiced *over the tribes of Israel when they were exiled for having worshipped idols, they in turn went astray after images* of wood.[9] 16. And he gave *as their punishment, to be delivered to* the hand *of the king of Babylon – this is the striking* of the sword – *this shall be their punishment* – delivering them into the hand of the killers.[10] 17. Cry and wail, O Son of Adam, for it surely shall befall My people, it shall befall all the princes of Israel who shall be slain by the sword. For they have gathered together and come against My people from all around. Therefore, slap the thigh! 18. Because, *the prophets prophesied to them, but they did not repent. And what will their end be? Say, also* the tribe *of the House of Judah and Benjamin*[d] shall surely be exiled; and because of their evil deeds they* shall not survive," says the Lord God.[11] 19. "And you, Son of Adam, prophesy, and strike hand upon hand. The sword shall strike twice, and a third time; it is the sword of the slayers,[e] the sword of *punishment* by the great slaughter, the sword which makes them tremble, 20. in order to crush their heart, and to increase their stumbling. On all their

[a] Lit. "wrinkled."
[b] Lit. "a maker of proverbs."
[c] Lit. "to slay, slaying."
[d] SP omits "and Benjamin."

[e] Other versions: "the slain."
[f] Lit. "wherever your face is ready."
[g] Lit. "falling."
[h] K: "years."

cities I have appointed *those who slay with* the sword. Alas, the sword is drawn, it is burnished for destruction. 21. Be sharp, and slay — from the south; and destroy — from the north towards any direction which you face.^f 22. Also, *I will bring punishment upon punishment,*[12] and I shall put My fury to rest. I the Lord have decreed it *by My Memra."* 23. The word of *prophecy from before* the Lord was with me, saying: 24. "You, Son of Adam, set for yourself two roads, by which might come the king of Babylon's *men who slay by* the sword. Let both come out of the same country; and fix a place; fix the place at the head of *the fork in* the road to the city. 25. Set a road by which *those who slay with* the sword might come *from* Rabbah of the Ammonites, against those of the House of Judah *who went out* of Jerusalem *to dwell* in fortified cities.[13] 26. For the king of Babylon is standing at a point at the fork in the road, at the head of the two roads, resorting to divination, shooting arrows, consulting the idols, inspecting the liver.[14] 27. In his right hand the divining rod was indicating^g to go to Jerusalem, to appoint commanders to open the gates so that the killers might enter through them; to make noise with the shrieking of the trumpet; to appoint commanders over the gates; to cast up mounds; and to build siege-towers. 28. But in their eyes the omens which he augured about them seemed to be false divinations; *for they did not know that forty nine*[15] *times*^h he *would conceal and return to the matter until the hour would come for him, when they would be delivered into his hand.*[16] 29. Therefore, thus says the Lord God, Because you have

Notes, Chapter 21 continued

[4]MT: "Ah, O Lord God ... Is he not a maker of proverbs?"
They do not understand what he is saying, because it is couched in allegorical language. So he explains the meaning of the allegory in unequivocal terms beginning with v. 7.

[5]MT: "and I will cut off from you the righteous and the wicked." *Tg.* departs from the simple meaning of MT, maintaining that God will preserve the righteous by exiling them, so that they are not destroyed together with the wicked. This is in line with the opinion of R. Oshaia who says, "The Holy One blessed be He acted charitably with Israel, in that He scattered them among the nations." *b. Pes.* 87b. The intent of the statement is that Israel can never be totally destroyed, since there will always be a righteous remnant somewhere in the world.
Theologically, it would be an injustice of God to destroy the righteous with the wicked. Abraham had already challenged God on that score in his plea for the inhabitants of Sodom, Gen. 18:25. The problem is discussed in *b. 'A.Z.* 4a. But cf. *Mek. Pisha* 11 (Lauterbach, I, p. 85.) Cf. Y. Komlosh, "Al Šiṭato Šel Targum Jonathan," p. 90.

[6]The Jewish commentators explain this as retaliation against the other nations who rejoiced at the downfall of Judah. Kimḥi: "Just as My sword shall cut you down from south to north, and you shall be exiled there, to be cut down by the sword of the king from the north (Nebuchadnezzar), so will the other nations be smitten by his hand; and after that he will be smitten by the hands of Media and Persia."

[7]MT: "a sword, a sword." The poetic repetition of "a sword" in MT provides the exegetical rationale of the *Tg.'s* interpretation that there are two swords, one Babylonian, the other Ammonite. See vv. 20 and 28, *infra.*

[8]MT: "to flash like lightning."

[9]MT: "or should we rejoice? my son's staff, scorning all wood." Verse 15b in the Hebrew is difficult, if not impossible. *Tg.* skillfully weaves a theological-historical interpretation, interspersed between several words in the biblical text.

[10]MT: "And he gave it to be polished, to be grasped in the hand. The sword — it has been sharpened and polished, to be placed in the hand of the killer."

[11]MT (uncertain): "Verily, a test. What if also the staff, scorning, it shall not be, says the Lord God."

[12]MT: "I will strike My hand against My hand."

[13]MT: "Set a road for the sword to come to Rabbah of the Ammonites, and to Judah, in Jerusalem the fortified."

[14]Three primitive methods of obtaining advice by divination. For a critical analysis see *ICC*, p. 232 f.; *IB*, p. 180.

[15]MT: "oaths of oaths were theirs." *Tg.* interprets *šebu'e šebu'ot* as numbers, 7 times 7, equalling 49. Cf. *Lam. R.* Pet. 23.

[16]MT: "oaths of oaths were theirs; but he brings their guilt to remembrance, so that they might be captured."

brought to mind your guilt, in that your rebellions are revealed, your transgressions made visible in all your deeds; because you have brought this to mind, you shall be turned over to the *hand of the king of Babylon.* 30. And you, who have *incurred the penalty of death,*[17] O wicked prince of Israel, whose day has come *to be broken,* the time *for punishment* for his sins has arrived. 31. Thus says the Lord God, *I will* remove the mitre *from Seraiah the High Priest*[18] and *I will* take off the crown *of Zedekiah the king. Say,* neither this one nor that one *shall endure in his place – they shall surely be exiled; Gedaliah son of Ahikam, although it was not his, he shall take it; it shall be removed from Zedekiah, to whom it belonged.*[19] 32. *Their sins, which they had sinned, according to their sins*[20] *will I exact payment from them.* Nor shall it be *established securely for him, until I bring upon him the punishment of Ishmael son of Netaniah and I will deliver him into his hand.*[21] 33. And you, Son of Adam, prophesy and say, Thus says the Lord God concerning the Ammonites and concerning their shameful deeds; yes say, a sword, a sword is drawn for the slaughter, it is burnished for destruction, so that it may flash;[i] 34. for *prophesying* falsely about you, for *teaching* deceptions concerning you, so as to deliver *your neck,* like the necks of the slain wicked, whose day has come *when they shall be broken,*[22] the time of visitation for their evils, when their end has come. 35. Return *the sword* to its sheath. In the place where you were created, *in the land of your sojourn I will exact payment from you.*[23] 36. And I will pour out My fury upon you; I *will overpower you*[24] with the fire of My punishment, and I will deliver you into the hand of wicked men who are artisans of destruction. 37. *You shall be delivered up for destruction to nations who are as fierce as fire, it shall be your death penalty,*[25] in the midst of the land where the memory of you shall not enter; for I the Lord have decreed it *by My Memra."*

CHAPTER 22

1. The word of *prophecy from before* the Lord was with me, saying: 2. "And you, Son of Adam, would you *admonish,*[1] would *admonish* the city, *in the midst of which one has shed innocent* blood? Then declare to her all of her abominable deeds. 3. And say, Thus says the Lord God: A city in the midst of which one[a] has shed *innocent* blood, the time has come for her to be crushed, together with those who worship idols within her, thereby defiling her. 4. You have become guilty by *the sin of* the *innocent* blood which you have shed, and you have become defiled by your

Apparatus, Chapter 21 continued

[i] Lit. "have flashes."

Apparatus, Chapter 22

[a] BM reads "she" or "it."   [b] Lit. "defiled of name."

worship of your idols. Now the day is near for you to be crushed, and *the time has come for evil to befall you.*[2] Therefore I have made you a reproach to the nations and a mockery to all countries. 5. Those who are near and those who are far from you shall mock you, who are ill-famed,[b] whose noisy crowds are many. 6. Behold, the princes of Israel in you, each has used his power in order to shed *innocent* blood. 7. Father and mother they have dishonored within you; the *proselyte* they have treated with oppression in your midst; orphans and widows they have wronged in you. 8. Towards My sacred things you have acted contemptuously; you have profaned My Sabbaths. 9. There were within you men who informed on others in order to shed *innocent* blood; and on the mountains *they worshipped idols*[3] within you; a *conspiracy of transgression*[4] have they made in your midst. 10. The father's nakedness they have uncovered in you; a woman during her period they have violated in you. 11. A man commits abomination with his neighbor's wife; and another man defiles his daughter-in-law in the *conspiracy of transgression;* and in you still another man violates his sister, his father's daughter. 12. Within you they have taken bribes in order to shed *innocent* blood; you have taken usury and interest, and made profit for your friend by oppression. But *the worship of* Me you have abandoned says the Lord God.[5] 13. Behold, I am *bringing My punishment*[6] upon you for the sins of monetary oppression which you have committed and for the *innocent* blood *which has been shed* in your midst. 14. Can your heart remain strong and can your hands remain firm for the days in the future that I will deal with you? I the Lord have decreed it *by My Memra* and I will fulfill it. 15. I will *exile* you among the nations and disperse you in the countries and I will remove your filthiness from you. 16. Then I shall be sanctified through you before the eyes of the nations, and you shall know that I am the Lord." 17. The word of *prophecy from before* the Lord was with me, saying: 18. "Son of Adam, the House of Israel has become dross before Me; all of them are like

Notes, Chapter 21 continued

[17]MT: "and you are fatally wounded."

[18]See 2K 25:18-26; Jer. 52:24-27.

[19]MT: "Thus says the Lord God: Remove the turban and lift off the crown; neither this nor that; exalt what is lowly, and bring down what is exalted."

[20]An interpretation of the triple *'awwah* of MT, which *Tg.* either reads or takes as *'awon,* "iniquity."

[21]MT: "until he comes, to whom it rightfully (or, to whom justice) belongs;" a perfect text for a Targumic Messianic interpretation, which *Tg.* Ezek. ignores. See S.H. Levey, *The Messiah: An Aramaic Interpretation,* p. 85 f. and "The Targum to Ezekiel," p. 144. Jerome's comment takes this passage as Christological.

[22]MT: "...to place you at the necks of the slain wicked ones, for their day has come..."

[23]MT: "in the land of your origin I will judge you."

[24]MT: "I will blow upon you."

[25]MT: "you shall be fuel for the fire, your blood shall be in the midst of the earth."

Notes, Chapter 22

[1]MT: "would you judge."

[2]*Tg.* reads *'et* for Masoretic *'ad.* So, too, LXX, V, and S. See 20:4, *supra,* and n. 1 thereto.

[3]MT: "they have eaten."

[4]*Tg.*'s rendering of the Hebrew *zimmah,* lit., a plan, device, or counsel of sins, which I have chosen to translate as "conspiracy of transgression., Ex. chs. 20-23; Holiness, Lev. ch. 18 ff.; and Deuteronomic, chs. 5 ff. The Rabbinic sources calculate 24 sins in this chapter, *b. Ta'an.* 4b-5a; *Ex. R.* 42:8. They posit these against the two cardinal sins mentioned in Jer. 2:10-13, forsaking God and practicing idolatry. Cf. *Lev. R.* 33:3.

[6]MT: "I strike My hand."

copper, tin, iron and led *mixed* in a crucible; they have become silver dross.[7] 19. Therefore, thus says the Lord God, Because you have all become dross, behold I will gather you into the midst of Jerusalem. 20. Like the gathering together of silver, copper, iron, lead, and tin into the midst of a crucible, *for the fire to overpower it*[8] in order to melt it, so will I gather you in My anger and in My wrath and I shall *finish you and destroy you.*[9] 21. And I will gather you and *overpower you*[10] with the fire of *My punishment*[11] and you will melt away in the midst of it. 22. As silver is melted inside a crucible, so you shall be melted in the midst of it, and you shall know that I the Lord have poured out My wrath upon you." 23. The word of *prophecy from before* the Lord was with me, saying: 24. "Son of Adam, say to her, You are the land *of Israel,* a land that is not cleansed, and *no good deeds have been performed in her, to protect her*[12] in the day of *curse.* 25. *Her fellow-travelling teachers*[13] in the midst of her are like lions roaring for the kill; they have *slain*[14] human beings; they have appropriated wealth and precious things; they have increased her widows in her midst. 26. Her priests *misinterpret*[15] My Torah and desecrate My holy things; they have made no distinction between the sacred and the non-sacred,[c] and they have not made known the difference between the unclean and the clean; and they have closed their eyes to My Sabbaths; so that *My will*[16] is profaned among them. 27. Her princes in the midst of her are like wolves snatching what they have robbed; shedding *innocent* blood, destroying lives in order to acquire dishonest wealth. 28. And the *false* prophets who are in the midst of her are *like one who builds a wall* and daubs it with plain mud[d] *without straw:*[17] they prophesy falsehood and teach them lies. They say, 'Thus says the Lord God,' whereas nothing had been spoken to them *from before* the Lord. 29. The people of the land have practiced oppression and committed robbery; they have wronged the poor and needy, and they have oppressed *the proselyte,* which is *not proper.*[18] 30. So I sought among them, before Me, a man *possessed of good deeds*[19] who would stand in the breach before Me, and *pray for mercy for the people of* the land,[20] not to suffer destruction; but I found none. 31. So I have poured out My fury upon them; with My *punishing*[21] fire I destroyed them; I have brought down upon their heads *the punishment for* their ways, says the Lord God."

CHAPTER 23

1. The word of *prophecy from before* the Lord was with me, saying: 2. "Son of Adam, *prophesy against two countries who are like* two women who were the daughters of one mother. 3. In Egypt they *went astray after the worship of their*

Apparatus, Chapter 22 continued

[c] Or "profane," "ordinary."

[d] SP omits "mud."

Apparatus, Chapter 23

[a] Or "she chose."

[b] RB, following MT. Other versions: "she."

idols, there *they worshipped idols* and *their deeds became corrupt*[1] there. 4. Their names were Oholah, the elder one, and Oholibah, her sister. *When they served before Me,*[2] they prospered with sons and daughters. As for their names, Oholah is Samaria and Oholibah is Jerusalem. 5. Now Oholah *strayed from My worship and it pleased her*[a3] *to stray* after her friends, after the Assyrians, *her* neighbors.[4] 6. Clothed to perfection — governors and officers — desirable young men — all of them, horsemen riding horses. 7. It pleased her[a] to stray after them — all of them young Assyrians; and with all those whom she chose, she defiled herself with all of their idol *worship.* 8. She did not give up *the idol worship* which remained with her from Egypt, *for they had made her worship idols* and *they had taught her evil practices* and had poured out *their idolatry* upon her.[5] 9. Therefore I[b] delivered her into the hand of her *friends,* into the hand of the Assyrians, after whom she had *chosen to go astray.* 10. They uncovered her shame; her sons and daughters they took *captive;* and

Notes, Chapter 22 continued

[7]Cf. Jer. 6:30. *Pes. R.* 7:7 quotes Zech. 4:2 to demonstrate that "all Israel is gold," not silver dross.

[8]MT: "to blow fire upon it."

[9]MT: "I will cast you in and melt you."

[10]MT: "I will blow upon you."

[11]MT: "My wrath."

[12]MT: "she has not been rained upon." *Tg.* takes rain as a metaphor, symbol of the blessing and protective power of good deeds, to counteract the day of curse, "the day of indignation" in MT. The latter is taken by the Sages to mean the Deluge in the days of Noah, with a disagreement as to whether the land of Israel was inundated at that time. *b. Zeb.* 113a; *Lev. R.* 31:10. The Samaritans believed that Mt. Gerizim was unaffected by the Deluge, citing this passage in Ezek. as prooftext. *Deut. R.* 3:6.

[13]A strange interpretation of the MT, which has "a conspiracy of prophets." But just as the prophets in MT must refer to false prophets, so the Targumic rendering must refer to teachers who expound false doctrines. Cf. *Tg.* Is. 9:14; MT: "and the teacher who teaches falsehood, he is the weakling." Cf. also *Tg.* Is. 3:2.

There must have been a proliferation of teachers who were teaching ideas that were unacceptable to the normative Jewish community. Testimony to that effect was given by R. Johanan, who said: "Israel did not go into exile until they produced twenty four sects of *Minim.*" *y. Sanh.* 29c. "*Minim*" were varieties of heretics and non-conformists of one kind or another, from the standpoint of the Jewish religion. See R.T. Herford, *Christianity in Talmud and Midrash,* p. 181.

[14]MT: "devoured."

[15]MT: "have done violence to."

[16]MT: "so that I am profaned." *Tg.* makes the will of God the surrogate.

[17]MT: "have daubed for them with whitewash." Cf. 13:10 *supra.*

[18]This is a most unusual rendering of the Hebrew *belo'mišpat,* "without justice." *Tg.*'s translation might have been *belo'dina'* "outside the law." However, there may be some legal questions pertaining to the proselyte's rights, and hence the reluctance to translate it in the usual manner. See *S-A,* p. 55 f.

[19]MT: "who would build up the wall." Not just anybody may intercede for the people. However, see *b. B.B.* 116a; *b. Šab.* 67a, for a different opinion.

[20]MT: "in behalf of the land."

[21]MT: "with the fire of My fury."

Notes, Chapter 23

[1]MT: "they played the harlot in Egypt, they played the harlot in their youth; for there they let their breasts be squeezed and their virgin nipples fondled." Note the euphemistic generalization. Throughout this chapter, as in ch. 16, *Tg.* renders the glaring specific sexual references in subdued tones and modified interpretaion, in terms of idolatry.

[2]MT: "they became mine."

[3]MT: "she played the harlot under Me, and she lusted after her lovers." Cf. BDB, p. 721, sub *'agab.*

[4]*Tg.* reads *q'robeha* for MT's *q'robim.* LXX does the same. Rashi follows the *Tg.*

[5]MT: "She did not give up her harlotry from Egypt, for they had lain with her in her youth, and had squeezed her virgin breasts, and poured out their lust upon her."

her *people* they slew with the sword. She became a byword for the *countries;*[6] and they executed *just punishment* upon her.[c] 11. Her sister Oholibah saw this, yet she corrupted her love more than her sister; and *her idols* exceeded *the idols* of her sister. 12. It pleased her to stray after the Assyrians, neighboring governors and officers, in full battle garb, horsemen riding on horses, desirable young men, all of them. 13. And *it was revealed before me* that she had become defiled; it was one way, alike for both of them. 14. But she added to her *idolatry,* when she saw men portrayed on the wall, figures of Chaldeans portrayed in colors, 15. girded with belts around their waists, helmets on their heads. All of them had the appearance of valiant men, the likeness of Babylonians from the country of the Chaldeans, the land of their birth. 16. And *it pleased her to stray* after them, after what she saw with her eyes; so she sent messengers to them, to *the country of the land of* the Chaldeans. 17. Now the Babylonians came to her to make love, and they defiled her *with their idolatry;* and she defiled herself with them until she became disgusted with them.[d] 18. *But her disgraceful conduct had been exposed,* and her shame was seen, so *My Memra* loathed her as *My Memra* had loathed her sister. 19. Yet she increased her *idolatry,* remembering the former days in which she had strayed with them when she was in the land of Egypt. 20. And it pleased her to be a servant[e] for them,[e] whose flesh was the flesh of asses, and whose offensive smell[7] was like that of horses. 21. And you recalled the sins of your previous *conspiracy of transgression,* you made love on account of the sins of your childhood, ever since Egypt. 22. Therefore, O Oholibah, thus says the Lord God, Behold I will *swiftly* bring against you, your friends with whom you became disgusted, and I will bring them against you from all around. 23. The Babylonianas and all the Chaldeans, those of Pekod, and of Shoa, and of Koa, and all the Assyrians with them, desirable young men, governors and officers, all of them, valiant men and ready, all of them riding on horseback. 24. And they shall come against you with armor, with chariots, and wheels, and with an encampment of peoples who will be armed with shields and helmets. They shall array themselves against you on all sides. And I will place before them the matter of *just punishment* and they shall *call you to account* according to their laws. 25. And I will *execute*[f] *My punishment* on you, and they shall *exact payment* from you with fury. *Your princes and your nobles shall be exiled* and your people shall be slain with the sword. They shall take your sons and daughters *captive,* and *the choicest of your land* shall be burned with fire.[8] 26. They shall strip you of your expensive clothes and remove your beautiful garments. 27. And I will put a stop to *the sins of your conspiracy of transgression* and *your worship of idols,* which had been with you when you were in the land of Egypt, so that your eyes shall not be lifted up to them and you shall never again recall *the idolatry of* the Egyptians. 28. For thus says the Lord God, Behold I will deliver you into the hand of those whom you hate, into the hand of those with whom you became disgusted. 29. They shall *call you to account* with animosity and

Apparatus, Chapter 23 continued

[c] SP. RB: "in her midst."
[d] Lit. "her soul loathed them."
[e] According to K. Or "prostitute." K offers alternative reading: "to be taken away by them."
[f] Lit. "give."

[g] K: "you shall be plucked up by your breasts (my RB reads, by your hair).
[h] K: "righteous."
[i] RB: "you."
[j] RB: "swallowed up by sins."

take away all that you have earned, and leave you *homeless* and *abandoned;* and the disgrace of *your idolatry* and *the sins of your conspiracy of transgression* and your *premeditated sins* shall be exposed. 30. *Your sins* have caused you all this, in that you *have strayed* after the nations and have become defiled by *worshipping* their idols. 31. You have walked in the way of your sister, and I wll place her cup *of punishment* in your hand. 32 Thus says the Lord God, "You shall drink your sister's cup *of punishment, the strong* one and the *hard* one. You shall be an object of derision and mockery. Much shall be the trouble which shall come over you. 33. *Behold,* you shall be filled with *pain* and sorrow. A cup of despair and desolation , a *cup of punishment* is that of your sister, Samaria. 34. You shall drink it and finish it; her *punishment you shall receive;* and you shall *tear your flesh,[8]* for I have decreed it by *\My Memra,* says the Lord God. 35. Therefore, thus says the Lord God, Because you have abandoned My *worship* and cast away My *faith* from before your eyes, you, too, shall be held accountable for *the sins of your conspiracy of transgression and your idolatry."* 36. The Lord said to me, "Son of Adam, Would you *admonish* Oholah and Oholibah, then declare their abominations to them. 37. For there are adulterers[h] among them; and they have shed *innocent* blood with their hands; and they have *strayed* after *the worship of* their idols; and even their children, from whom there should have descended offspring sacred before Me, they passed them through the fire *in pagan ritual.[9]* 38. Also in this they caused anger *before* Me: they defiled My Holy Temple on that day and they profaned My Sabbaths. 39. For when they had slaughtered their children *in worship of* their idols, on that same day they came into My Holy Temple, desecrating it. Behold, this is what they did within My Holy Temple! 40. Moreover, they[i] sent for men who came from afar, to whom a messenger was sent, and behold, they came to the place which you *had arranged; you made ready the markets and appointed market overseers.[10]* 41. *You set up* fashionable couches with expensive pillows, and tables *full of many good things* you spread before them;[11] and My incense and My oil you placed upon them. 42. The sound of their noisy crowds was that of thoughtless unconcern in her midst; and strong men, and numerous people came from all around — from the desert; and they put bracelets on their hands and a beautiful crown on their heads. 43. And I said *to the Congregation of Israel whose people* were worn out by *sins,[j][12]* now *she will give up her idolatry* and

Notes, Chapter 23 continued

[6]MT: "women."

[7]*Tg.*'s rendering, *wesaḥnat,* is a homonym, meaning either "issue" or "offensive smell." The exegesis is challenging, because here again the Targumic line is to circumvent the sexual references by its own refinement. On the other hand, it can conceivably be read according to MT: "issue."

[8]MT: "I will set My jealousy against you, and they shall deal with you in fury. They shall cut off your nose and your ears, and the last of you shall fall by the sword. They shall take away your sons and your daughters, and your residue shall be devoured by fire."

[9]MT: "to be consumed." *Tg.* renders it, "in (pagan) ritual." LXX: "they passed them through the fire." V: "to be devoured." Some English translations: "for food."

[10]An economic interpretation of MT's description of female make-up. MT: "you bathed, painted your eyes, and adorned yourself with finery."

[11]*Tg.*'s language seems to reflect the luxurious Roman and Hellenistic dining room atmosphere. See *S-A,* p. 110.

[12]*Lam. R.* 33:6 makes an interesting observation. "Aquila translates Ezek. 23:43a, I said to the *panaia porne* (worn out prostitute)." Aquila reflects the views of his teacher, who, according to Jerome, was R. Akiba. See article "Aquila" in *JE.* II, p. 34 f.

return to My worship; but she did not return.[k13] 44. But they went in to her, as men go in to a woman *brothelkeeper,*[14] so did they go in to Oholah and to Oholibah, *countries with their conspiracies of transgression.*[15] 45. But righteous men, who are opposed to them, shall *exact payment* from them, punishment of adulteresses and punishment of women who shed blood; for there are adulterers among them and *innocent* blood they have shed with their hands." 46. For thus says the Lord God, "*Prophesy* that armies might go up against them, and deliver them for crushing and spoil. 47. And the armies shall pelt them with stones from the *sling,* and split them with their swords;[m] and they shall slay their sons and daughters, and burn their houses with fire. 48. And I will bring to an end *the sins of the conspiracy of transgression* from the land and *all countries* shall be subjugated, so that they shall not act in accordance with your *conspiracy of transgression.* 49. And *the sins of your conspiracy of transgression* shall be visited upon you, and you shall bear the penalty for the transgressions of your idolatry; and you shall know that I am the Lord God."

CHAPTER 24

1. The word of *prophecy from before* the Lord was with me in the ninth year in the tenth month, on the tenth day of the month,[1] saying: 2. "Son of Adam, write for yourself the name of the day, of this very day; on this very day the king of Babylon has besieged[2] Jerusalem. 3. And *proclaim a prophecy*[3] to the rebellious people and say to them, Thus says the Lord God, *Prophesy that armies shall go up against the city* and *also that an ultimatum*[a] *shall be*[b] *given to her to surrender.*[c4] 4. *Gather her princes in the midst of her, every valiant, fear-inspiring man and warrior; fill her with the armies of nations.* 5. *Bring near the kings of the nations, and also equip the siege-troops together with them; announce her time,*[d] *and also let her slain be piled up in her midst.*[5] 6. Therefore, thus says the Lord God, Woe to the city in whose midst *innocent* blood was shed, for she is *like* a pot whose filth is in it, whose filth has not gone out of it. *Exile upon exile, her people has been driven out because no repentance was practiced in her.*[6] 7. For the *innocent* blood which has been shed in the midst of her, *with premeditation, with arm held high did she shed it; she did not shed it by mistake, so that she might be repentant for it.*[7] 8. *To effect punishment,* to take vengeance *with force, have I uncovered their sins,* because they shed *innocent*

Apparatus, Chapter 23 continued

[k] Or "repent."

[m] RB and K. SP: "at their end."

Apparatus, Chapter 24

[a] Lit. "a time limit."
[b] SP: "has been."
[c] Lit. "accept the siege."

[d] K and MM: "four times."
[e] Or "false accusations."
[f] Lit. "let them be on your head."

blood so *swiftly, that it cannot be forgiven.*[8] 9. Therefore, thus says the Lord God, Woe to the city in whose midst one shed *innocent* blood; I, too will make *her misfortune*[9] great. 10. *Make numerous the kings, gather the armies, equip the siege-troops, and invite warriors against her, so that her valiant men shall be confounded.*[10] 11. *And I will leave the land desolate, so that the gates of her cities shall be desolate and demolished; and those who do unclean things* shall melt away in the midst of her; *her sin shall be destroyed.*[11] 12. *She has become filled with intrigue;*[e] *and those who do evil have not left her.* She shall be burned with fire *because of her many sins.*[12] 13. *When you became unclean by your conspiracy of transgressions,*[13] because I tried to cleanse you but you would not be cleansed from your defilement, you shall not be cleansed again until I have accomplished My fury upon you. 14. I the Lord have decreed it by *My Memra.* It has come and shall be fulfilled! I will not hold back, and I will not spare, and will have no pity![14] According to your evil ways and your rotten deeds *will I call you to account,*[15] says the Lord God." 15. The word of *prophecy from before* the Lord was with me, saying: 16. "Son of Adam, behold I am taking away from you the delight of your eyes by plague, but you must not mourn nor weep, nor shed tears. 17. Sob quietly; do not perform the rites of mourning for the dead. Wear your *phylacteries,*[16] put your shoes on your feet, do not cover

Notes, Chapter 23 continued

[13]MT (uncertain): "now they shall take advantage of her harlotry, but she ..."
[14]MT: "harlot."
[15]MT: "women (?) of lewdness."

Notes, Chapter 24

[1]*b.R.H.* 18b. associates this date with Zech. 8:19, which mentions the fast days of the fourth, fifth, seventh and tenth months. All four are based on historical events connected with the tragedy of the destruction of the first Temple. According to R. Akiba, these fast days are the ninth of Tammuz, the ninth of Ab, the third of Tishri, and the tenth of Tebet, the date indicated in this v. In subsequent Jewish practice, the seventeenth of Tammuz, related to the siege of the second Temple by Titus, is observed, in preference to the ninth. *b. Ta'an* 26b. According to *y. Ta'an.* 68c, the fast of Tammuz is, to begin with, on the seventeenth, not the ninth, even according to R. Akiba.

[2]*smk,* lit., "leaned on," "pressed against." *Tg.* employs same verb as the Hebrew.

[3]MT: "propound a parable."

[4]MT: "put on the caldron, put it on, and also pour water into it, etc., etc." Cf. Ezek. 11:3, 11 and Jer. 1:13 ff. In vv. 3-12 of this chapter *Tg.* departs from the poetic allegory of MT and provides an interpretation in terms of the conditions of siege which *Tg.* sees in the poetic language.

[5]MT (vv. 4, 5): "put into it the pieces, all the good pieces, the thigh and the shoulder, fill it with the choicest bones. Take the most select of the flock, and arrange the bones at the bottom of it. Seethe it thoroughly, so that even the bones are boiled."

[6]MT: "empty it piece after piece; no lot has fallen on her."

[7]MT: "she set it upon a bare rock; she did not pour it out on the ground, to cover it with dust."

[8]MT: "to rouse fury, to take vengeance, I have placed her blood on a bare rock, that it might not be covered."

[9]MT: "her pile."

[10]MT: "pile on the wood, kindle the fire, boil the meat thoroughly, add spices, and let the bones be burned."

[11]MT: "stand it empty on the coals, in order that it may become hot, that its copper might glow; then its filthiness shall melt away in it, and its rust shall be consumed."

[12]MT (uncertain): "... its abundant filthiness cannot leave it except by fire."

[13]MT: "because of your filthy lewdness."

[14]MT: "I will not relent." *Tg.* reads *'arahem* instead of *'ennahem.*

[15]MT: "they have judged you."

[16]MT: "bind your head-dress upon you."

your upper lip, and do not eat the bread of *mourners.*"[17] 18. So I *prophesied* to the people in the morning, and my wife died in the evening. The next morning I did as I had been commanded. 19. And the people said to me, "Will you not tell us what these things which you are doing mean for us?" 20. Then I said to them, "The word of *prophecy from before* the Lord was with me, saying: 21. 'Say to the House of Israel, Thus says the Lord God, Behold I am about to desecrate My Holy Temple, the glory of your strength, the delight of your eyes, and the love of your life;[g] and your sons and daughters, whom you had abandoned, shall be slain by the sword. 22. And you shall do as I have done. You shall not cover your upper lip, nor eat the bread of *mourners.* 23. Your *phylacteries* shall be on your heads and your shoes on your feet; you shall not mourn and you shall not weep, but you shall melt away because of your sins, and you shall sob to one another. 24. Ezekiel shall be a sign for you. You shall do according to all that he has done, when it comes. And you shall know the I am the Lord God.' 25. And you, Son of Adam, will it not be, on the day when I take away from them and *from* their sons and *from* their daughters, *their Holy Temple,* the glory of their strength, and their crowning joy, the delight of their eyes[h] and the love of their life *which is so good for them,* shall be taken from them. 26. On that day the fugitive shall come to you to give you[i] the report. 27. On that day, when the fugitive comes, your mouth shall be opened and you shall *prophesy,* and no longer be silent. So you shall be a sign for them, and they shall know that I am the Lord."

CHAPTER 25

1. The word of *prophecy from before* the Lord was with me, saying: 2. "Son of Adam, *hear this prophecy concerning* the Ammonites, and prophesy against them. 3. And say to the Ammonites, Hear the word of the Lord God. Thus says the Lord God, Because you said 'Hurrah'[a] over My sanctuary, that it was desecrated; and over the land of Israel, that it had become desolate; and over those of the House of Judah, that they went into exile. 4. therefore, behold, I am handing you over to the sons of the East[b1] as a possession, and they shall occupy their castles within you, and shall spread[c] their encampments within you. They shall eat *the best of your land* and *take*

Apparatus, Chapter 24 continued

[g] Or "soul."
[h] SP omits these two clauses.

[i] Lit. "to let you hear."

Apparatus, Chapter 25

[a] Lit. "O joy!"
[b] Or "easterners."
[c] RB and AP: "dwell."
[d] SP: "with puffed up spirit."

[e] Lit. "How are those of the House of Judah different."
[f] Other versions: "to the sons of Qedem."

your property as spoil.[2] 5. I will make Rabbah a dwelling place for camels and the Ammonites a resting-place for flocks of sheep; and you shall know that I am the Lord. 6. For thus says the Lord God, Because you have clapped with your hands and stamped with your foot and rejoiced with *utter recklessness*[d] over the land of Israel; 7. therefore, behold, I am lifting up *My striking power*[3] against you, and I will give you as a spoil[4] to the nations; I will cut you off from among the peoples, and I will destroy you; I will make you a desolation among countries, and you shall know that I am the Lord." 8. Thus says the Lord God: "Because the Moabites and Seir say, *'Why should those of the House of Judah fare differently*[e] *from all the nations?'* [5] 9. therefore, behold, I am *shattering the might* of Moab, from its cities, its villages, to its open towns, the delight of their land Beth-Jeshimoth, Baal-Meon, and Kiria-thaim. 10. The sons of the East shall come against the Ammonites,[f] and I will turn her over as a possession, so that there shall be no remembrance of the Ammonites among the nations. 11. And I will inflict *just punishment* on Moab, and they shall know that I am the Lord. 12. Thus says the Lord God: Because the Edomites acted with powerful vengeance towards the House of Judah and have committed a grievous sin by taking revenge upon them, 13. therefore, thus says the Lord God, I will lift up *My striking power*[3] against Edom and destroy from it man and beast, and I will make it a ruin *from the south;* and the inhabitants of Dedan shall be slain by the sword. 14. And I will inflict My punishment upon Edom; they shall be delivered into the hand of My people Israel, and they shall take vengeance upon Edom according to My wrath;[6] and they shall know *My punishment,*[7] says the Lord God. 15. Thus says the Lord God: Because the Philistines acted with hatred and took vengeance *with utter recklessness,*[d] so as to destroy with everlasting hatred, 16. therefore, thus says the Lord God, I will lift up *My striking power*[3] against the Philistines and I will destroy *the nation that deserves to be destroyed*[8] and I will demolish the rest of the seacoast. 17. I will execute great vengeance upon them with mighty fury; and they shall know that I am the Lord, when I inflict *My punishment*[7] upon them."

Notes, Chapter 24 continued

[17]The Halakah forbids the mourner to do certain things as the signs of mourning. Though he has lost his wife, Ezekiel is enjoined by God to disregard those prohibitions. Cf. *b.M.K.* 15a. *Tg.*'s rendering agrees with the Halakah. Cf. *b. Suk.* 25b; *b. Ber.* 11a.

Notes, Chapter 25

[1]*Tg.* understands *qedem* geographically, not as a proper noun.

[2]MT: "they shall eat your fruit and drink your milk."

[3]MT: "My hand."

[4]*Tg.* follows Q, *lbz.* The Ket., *lbg,* is unintelligible. Kimhi ingeniously explains it by the method of A"T B"H, in which the letters G and Z are interchangeable.

[5]MT: "the House of Judah is like all other nations."

[6]This v. is used in a curious way in Talmudic legend. "The emperor sent Nero Caesar against the Jews. As he was coming, he shot an arrow to the east and it fell in the direction of Jerusalem; to the west , and it fell towards Jerusalem; in all directions, and it still fell towards Jerusalem. He said to a youngster, Quote me your verse. He replied, I shall take my vengeance upon Edom by the hand of My people Israel (Ezek. 25:14). Whereupon Nero said, The Holy One blessed be He wants to detroy His Temple, but He wants to clear Himself by blaming me. So he ran away, and went and became a proselyte; and R. Meir descended from him." *b. Git.* 56a.

[7]MT: "My vengeance."

[8]MT: "I will cut off the Kerethites." a play on words. *Tg.* takes up the play, but interprets the last word not as a proper noun.

CHAPTER 26

1. It was in the eleventh year, on the first day of the month, that the word of *prophecy from before* the Lord was with me, saying: 2. "Son of Adam, because Tyre said about Jerusalem, 'Hurrah! She is broken, *who used to supply merchandise to the nations.*[1] She has come around to me;[a] *she who was full*[2] lies in ruins,' 3. therefore, thus says the Lord God, Behold, I am *sending My wrath* against you, O Tyre, and I will make *the armies of* many nations rise against you as the sea rises with *the roaring of* its waves. 4. They shall destroy the walls of Tyre, and break down her towers; I will denude[b] her of her soil, and make her as smooth as a bare[c] rock. 5. She shall be a place for spreading of nets in the midst of the sea, for I have decreed it *by My Memra,* says the Lord God, and she shall become spoil for the nations. 6. And *those who inhabit her villages*[3] which are in the field shall be slain by the sword, and they shall know that I am the Lord. 7. For thus says the Lord God, Behold, I am bringing against Tyre, Nebuchadrezzar,[d] king of Babylon from the north, a king of kings, with horses and chariots, and horsemen, and armies with many people. 8. He shall slay by the sword *the inhabitants of your villages*[3] which are in the field; he will build a siege tower against you and pile up a mound against you, and raise against you those who are armed with shields. 9. And a striking force of his battering rams he shall place against your walls, and your towers he will smash with his *projectiles*[e] *of iron.*[4] 10. From the *stamping*[f][5] of his horses their dust shall cover you; your walls shall shake from the noise of horsemen, wheels and chariots, when he enters your gates, like those who enter a city which has been breached *from its wall.* 11. With the hoofs of his horses he shall trample all your streets; he shall slay your people with the sword; and your mighty pillars he shall pull down to the ground. 12. They shall take your property as spoil and capture your merchandise; they shall break through your walls and break down your pleasant houses; your stones and timber and soil they shall cast into the midst of the water. 13. I will put a stop to your noisy songs, and the *melodious* sound of your harps shall be heard no more. 14. I will make you bare as a smooth rock; you shall be a place for the spreading of nets; you shall never be rebuilt; for I the Lord have decreed it *by My Memra,* says the Lord God." 15. Thus says the Lord God to Tyre: "Will not the port cities quake from the sound of the fall *of your slain,* at the groan of those wounded by the sword, when the slain are piled up in the

Apparatus, Chapter 26

[a] Lit. "she has been turned coming to me."
[b] Lit. "uproot."
[c] Lit. "uncovered."

[d] Some versions: "Nebuchadnezzar."
[e] Or "catapults." Lit. "stones."
[f] MM: "hoofs."

Apparatus, Chapter 27

[a] Or, "architects."

midst of you? 16. Then all the princes of the sea shall descend from their thrones, and remove their robes, and throw off their embroidered garments. They shall clothe themselves with trembling; they shall sit on the ground and shudder *because of their misfortunes,* and they shall be desolate on account of you. 17. And they shall take up a lamentation over you and say to you, How you have perished, you who had dwelt in the midst of the seas, O renowned city, that resided by the might of the sea, both she and her inhabitants. How have all her inhabitants *been delivered to misfortune!*[6] 18. Now the port cities shall tremble on the day when *your slain* shall fall; the islands of the sea shall be appalled by your departure into exile. 19. For thus says the Lord God: When I make you a devastated city, like the cities that are uninhabited, when I bring up against you *the armies of nations who are as numerous as* the waters of the deep; and *many nations*[7] shall cover you; 20. then I will bring you down, with those who descend to the Pit *of Hell,*[8] to a people from ancient times, and I will make you desolate, in the nether-world, like the ruins of antiquity, with those who descend to the Pit *of Hell;* so that you shall remain uninhabited. But I will give *joy* to the *land of Israel.*[9] 21. I will make you *as though you had never been,* and *so you shall be.*[10] You shall be sought, but you shall never be found again, ever, says the Lord God."

CHAPTER 27

1. The word of *prophecy from before* the Lord was with me, saying: 2. "Now you, Son of Adam, take up a lamentation over Tyre. 3. And say to Tyre, which sits at the entrance *of the harbors* of the sea, which supplies the nations with merchandise on many coast-lands, Thus says the Lord God: O Tyre, you have said, 'I am perfect in my beauty.' 4. Your borders are in the midst of the seas, your artisans[a] have perfected *your buildings.*[1] 5. Of cypress trees of Senir they built all of your planks for you; they

Notes, Chapter 26

[1]MT: "the gateways of the peoples."
[2]MT: "I shall be filled." *Tg.,* as LXX, reads *hammle'ah,* instead of MT's *'immal'ah.*
[3]MT: "her daughters."
[4]MT: "his swords."
[5]MT: "the abundance."
[6]MT: "who struck terror upon all its inhabitants."
[7]MT: "many waters."
[8]*gob bet'abdana',* which can mean either "the pit of the place of destruction" or "the pit of the place of perdition." I have rendered it "the Pit of Hell," following Rashi, who interprets MT "with those who descend to Gehenna."
[9]MT: "but I will give beauty in the land of the living."
[10]MT: "I will bring you to a horrible end, and you shall be no more." Rashi explains *Tg*'s exegesis as dividing the word into *bal hawat,* "not have you been." V's translation is similar: "I will bring you to nothing, and you shall not be."

Notes, Chapter 27

[1]MT: "your beauty."

took cedars from Lebanon to make masts for you. 6. Of oaks from Bashan they made the oars *of your ships; the frames of your doors* they made of boards of box-wood,[2] inlaid with ivory; *a canopied house for a theatre,*[3] from the country of *Apulia.*[4] 7. Of linen and embroidery from Egypt was your sail, to serve as your ensign; blue and purple from the *country of Italy*[5] was your awning. 8. The inhabitants of Sidon and Arvad were oarsman *and brought merchandise to your midst.* Your wise men, O Tyre, were in you; they were your pilots.[b] 9. The elders of Gebal and her wise men were in you, making your repairs. All *those who go down to* the ships of the sea and their sailors *were oarsmen,* bringing merchandise into your midst. 10. Men of Persia, Lud and Put were in your army, your warriors; they hung shields and helmets in you; they enhanced your splendor. 11. The sons of Arvad and your army were upon your walls round about; they perfected[c] your beauty. 12. *From the sea*[6] they brought merchandise to your midst; an abundance of all kinds of wealth, in silver, iron, tin and lead, *they placed in your storehouses.*[d] 13. Greece,[7] Tubal and Meshech, they were your merchants; they brought merchandise into your midst, human lives[8] and copper utensils.[9] 14. From the country of Garmamia,[10] horses, horsemen and mules brought merchandise into your midst. 15. The people of Dedan were your merchants; the inhabitants of many islands brought merchandise into your midst; with horns *of wild goats,* tusks of *ivory,*[11] and *peacocks,*[12] they brougth back an offering[13] to you. 16. *From* Aram they brought merchandise into your midst, because of your great *wealth;*[14] *purple robes,*[15] embroidery, fine linen, precious stones and pearls *they placed in your store-houses.* 17. Judah and the land of Israel, they were your merchants, in wheat *pastry and parched grain,*[16] honey, oil, and balm, which they placed *in your shops.* 18. From Damascus they brought merchandise into your midst, because of your great wealth, great wealth of every kind, in wine, vinegar sauce, and soft fluffy[e] wool of fine sheep. 19. Vedan and Javan[17] brought your wares *in caravans,*[18] baled with iron bands; cassia and calamus spice *they placed in your shops.* 20. From Dedan they brought merchandise into your midst — expensive outfits for riding. 21. Arabia and all the princes of Nabataea, they were your merchants, in *oxen,* rams and goats; in them was your trade. 22. The merchants of Sheba and Raamah, they were your merchants, in the finest of all spices and in all precious stones and gold. *They placed these in your store-houses.* 23. Haran and *Nisibis* and *Hadyab,* the merchants of Sheba, the country of Assyria and *Media,*[19] they were your merchants. 24. They were your merchants in the very finest kinds of valuable things; in cut woolens of blue; in cloaks embroidered with a design of roses;[f] in official garments of crimson *laid out in wooden chests covered with leather,* bound with cords of hemp and sealed *with an engraved signet ring made of a marine substance, deposited in towers of myrtle-wood.* In them was your trade. 25. They would travel in *ocean-going*[20] ships and bring merchandise into your midst. So *you became rich and very powerful*[21] in the midst of the seas. 26. In many waters have they swept in upon you, *they who have plundered you; a king as mighty as* the east

Apparatus, Chapter 27 continued

[b] Lit. "chiefs," "leaders."
[c] Lit. "completed."
[d] Or "treasuries."

[e] Lit. "downy."
[f] RB: "cedars."

wind has crushed you in the midst of the seas. 27. Your riches and your property, your merchandise, your mariners and your pilots, your repairmen and those who bring the wares of your shops, and all the valiant warriors who are in you and in all the armies in you, shall fall into the midst of the seas, on the day of the downfall *of your slain*. 28. At the sound of the outcry of your pilots, your port-cities shall quake. 29. And all the oarsmen, the mariners, all the maritime administrators, shall come down from their ships and stand upon the land. 30. And they shall raise their voices

Notes, Chapter 27 continued

[2]MT's *bat 'ašurim* is read as one word *bet'ašurim* by *Tg.*, which translates it as "with box-wood." Rashi and Kimhi follow suit. So does BDB, p. 81, sub *te'aššur.*

[3]*bet ḥufa'ah l'atiṭron.* Rashi understands the latter as two words, and renders the phrase "a covered house that cannot collapse," (from the root, *try,* "to move" or "to shake"). Kimhi confesses that he does not understand the meaning of the *Tg.*, and he cites some versions that read *l'atar naṭron,* "guard-house." The simple fact is that the word, undivided, is an Aramaic variant of the Greek *theatron,* "theatre." See Levy, II, p. 525; Jastrow, I, p. 61, sub *'ityatron.*

As it stands, the phrase in the *Tg.*, seems to be an additional feature of Tyre, which *Tg.* provides on its own. Since the symbolism is that of a ship, and since the *Tg.* was familiar with Greco-Roman culture, this may indicate that there was a theatre of some kind on Roman galleys for the entertainment of the ship's administrators. LXX: "shaded houses of wood."

[4]MT: *kittiyyim.* Cf. *Tg.* Onq. Num. 24:24. Apulia was a province in the southeast of Italy. While LXX carries over the Hebrew, V renders "Italy." The identity of some of the geographic locales in the *Tg.* is problematic, even questionable. However, what is certain is *Tg.*'s exegetical effort to provide names of places which would be familiar to its contemporaries. Cf. M. McNamara, *Targum and Testament,* p. 196, sub "Italy." For a further critical analysis of place names, see *IB,* p. 213 f.

[5]MT: "the isles of Elishah." The ships's furnishings mentioned here are the subject of halakic discussion in *m.B.B.* 5:1 and *b.B.B.* 73a.

[6]MT: "*taršiš.*"

[7]MT and *Tg.: yawan.* The word may mean Greece, and is so rendered both by LXX and V.

[8]As slaves and chattel.

[9]The poetic ring of *Tg.*'s rendering is worth noting: *benafša' de' anaša' umane nehaša',* with the unmistakable intimation that in Tyre human life was looked upon as being as valuable as a piece of copper. That Jewish slaves were part of the stock-in-trade of the Greeks is evident from Joel 4:6.

[10]The identity of Garmamia is in some doubt. Jastrow I, p. 270, is of the opinion that it is the land of the Cimmerii. Levy identifies it as the Roman province of Germania, modern Germany, I. p. 155. See *S-A,* p. 118 and n. 375; M. McNamara, *Targum and Testament,* p. 194, sub Germania.

[11]MT: *qarnot šen. Tg.* feels that the Hebrew is laconic, and supplies what is missing: horns *of wild goats* and tusks *of the elephants* (ivory).

[12]MT (Q): "ebony." Rashi follows *Tg.*

[13]*qurbanak. Tg.* uses the same word that is used for the sacrifices offered to the deity. In this context it may have the force of "tribute," or "gift."

[14]*Tg.* read *m'ašrayik,* instead of MT's *ma'asayik.*

[15]MT: *benofek.nofek* is a precious stone which was in the breast-plate of the high priest, Ex. 28:18; 39:11. *Tg.*'s rendering, "robes," or "cloaks," or simply "garments," is rather strange. Kimhi: "I am surprised at *Tg.*'s translation, because *nfk* is the name of a precious stone mentioned in the Torah." I suggest that *Tg.* may have had a text of the Hebrew at variance with MT that we possess. That text may have read *bnsk,* with *Samek* instead of *Pe,* based on the verb *nsk,* one meaning of which is "to weave." See BDB, p. 651, sub *nsk* II.

[16]These terms, like the Hebrew, are uncertain. Both Rashi and Kimhi find the text difficult, and do not understand the meaning of the *Tg.* Rashi's comment is of interest in that he quotes a R. Shimeon, that he found in a volume of Scripture a Targum Yerushalmi which translated *b'ḥitte minnit ufannag,* "of milled grain and corn, milled barley." He also quotes the same source as having a slight variant of *Tg.* Ezek. 39:16.

My translation is according to Jastrow, II, p. 1474, sub *rihuš,* and p. 1328, sub *qulya'.*

[17]*Tg.* follows MT, which may be corrupt, since *yawan* was already mentioned in v. 13.

[18]MT: *m'uzl,* which *Tg.* takes as a passive from the Aramaic *'azl,* hence, "to be brought," i.e., "in caravans."

[19]MT: *kilmad. Tg.* reads *kal madai,* "all of Media."

[20]MT: *taršiš.*

[21]MT: "so you became full and heavy (or honored)."

over you, and cry out bitterly: they shall place[g] dust upon their heads and they shall be covered[h] with ashes. 31. They shall pluck their hair on your account, and gird themselves with sackcloth, and weep over you in bitterness of soul and they shall observe bitter mourning. 32. In their affliction they shall raise a lamentation over you and they shall wail over you, 'Who was like Tyre? There was none *compared to her*[22] in the midst of the seas!' 33. When your merchandise came from among the seas you satisfied many nations; with your abundant wealth and property you enriched the kings of the earth. 34. *Now* you *who dwelt in the midst of the seas*[i] are broken;[23] in the midst of the seas, into the depths of the waters have fallen your merchandise and all of your armed forces within you. 35. All the inhabitants of the islands are confounded over you, and their kings are trembling convulsively; their faces have become drawn. 36. The merchants among the nations are appalled[24] at you; *they regard* you as *though you had never* existed;[25] and so you shall be, forever."

CHAPTER 28

1. The word of *prophecy from before* the Lord was with me, saying: 2. "Son of Adam, say to the *king* of Tyre,[1] Thus says the Lord God: Because you are arrogant and have said, 'I am a god.[2] I sit in the seat of *the mighty*[3] in the midst of the seas;' whereas you are a man, *and not indispensable,*[a4] although you think in your heart that you are a god. 3. Behold, are you wiser than Daniel?[5] Is no secret concealed from you?[6] 4. By your wisdom and your understanding you have acquired for yourself material possessions, and you have gathered gold and silver into your treasuries. 5. By your great wisdom in your commerce you have enlarged your *armies,*[7] and because of your *armies* you have become arrogant.[8] 6. Therefore, thus says the Lord God, Because you have thought in your heart you are a god, 7. therefore, behold, I am bringing strangers against you, the mightiest of nations, and they shall draw their swords against the *adornment of your wisdom,*[9] and they shall demolish your awe-inspiring splendor. 8. They shall bring you down to destruction, and you shall die the death of those who are struck by the sword, in the midst of the seas. 9. Will you continue to say, 'I am a god,' before those who slay you, you being a man, *and not indispensable,*[a] in the hand of those who destroy you? 10. You shall die the death of *the wicked*[10] at the hand of strangers, for I have decreed it *by My*

Apparatus, Chapter 27 continued

[g] Lit. "lift," "raise."
[h] MM. SP: "rubbed."

[i] RB: "who supplied merchandise to the nations."

Apparatus, Chapter 28

[a] Lit., "and there is no need of you."

[b] Or, "the format of a picture."

Memra, says the Lord God." 11. The word of *prophecy from before* the Lord was with me, saying: 12. "Son of Adam, take up a lamentation over the king of Tyre, and say to him, Thus says the Lord God, You were *like the sculptural mold,*[b][11] *fashioned* in wisdom and perfect in its beauty. 13. *In abundant prosperity and luxuries you delighted yourself, as though you were residing* in Eden,[12] the garden of *the Lord.*[13] *Wealth, grandeur and honor were given to you.* Your robe was adorned with all kinds of jewels, carnelian, topaz and diamonds; beryl of the sea and spotted stones; sapphire, emerald and smaragd; *inlaid in* gold. *All these were made for your adornment; as a result, you have become arrogant; however, you did not reflect wisely on*

Notes, Chapter 27 continued

[22]MT: "when she was silenced." cf. Ps. 115:7. *Tg.* reads *kedomeh* (The vocalization is essential to an understanding of *Tg.*'s exegesis.), "compared to."

[23]MT: *'et nisheret, Tg.* reads *'attah nishart.*

[24]MT: "they hiss."

[25]Cf. *Tg.* Ezek. 26:21 *supra* and note 8 thereto.

Notes, Chapter 28

[1]The Rabbinic Tradition understood this as referring to Hiram, king of Tyre, who is a fascinating subject of Rabbinic legend. *b. Hul.* 89a; *b. B.B.* 75a; *Gen. R.* 96:5; *passim.* MT: "prince."

[2]MT: *'el. Tg. dahla',* one of the terms used by *Tg.* to designate deity other than Yahweh. It is not as deprecating as *ta'wa* which *Tg.* employs for idolatrous practice. Cf. Churgin, p. 112, f.

[3]MT: *'elohim,* which *Tg.* renders *taqifin,* thus averting even a remote resemblance of the king of Tyre to the God of Israel. For an identical rendering of *'elohim,* see *Tg.* on Ps. 82:1. But, cf. 2c, where *Tg.* has *dahla'* for *'elohim. Yal. Sim.* #367 *ad. loc.* has Hiram comparing himself to God, impregnable both in the sea and in a citadel which he had built into the heavens.

[4]MT: *welo' 'el,* "and not a god."

[5]This v. can be understood either as a statement or as a question. LXX takes it interrogatively, and the context would indicate a note of sarcasm, a response to the king of Tyre's claim to be all wise. Daniel is depicted in 14:14, 20 as a paragon of righteousness. Here he seems to be the ultimate in wisdom. The Sages interpret this verse as God ridiculing Hiram concerning his claim to divinity and omniscience. *Gen. R.* 96:5.

[6]MT: "they have not kept you in the dark," or read as a question. *Tg.* here renders the phrase in passive.

[7]MT: *heleka,* which *Tg.* understands in the sense of "valor," although in v. 4 *Tg.* takes it as "material possessions."

[8]Mundane and commercial wisdom are no substitute for ethics and morality, and have led only to military power and megalomania.

[9]MT: "the beauty of your wisdom."
The implication of *Tg.*'s rendering is that the king of Tyre's sophistication is merely a facade, skin-deep, the Hebrew *yefi* would lend itself to the *Tg.*'s exegetical thrust.

[10]MT: "the uncircumcised."

[11]The MT is uncertain. It could mean "the seal of measurement," or "model of perfection," but the exact meaning is unclear. *taknit* occurs only twice in Scripture, here and in 43:10 *infra. Tg.,* however, reads *tabnit,* "a structural pattern," and renders the entire phrase as an allegorical reference, "like the (original) sculptural mold," i.e. the Primal Adam. In fact, the Rabbis understand this v. as referring to Adam. *b. B.B.* 75a; *Eccl. R.* 7:36; *Pes. R.* 14:10.

[12]*Tg.* continues to interpret the Hebrew metaphorically, not literally. The king of Tyre was not actually in the Garden of Eden, but he was provided with the luxuries that equalled those of Paradise. In this respect, Targumic exegesis departs from some Rabbinic legend, which maintained that Hiram actually resided in the Garden of Eden, and lived a fantastically long life, outliving all the kings of Israel and Judah combined, fifty prophets and ten high priests. Hiram's haughtiness derived form his having given Solomon the cedars for the building of the Temple, and God destroyed the Temple in order to make him humble. *Yal. Sim.* #367. However, Hiram is also numbered among the seven, or nine, who entered alive into Paradise-Eden. *Kallah Rab.* 3:25; *Der. Er. Zut.* 1:18. However, some Rabbinic authorities deny that Hiram was ever in the Garden of Eden. *Gen. R.* 9:5.

[13]MT: *'elohim,* "God."

your body, which consists of orifices and organs[c][14] *of which you have need, for it is impossible for you to survive without them.* They were designed for you from the day on which you were created.[d][15] 14. You are *a king anointed for the kingdom,*[16] and I have given you greatness, but *you looked with contempt* upon the holy mountain of *the Lord,*[13] *and you planned to exercise dominion over the holy people.*[17] 15. You were perfect in your ways from the day you were created, until *falsehood* was found in you. 16. Because of your abundant commerce, your treasuries were filled with *what you had taken by* violence. You sinned; and I made you profane, because you *looked upon* the holy mountain of *the Lord*[13] *with contempt;* and I destroyed you, *O noble king, because you planned to exercise dominion over the holy people.* 17. You grew arrogant because of your might; your wisdom was ruined[e] because of your awesome splendor, *I have*[f] *driven you out over the earth;*[g] I have given you as a warning to kings to ponder over you. 18. Through the multitude of your sins in dishonest trade you have profaned your sanctuary; *and because of your deliberate sins* I brought *nations who are as strong as* fire. *They* shall destroy you; and I will reduce you to ashes on the ground in the eyes of all who see you. 19. All who know you among the nations are astounded over you. *I will make you as though you had never been, and so you shall be,* forever."[18] 20. The word of *prophecy from before* the Lord was with me, saying: 21. "Son of Adam, *hear the prophecy concerning*[19] Sidon, and prophesy against her. 22. And you shall say, Thus says the Lord God, Behold I am *sending My wrath* against you, O Sidon, and I will be glorified in the midst of you. And they shall know that I am the Lord when I visit *just punishment* upon her and I will be sanctified through her. 23. And I will send pestilence into her, and *killing,*[20] into her streets, when the slain shall be flung within her, when I bring against her *those who slay by* the sword, from all around; and they shall know that I am the Lord. 24. Then for the House of Israel there shall no longer be *a wicked king or an annoying ruler*[21] from all who surround and plunder them, and they shall know that I am the Lord God." 25. Thus says the Lord God: "When I gather the House of Israel from among the nations in whom they have been scattered, I will be sanctified

Apparatus, Chapter 28 *continued*

[c] Lit., "holes."

[d] A marginal note in CR cites another Targum on v. 13: "You were in Eden, the garden of the Lord. All kinds of jewels adorned your robe. You saw with your own eyes the ten canopies which I made for the Primal Adam, made of carnelian, topaz and diamonds; beryl of the Mediterranean Sea and spotted stone, sapphire, emerald, smaragd, and fine gold. They showed him at his wedding all the works of Creation, and the angels were running before him with timbrels and with flutes. So, on the day when Adam was created they were prepared to honor him, but after that he went astray and was expelled from there. You, too, did not take a lesson from him but rather, your heart became haughty and you did not reflect wisely on your body, that you are made of orifices and organs which you need for excretion, and it is impossible for you to survive without them. These were designed for you from the day on which you were created."

[e] RB and AP: "you have been ruined by your wisdom."

[f] RB. SP: "it has."

[g] Or, "I have flung you to the ground."

Apparatus, Chapter 29

[a] Or "rings."

[b] Or "destroy you."

through them in the eyes of the nations, and they shall dwell on their land, which I have given to My servant Jacob. 26. And they shall dwell securely on it, and they shall build houses, and plant vineyards. They shall dwell securely when I inflict *just punishment* upon all those around them who have plundered them. Then they shall know that I am the Lord their God."

CHAPTER 29

1. In the tenth year, the tenth month, on the twelfth day of the month, the word of *prophecy from before* the Lord was with me, saying: 2. "Son of Adam, *hear the prophecy* concerning Pharaoh, king of Egypt and prophesy against him and against the *Egyptians,*[1] all of them. 3. *Prophesy,* and say, Thus says the Lord God, Behold I am *sending My wrath* against you, Pharaoh, king of Egypt, *you who are like* the great monster which *dwells* in the midst of the rivers, who said, 'Mine is the *kingdom,* and it is I who have *conquered.*'[2] 4. I will put chains[a] in your jaws and *I will slay your mighty rulers, together with your valiant men, and I will remove you*[b] *from your kingdom; your mighty rulers, together with your valiant men, shall be slain.*[3] 5. And I will banish you to the wilderness, you and *all your mighty rulers,*[4] *your carcass shall be flung* on the open field; you shall not be gathered in, nor shall you be *buried.*[5]

Notes, Chapter 28 continued

[14]MT: *tuppeka uneqabeka,* which BDB p. 666 sub *nqb,* translates "thy sockets and thy grooves." *Tg.* interprets these as the functioning apparatus of the body, which mark the human being as mortal, hence applicable to the king of Tyre, scoffing at his claim to immortality. Commenting on this v., R. Judah quoted Rab: "The Holy One blessed be He said to Hiram king of Tyre, I foresaw concerning you (that you would consider yourself a god), so I created very many orifices in Adam. There are some who say, that this is what God said to Hiram, I foresaw you (that you would consider yourself immortal), so I decreed death upon the Primal Adam." *b. B.B.* 75a, b.

[15]Reference to the ten canopies mentioned in the marginal note in CR is found in *b. B.B.* 75a; *Lev. R.* 20:2; *Pes. R.* 14:10; *Pirq. d'R. El.,* 12.

[16]MT: "you were a protective, anointed cherub."

[17]MT: "you walked among stones of fire."

[18]MT: "you have come to a dreadful end, and shall be no more, forever."

[19]MT: "set your face towards."

[20]MT: "blood."

[21]MT: "a piercing brier or a pain-inflicting thorn." *Tg.* expounds the poetic imagery in terms of the Jewish ideal of peace and independence, enlightened rule for the nation. Cf. *Est. R.,* 9:2.

Notes, Chapter 29

[1]MT: "Egypt." *Tg.*'s rendering implies that God has no quarrel with the land as such, but with its people.

[2]MT: "My Nile is mine, I made it for myself." The marine symbolism of the Hebrew is translated in terms of the political application and ramifications, throughout this prophecy.

[3]MT: "and I will make the fish of your streams cling to your scales; and I will pull you up from the midst of your streams, with all the fish of your streams clinging to your scales."

[4]MT: "the fish of your streams."

[5]*Tg.* reads *tiqqaber* for MT's *tiqqabes.*

To the beasts of the earth and to the birds of the sky have I delivered you, to be consumed. 6. Then all the inhabitants of Egypt shall know that I am the Lord. Because they were as supportive as a *crushed* reed[6] to the House of Israel; 7. *when they formed an alliance[c] with you, you were delivered into the hand of a powerful king,[d] and their secure abode was lost; and when* they relied upon you, you broke, and you *could not be a dependable protector[e] for them.*[7] 8. Therefore, thus says the Lord God, Behold I am bringing against you *those who slay by* the sword and I will cut off man and beast from you. 9. And the land of Egypt shall become a desolation and a ruin. And they shall know that I am the Lord. Because he said, '*The kingdom* is mine and it is I who have *conquered,*' 10. therefore, behold, I am *sending My wrath* against you and against your *kingdom,* and I will make the land of Egypt a ruin, a desolation and a wasteland, from Migdol Syene as far as the border of Ethiopia. 11. The foot of man shall not pass through it, nor shall the foot of beast pass through it, and it shall remain uninhabited for forty years. 12. And I will make the land of Egypt the most desolate among desolate countries; and her cities shall be the most desolate among cities that have been ruined, for forty years. And I will *exile* the Egyptians among the nations and scatter them among the countries. 13. For thus says the Lord God, At the end of forty years I will gather the Egyptians from among the nations where they had been scattered. 14. And I will bring back the captivity of Egypt, and I will return them to the land of Pathros, to the land *where they had dwelt,*[8] and there they shall be a *feeble* kingdom. 15. It shall be the *weakest* of kingdoms,[9] and never again lord it over the nations; and I will reduce them so that they cannot subjugate[f] the nations. 16. They shall never again be trustworthy for the House of Israel to rely on, but it shall be a reminder of their sins in having turned to follow after them. Then they shall know that I am the Lord God." 17. It was in the twenty-seventh year, in the first month, on the first day of the month, that the word of *prophecy from before* the Lord was with me, saying: 18. "Son of Adam, Nebuchadrezzar king of Babylon, compelled his army to exert a major thrust[g] against Tyre. Every hair of the head was plucked, and every shoulder was peeled bare, yet neither he nor his army gained anything from Tyre for the effort which they put forth against her. 19. Therefore, thus says the Lord God, Behold I am giving the land of Egypt to Nebuchadrezzar king of Babylon, and he shall carry off into captivity her *noisy crowds,* and take her as spoil, and completely deplete her. It shall be payment for his army. 20. I have given him the land of Egypt, *which has sinned before Me,* as his compensation, *thus exacting payment from them,* says the Lord God. 21. At that time *I will raise up liberation*[h10] for the House of Israel, and *upon you I will bestow the freedom of speech[i] to prophesy among them.*[11] And they shall know that I am the Lord."

Apparatus, Chapter 29 *continued*

[c] K cites variant: "when you humbled yourself."
[d] K adds: "the king of Babylon."
[e] Lit. "a house of reliance."
[f] Or "enslave."

[g] Lit. "a great labor."
[h] Or "redemption"
[i] Lit. "opening of the mouth."

Apparatus, Chapter 30

[a] Or "from before."

[b] SP. Other versions omit.

CHAPTER 30

1. The word of *prophecy from before* the Lord was with me, saying: 2. "Son of Adam, prophesy and say, Thus says the Lord God, Wail, and woe, in *the presence of*[a] the day. 3. For near is the day *which is destined to come from before* the Lord; it will be a day of cloud, *earth-shaking;* it shall be a time *of the crushing* of the nations. 4. A sword shall come to Egypt and there shall be trembling in Ethiopia, when the slain are flung in Egypt and her *noisy crowds*[1] shall be taken *captive,* and her walls shall crumble. 5. The people of Ethiopia and of Put and of Lud, and all of *her allies,*[2] and Cub, and the people of the land with whom they have a covenant, together with them shall *be slain* by the sword. 6. Thus says the Lord, Those who support Egypt shall be slain, and the glory of her might shall come to naught. From Migdol to Syene, they shall *be slain* by the sword within her, says the Lord God. 7. And they shall be desolate in the midst of countries that are desolate; and their cities shall be among cities that have been laid waste. 8. And they shall know that I am the Lord, when I have brought *nations that are as fierce as* fire against Egypt, and all those who support her are broken. 9. At that time messengers shall go forth from *before* Me *by legions,*[3] to bring trembling upon Ethiopia, which is dwelling securely; and there shall be a quaking within them on the day of *punishment*[b] *of* Egypt; for behold, it is coming. 10. Thus says the Lord God: I will put an end to *the noisy crowd* of Egypt by the hand of Nebuchadrezzar king of Babylon. 11. He and his people with

Notes, Chapter 29 continued

[6]Cf. *Tg.* Isa. 36:6; 2K 18:21.

[7]MT: "when they grasped you by the hand, you splintered, and tore every shoulder; and when they leaned upon you, you would break and make their loins stand forth."

[8]MT: "of their origin." Cf. Ezek. 20:38.

[9]"Antoninus asked our saintly teacher (Judah the Prince): I am seeking to go to Alexandria, but perhaps it will raise up a king against me and he will vanquish me. He replied to him, I do not know; but nevertheless, we do have a Scripture to the effect that the land of Egypt will be unable to raise up neither ruler nor prince, as it is said, There shall never again be a prince from the land of Egypt (Ezek. 30:13). It shall be the lowliest of the kingdoms (Ibid. 29:15)." *Mek. Širata* 6 (Lauterbach, II, p. 50. English translation is mine.)

[10]MT: "I will cause a horn to sprout." The Aramaic text reads *purqan. Tg.* Ezek. consistently steers clear of using the Messianic designation, *mešiha',* which would have been in order here.

[11.]MT: "I will open your lips among them."

Notes, Chapter 30

[1]MT: "multitude" or "wealth."

[2]MT: *ha'ereb,* which could mean Arabia, but which *Tg.* probably takes in the sense of "a mixed multitude," (Ex. 12:38) and as applied to Egypt, its allies. Cf. *Tg.* Jer. 25:20. Cf. also *JPS* [*N*]*, ad loc; S-A* p. 197; *IB,* p. 229.

[3]MT: *baṣṣim,* "in ships," which *Tg.* understands as "legions" or "forces." This is in line with both *Tg.* Onq. and Ps.-J. on Num. 24:24. See S.H. Levey, *The Messiah,* pp. 22 ff.; M. McNamara, *Targum and Testament,* p. 196 sub Italy.

him, the most powerful of nations, are coming to destroy the land. They shall draw their swords against Egypt and fill the land with the slain. 12. I will make dry land of their rivers, and *deliver*[4] the land into the hand of evil-doers; and I will render the land and all that is in it a desolation, by the hand of strangers. I the Lord have decreed it *by My Memra.* 13. Thus says the Lord God, I will destroy *those who worship* idols and put an end to *those who worship* images from *Memphis,*[5] and there shall no longer be a *king*[6] in the land of Egypt. Thus will I strike fear in the land of Egypt. 14. I will make Pathros desolate, and I will bring *nations who are as fierce as* fire against *Tanis,*[7] and I will execute *just punishment* in *Alexandria.*[8] 15. And I will pour out My fury upon *Sin,*[9] the stronghold of Egypt, and I will put an end to *the noisy crowd* of *Alexandria.* 16. I will bring *nations who are as fierce as* fire against Egypt; Sin shall shake convulsively; and *Alexandria* shall be a crumbled wall; and as for *Memphis,* enemies shall encircle her day in and day out. 17. The young men of Aven[c] and Pibeseth[10] shall be slain by the sword and *those who serve them*[11] shall go into captivity. 18. And over Tahpanhes *I will bring darkness*[12] during the day, when I break the *might*[13] of Egypt there, and the glory of her strength is demolished in her. *A king* shall cover her *with his armies,* like a cloud *that rises and covers the earth;* and *the inhabitants of her towns* shall go into captivity.[14] 19. I will execute *just punishment* upon Egypt, and they shall know that I am the Lord." 20. It was in the eleventh year, in the first month, on the seventh day of the month, the word of *prophecy from before* the Lord was with me, saying: 21. "Son of Adam, I have broken the *might*[d15] of Pharaoh, king of Egypt. And behold he is not strong enough to heal, or to give *counsel,* to be wise, nor to provide the strength *to hold on to the kingdom.*[16] 22. Therefore, thus says the Lord God, Behold I am *sending My wrath* against Pharaoh king of Egypt, and I will break his *auxiliaries and his mighty rulers who are in them. He crushed the kingdoms.*[e] but I will remove the power[f] from him.[17] 23. I will *exile* the Egyptians among the nations and scatter them throughout the countries. 24. And, I will strengthen the *kingdom*[18] of the king of Babylon and I will put My *power*[19] into his hand, and I will break *the power*[20] of Pharaoh, and he shall groan before him, like the groan of those wounded by the sword. 25. I will strengthen the *kingdom*[18] of the king of Babylon, but the *kingdom*[18] of Pharaoh shall *be abolished;* and they shall know that I am the Lord when I place *My power*[19] into the hand of the king of Babylon and *he executes punishment*[21] on the land of Egypt. 26. And I will *exile* the Egyptians among the nations and I will scatter them throughout the countries, and they shall know that I am the Lord."

Apparatus, Chapter 30 continued

[c] RB. SP: (more correctly) *'on.*
[d] RB. SP: "the kingdom."

[e] RB and others. SP reads sing.
[f] RB and SP. K: "his power."

Apparatus, Chapter 31

[a] BM: "Assyria."

[b] Lit. "kingdom."

CHAPTER 31

1. It was in the eleventh year, in the third month, on the first day of the month, the word of *prophecy from before* the Lord was with me, saying: 2. Son of Adam, "Say to Pharaoh king of Egypt and to his *noisy crowd:* To whom can you be compared in your *might?* 3. Behold, the Assyrian[a1] was like a cedar in Lebanon whose branches are fair, with swinging boughs, lofty in stature, and *sending its roots by the water-courses.*[2] 4. *With numerous peoples and powerful auxiliaries he subjugated the kings under his dominion,*[b] *and he appointed his governors over all the countries.*[3] 5.

Notes, Chapter 30 continued

[4]MT: "and I will sell."

[5]MT: *minnof,* "from Noph." *Tg.* renders the name of the city by its Hellenistic designation. See *S-A,* p. 116. So, too, with other Egyptian cities. For the modern names of places mentioned here, see *IB,* p. 230 f.

[6]MT: "prince."

[7]MT: *so'an.*

[8]MT: *no'.* BDB identifies the place as Thebes, p. 609 sub *no'.* LXX renders it Diospolis. V: Alexandria. Cf. *Tg.* Nahum 3:8.

[9]*Tg.* carries this over exactly as in MT. V: Pelusium.

[10]*Tg.* renders both of these places the same as MT. LXX: "Heliopolis and Bubastum." Cf. Y. Komlosh, "*'Al Šiṭato,*" p. 88.

[11]MT: *wehennah,* "and they (f.)." The Aramaic word also means "those who worship them."

[12]MT: *hasak* with variant MSS. *hašak.* *Tg.* reads the latter, but renders a causative, that the darkness during the daytime will be God's doing, probably a reference to and a recurrence of the plague of darkness mentioned in Ex. 10:21 ff.

[13]MT: "the rods" or "scepters."

[14]MT: "a cloud shall cover her, and her daughters shall go into captivity."

[15]MT: "the arm."

[16]MT: "it has not been bound up, to give it healing by binding it with a bandage, to give it strength to hold a sword."

[17]MT: "I will break his arms, both the strong one and the borken one; and I will make the sword fall from his hand."

[18]MT: "the arms."

[19]MT: "My sword."

[20]MT: "the arms."

[21]MT: "and he extends it."

Notes, Chapter 31

[1]MT: *Aššur,* which perplexes the modern translators and interpretors, since the subject was supposed to be Pharaoh, king of Egypt. However, all of the ancient versions subscribe to the Hebrew of MT. V. 2b does ask for a comparison, and the comparison is to Assyria, from which presumably Egypt might take a lesson. *ICC,* p. 339 emends to *teaššur,* "box-tree" or "pine," *IB,* p. 234 reads *'ašweka,,* "I will liken you."

[2]MT: "its top was among the thick branches."

[3]MT: "water made it grow, the deep made it lofty, its streams encircling the place where it was planted. Its streams it sent forth to all the trees of the field."

Consequently, by virtue of his might, he became loftier than all the kings of the nations, and his armies were numerous, and his auxiliaries were victorious[4] *over many nations because of his brilliance.*[5] 6. *With his armies he conquered all strongly fortified cities, and under his governors, he subjugated all the countries of the earth* and in the shadow *of his kingdom* dwelt all the many[c] nations.[6] 7. *With his auxiliaries and many valiant men he was victorious, for the fear of him was over many nations.*[7] 8. *Mighty kings could not succeed against him, because of the mighty power which was with him from before the Lord; rulers could not stand up before his armies, and could not stand up before his armies, and valiant men could not prevail over his auxiliaries, because of the mighty power which was with him from before the Lord; no king was like him in his might.*[8] 9. *I made him handsome by reason of his many valiant men, and all the ancient*[d] *kings trembled before him, because of the mighty power which was with him from before the Lord.*[9] 10. Therefore, thus says the Lord God, Because *you have acted high and mighty;*[10] he *imposed his tyranny on the kingdoms* and his heart was haughty because of his *might,* 11. I will deliver him into the hand of the most powerful of nations; it shall[e] surely punish him[11] according to his sin. I have banished him. 12. Strangers, the most ruthless of nations, have destroyed him and cast him off. On the mountains and in all the valleys *his armies* have fallen; his *auxiliaries* have been scattered among all the rivulets of the land; all the nations of the world have come down from the shadow *of his kingdom* and have abandoned him. 13. On the *fallen heap of his slain*[12] dwell all the birds of heaven, and on *the corpses of his armies*[13] rest all the beasts of the field. 14. So that *no ancient kings* should exalt themselves because *of their might, nor impose their tyranny on the kingdoms; nor should all those who serve the state*[f] *lord over people by virtue of their power;*[14] for all of them are doomed[g] to death, to the nether world, among mortal men, with those who go down to the Pit *of Hell.* 15. Thus says the Lord God: On the day that I brought him down to Sheol,[15] *they mourned for him. Trouble covered the world; countries were laid waste and many nations trembled; I turned the faces of kings* dark over him, and *all the kings of the nations smote the shoulder over him.*[16] 16. I made the nations tremble from the sound of his fall, when I brought him down to Sheol with those who go down to the Pit *of Hell; and all the ancient kings, the governors, and those rich in material possessions, all who serve the state*[f17] were comforted in the nether world. 17. They, too, were brought down to Sheol with him, with those who were slain by the sword; and *his governors were broken of their power among the kingdoms.*[18] 18. Now then, to whom are you comparable in glory and in greatness among *the ancient kings?*[19] For you shall be brought down to the nether-world with *the ancient kings;*[19] you shall lie among *the sinners,*[20] with those who are slain by the sword. This is Pharaoh and all of his *noisy crowd,* says the Lord God."

Apparatus, Chapter 31 continued

[c] Or "great."
[d] Or "former."
[e] RB and AP: "I will."

[f] Lit. "the kingdom."
[g] Lit. "delivered," "handed over."

CHAPTER 32

1. It was in the twelfth year, in the twelfth month, on the first day of the month, the word of *prophecy from before* the Lord was with me, saying: 2. "Son of Adam, take up a lamentation over Pharaoh king of Egypt and say to him, You *were the mightiest*[1] of the nations, and you were like a monster in the seas, and you broke forth *with your armies, and you made the nations tremble by your auxiliaries, and you destroyed their countries.*[2] 3. Thus says the Lord God, I will spread My net over you in the assembly of many nations, and you *will be caught* in My snare. 4. I will abandon you in the land; I will fling your carcass on the open field; and I will make all the birds of the sky to settle on you, and from you I will satisfy the hunger of all the

Notes, Chapter 31 continued

[4]See Levy, II, p. 125, sub *nesah.*

[5]MT: "for that reason, its stature towered above all the trees of the field. Its branches became numerous, and its boughs grew long, because of the abundant water which spread around it."

[6]MT: "in its branches all the birds of the sky make their nests, and under its boughs all the beasts of the field bore their young, and in its shadow dwelt all great nations."

[7]MT: "it was beautiful in its growth, in the length of its branches, because its roots went down to abundant waters."

[8]MT: "cedars in the Garden of God could not eclipse it, cypresses could not compare with its boughs, and plane-trees were not like its branches. None of the trees in the Garden of God could compare with it in its beauty."

[9]MT: "I made it beautiful in the multitude of its branches, and all the trees of Eden that were in the Garden of God envied it."

[10]I have translated the Aramaic (and Hebrew) idiom, "high in stature" or "in exaltation," into a familiar English idiom which conveys the meaning as forcefully as possible.

[11]The theological implication is that God is manifest in the historical situation and nations are His agents, carrying out His will.

[12]MT: "upon its fallen heap."

[13]MT: "its branches."

[14]MT: "so that no trees by the water should exalt themselves because of their height, or push their tops through the thick boughs, and that no trees that drink water should stand up to them in height."

[15]*Še'ol* is one of the seven designations of Gehenna. *b. 'Erub.* 19a. *Tg.* retains the Hebrew designation, then interprets.

[16]MT: "I made them mourn. I covered the depths and withheld its rivers, so that its abundant waters ceased. I darkened Lebanon over it, and all the trees of the field languished over it."

[17]MT: "and all the trees of Eden, the choicest and best of Lebanon, all the well-watered trees."

[18]MT: "and his arm, those who lived under his shadow among the nations."

[19]MT: "among the trees of Eden."

[20]MT: "the uncircumcised."

Notes, Chapter 32

[1]MT: "a young lion."

[2]MT: "you burst forth in your rivers, stirring up the water with your feet, and fouling their rivers." The Targumic exegesis translates the poetic allegory of Scripture into political and historical reality, as it does with the rich metaphor of the preceding chapter.

beasts of the earth. 5. I will strew the flesh *of your slain* upon the mountains, and the valleys shall be filled with *the corpses of your armies.*[3] 6. I will saturate the earth, even upon the mountain, with *fertilizer*[4] *from* your blood, and the rivulets will be full of you. 7. *Trouble shall cover you* when I dim *the glorious splendor of your kingdom from* the heavens; *and the people of your armies, who were as numerous* as the stars, *shall be reduced. A king shall cover you with his armies* like a cloud that rises and covers the sun, and like the moon, whose light does not shine during the day.[5] 8. *All the lanes of your roads, which are kept in good repair and guarded in the midst of you,*[a6] behold, they are like the shining lights in the heavens; I will ruin them for you, and trouble shall cover your land like thick darkness, says the Lord God. 9. I will make the hearts of many peoples *tremble,* when I bring those broken by your war among the nations, to countries which you have not known. 10. I will make many nations astounded over you, and their kings shall be utterly perplexed over you, when I *bring against you those who slay with* the sword; they shall see and tremble, in the presence of their misfortune, each man for his own life, on the day of the fall *of your slain.* 11. For thus says the Lord God, the king of Babylon's *men who slay with the* sword shall come upon you. 12. I will cause the downfall of your armies by the sword of heroic men, all of them the most ruthless among the nations. They shall despoil the might of Egypt, and all of her *noisy crowd* shall be wiped out. 13. I will destroy all her cattle from beside many waters, and the foot of man shall not *frighten* them any more, nor shall the hoofs of cattle *frighten* them any more. 14. Then *I will bring tranquillity to the nations, and I will lead their kings with gentleness,*[7] says the Lord God. 15. When I have made the land of Egypt a desolation, and the land has been wasted of all that fills it, when I strike[b] a blow against all of its inhabitants, then they shall know that I am the Lord." 16. *The prophet said,* "This *prophecy* is a lamentation and it shall become a dirge of the *villages*[8] of the nations. They shall raise it as a howl over Egypt, and they shall raise it as a howl over all her *noisy crowds,* says the Lord God." 17. It was in the twelfth year, on the fifteenth day of the month,[9] the word of *prophecy from before* the Lord was with me, saying: 18. "Son of Adam, *prophesy* concerning *the noisy crowd* of Egypt, and bring it down.[c] And to the *villages*[8] of the mighty nations *prophesy* that they shall be delivered to the netherworld, along with those who go down to the Pit *of Hell.* 19. To whom are you superior in *might?* Go down and sleep[d] with the *wicked.*[10] 20. Among those slain by the sword they shall *be flung;* they shall be delivered to the sword, which shall destroy them and all their *noisy crowds.* 21. The mightiest of warriors shall speak with him and with his helpers from the midst of Sheol; *the wicked* have gone down, they have died, slain by the sword. 22. Assyria is there and his entire army, their graves all around them; all of them are the slain, who were slain by the sword; 23. who were delivered to the grave at the farthest ends of the Pit *of Hell,* and their armies, their graves round about them; all of them are the slain, who were slain by the sword, who *were delivered to destruction,*[e] because they *exercised tyrannical*

Apparatus, Chapter 32

[a] RB. SP: "before me."
[b] Lit. "bring."
[c] RB. K and SP: "crush it."

[d] Or "die."
[e] Lit. "breaking," "crushing."
[f] Or "upon themselves."

dominion over the *land of Israel.*[11] 24. Elam is there, and all here *noisy crowd,* round about them, their graves; all of them are the slain, who were slain by the sword, who were brought down *wicked* to the nether-world, who *were delivered to destruction because they exercised tyrannical dominion over the land of Israel;* and they have been humbled, along with those who go down to the Pit *of Hell.* 25. Among the slain has their sleeping *chamber* been *appointed* for them, with all their *noisy crowds,* their graves round about them; all of them are *wicked,* slain by the sword, who were *delivered to destruction, because they exercised tyrannical dominion over the land of Israel;* they have been humbled along with those who go down to the Pit *of Hell;* they have been delivered among the slain. 26. Meshech and Tubal and all their *noisy crowd* are there, their graves round about them; all of them are *wicked,* slain by the sword, who *have been delivered to destrucion* because *they exercised tyrannical dominion* over the *land of Israel.* 27. They shall not lie with the heroic warriors, who were slain by the *wicked,* who were brought down to Sheol with their battle gear, and who put their swords beneath their heads. Their sins be upon their bones;[f] surely *they have been delivered to destruction* by the warriors, because they *exercised tyrannical dominion over the land of Israel.* 28. So you shall be broken among *the wicked,* and you shall lie with those who are slain by the sword. 29. Edom is there, her kings and all her princes, who have been delivered, with their might, among those who are slain by the sword. They shall lie with *the wicked,* with those who go down to the Pit *of Hell.* 30. The princes of the north are there, all of them, and all the Sidonians, who were brought down with the slain when they were broken of their might in disgrace; and they lie *wicked,* with those slain by the sword; they have been humbled, with those who go down to the Pit *of Hell.* 31. When Pharaoh sees them, he shall be comforted for all of his *noisy crowd;* Pharaoh and all of his armies shall be slain by the sword, says the Lord God. 32. Surely they shall be delivered to destruction by the warriors, because *they exercised tyrannical dominion in the land of Israel,* and they shall lie among the *wicked,* with those slain by the sword, Pharaoh and all his *noisy crowd,* says the Lord God."

Notes, Chapter 32 continued

[3]MT: *ramuteka,* is obscure. *Tg.* may have understood it as an Aramaism from *rema',* "to fling, cast away," hence, "those that are flung or cast away," i.e., "corpses." Or, it could have read a variant, *rimmateka,* "your worm," "decay" as S, V, and Symm. See *IB ad loc.,* p. 239.

[4]The rationale for this midrashic interpretation may be that while all other blood, even of animals, is regarded as sacred, this blood of ruthless killers is fit to be desecrated. *Tg.* reads *so'ateka* for MT's *safateka.* See K-B, p. 811 f. sub *safah.*

[5]The exegetical interweaving of the interpretive complement with the Hebrew text, in this v. and in v. 16 is a remarkable illustration of *Tg.* at its best.

[6]This is a perfect description of the pride of Roman military engineering, the Roman road, which Judaea knew only too well, and with which *Tg.* was all too familiar.

[7]MT: "then I will let their waters settle, and make their rivers flow like oil."

[8]MT: "daughters."

[9]Which month is not specified in *Tg.,* nor in MT. Kimhi suggests that this might be a referral back to v. 1, i.e., the twelfth month. LXX: "in the first month."

[10]MT: "the uncircumcised." *Tg.* translates this as *hayyabaya',* "the wicked" or "the guilty ones," throughout this chapter.

[11]MT: "who struck terror in the land of the living," which *Tg.* understands and interprets as the land of Israel, thus expounding the reality of foreign repressive dominion over Palestine. Psychologically and theologically, *Tg.*'s rendering expresses affectionately how the Jewish people feel about the holy land. It is the land of life, in contrast to exile and the Diaspora. This rendering prevails throughout the chapter. Cf. *Tg.* Ezek. 26:20 *supra.*

CHAPTER 33

1. The word of *prophecy from before* the Lord was with me, saying: 2. "Son of Adam, *prophesy* to the children of your people, and say to them, If I bring *those who slay by* the sword against a land, and the people of the land take one man from among them and appoint him as *the one to give warning.* 3. And if he should see *those who slay by* the sword coming against the land, he shall blow the trumpet and warn the people. 4. Then anyone who hears the sound of the trumpet and does not take warning, and *those who slay by* the sword come and take him away, *the responsibility[a] for his death*[1] shall be upon his own head. 5. He heard the sound of the trumpet but did not take heed, the responsibility for his death shall be on him; for had he heeded the warning, he would have saved his life. 6. But if the one who gives warning shall see that *those who slay by* the sword are coming, but does not blow the trumpet, so that the people have not been warned; and *those who slay by* the sword come and take one of them away, he has been taken away in his own sin; but I will demand an accounting for his blood from the hand of the one who gives warning. 7. Now you, Son of Adam, I have appointed you *teacher*[2] to the House of Israel, and when you hear a word from *My Memra* you must warn them *not to sin against[b] Me.* 8. When I say to the wicked, O wicked man you shall surely die, but you have not spoken so as to warn the wicked man from his way, he, the wicked man, shall die for his sin, but I will demand *an accounting* for his blood from your hand. 9. But you, if you have warned the wicked man from his way, to turn back from it, but he did not turn back from his way, he shall die for his sin, but you will have saved your life. 10. And you, Son of Adam, say to the House of Israel, Thus have you said, saying, 'Surely, our sins and our iniquities are heaped upon us, and because of them we melt away; how then can we survive?"[c] 11. Say to them, As I live, says the Lord God, I do not desire the death of the wicked, rather, when the wicked shall turn back from his way, then he shall live. Repent,[d] repent of your evil ways; for why should you die, O House of Israel?[3] 12. And you, Son of Adam, say to the children of your people, the merit of the righteous shall not save him on the day that he sins;[e] and as for the sin of the wicked, he shall not stumble[f] because of it on the day that he turns back from his sin. And the righteous shall not be able to save his life on the day that he sins. 13.

Apparatus, Chapter 33

[a] Lit. "guilt."
[b] Lit. "before Me."
[c] SP. RB: "live."
[d] Or "turn back."
[e] Lit. "of his sinning."
[f] Most versions. SP and BM: "shall not be put to death."

[g] Lit. "trusts," "relies on."
[h] Or "straight."
[i] Lit. "them."
[j] SP and MM, but omitted in the other versions. The phrase could have been a marginal gloss, explaining the reason for God's choice of Abraham, in that he was a mortal counterpart of the unique deity.

When I say to the righteous that he shall surely live, but *he tries to get by*[8] *on his merits and acts perfidiously,*[4] none of his good deeds shall be remembered, and he shall die because of the *perfidy* which he committed. 14. And when I say to the wicked, 'You shall surely die,' but he turns back from his sins and does what is truly just and righteous, 15. if the wicked returns a pledge, repays a robbery, and walks according to the decree of life so as not to *act perfidiously,* he shall surely live, he shall not die. 16. None of the sins that he has committed shall be remembered against him; he has done what is truly just and righteous, he shall surely live. 17. But the children of your people shall say, 'The good ways of the Lord *have not been explained to us;'*[5] when it is they whose ways are not right.[h] 18. When the righteous turns back from his good conduct and *acts perfidiously,* he shall die for it.[i] 19. And when the wicked turns back from his sins and does what is truly just and righteous, he shall live because of it.[i] 20. Yet you say, 'The good ways of the Lord *have not been explained to us!'* I will *demand an accounting*[6] from each one of you according to his ways, O House of Israel." 21. It was in the twelfth year of our exile, in the tenth month, on the fifth day of the month, a fugitive from Jerusalem came to me saying, "The city has been breached." 22. Now a *prophecy from before* the Lord *had been with me* in the evening before the coming of the fugitive; and He had opened my mouth before he came to me in the morning; and when my mouth was opened, I was no longer silent. 23. And the word of *prophecy from before* the Lord was with me, saying: 24. "Son of Adam, those who dwell in these ruins on the land of Israel are saying thus: 'Abraham was one man, *unique in the world,*[j7] yet he was given possession of the land; we are many, to us the land is surely given to possess it.'[8] 25. Therefore, say to them, Thus says the Lord God: You eat over the blood of the *innocent,* and you *imagine yourselves* possessing the land? 26. *You have endured because of your might,*[9] you have committed abomination, and every one has defiled his neighbor's wife; and you *imagine yourselves* possessing the land? 27. Thus you shall say to them, Thus says the Lord God: As I live, those who are in the ruins shall be slain by the sword; and him who is out in the open field I have delivered to the wild beasts for his destruction; and those who are in the strongholds and the caves

Notes, Chapter 33

[1]MT: "his blood."

[2]MT: *sofeh. Tg.* equates the prophet as teacher with the one who is appointed to give warning.

[3]The efficacy of repentance is one of the basic principles and cardinal doctrines of Rabbinic Judaism, and the repentant sinner is welcomed back into the faith, and regarded as the most highly prized member of the congregation. Cf. *b. Ber.* 34b; *Sanh.* 99a. *Lam. R. 3:44; Pes. R.* 44:1 ff.

[4]MT: "but he relies on his righteousness and commits iniquity."

[5]MT: *lo' yittaken,* "the way of the Lord is not right." *Tg.* hesitates to make this assertion, even though it is attributed to the non-righteous. *Tg.* interprets in such fashion that its theology remains intact, but that the populace does not understand God's way because of their claim that it has not been properly explained to them. Cf. 18:25 and note 10 thereto, *supra.*

[6]MT: "I will judge."

[7]The idea of the uniqueness of both God and Abraham, using this v. as proof-text, is found in *Gen. R.* 38:6. Cf. *Pes. R.* 11:4; *Mid. Teh.* 117:3.

[8]The ridiculous logic of their argument is imaginatively exposed in *t. Sot.* 6:9. "Now if Abraham, who worshipped only one God, possessed the land, we who worship many gods, is it not logical all the more that we should possess the land? etc."

[9]MT: "you rely on your sword." The evils enumerated in these vv. are translated into violations of the Halakah. *t. Sot.* 6:9.

shall die by pestilence. 28. And I will make the land a desolation and a waste; and her glorious might shall cease; and the mountains of Israel shall be desolate, without anyone passing through. 29. And they shall know that I am the Lord, when I make the land a desolation and a waste because of all their abominations which they have committed. 30. And you, Son of Adam, your fellow-countrymen who murmur against you by the side of the walls and at the doors of the houses, speak with one another, each to his brother, saying, 'Come now and hear what the word is that issues from *before* the Lord.' 31. And My people shall come to you as *students*[10] might come and sit before you; and they listen to your words but they will not obey them, because they act with *scorn* in their mouths;[11] their heart goes astray after their ill-gotten wealth. 32. And, behold, you are to them like the song of *the flutes,*[12] the sound of which is pleasant, and the musical performance excellent, for they hear your words, but they are not willing to do them. 33. But when it comes — and behold, it is coming — they shall know that a prophet has been among them."

CHAPTER 34

1. The word of *prophecy from before* the Lord was with me, saying: 2. "Son of Adam, prophesy against *the leaders*[1] of Israel. Prophesy and say to them, to *the leaders,* Thus says the Lord God: Woe *to the leaders* of Israel who have been providing for themselves. Have they not *been appointed leaders* to provide for the *people?*[2] 3. You eat *the best* and clothe yourselves with *pure* wool; you slaughter the fatlings, but you do not provide for the *people.* 4. You have not strengthened the weak, nor have you healed the ailing; the injured you have not bandaged; those that have wandered off you have not brought back and you have not searched for those who were lost; and by force and with hardheartedness you have ruled over them.[a] 5. So they were scattered for want of *a leader, and they have been handed over for destruction to all the kingdoms of the nations; and they have been pushed around.*[b3] 6. *My people have strayed* on all the mountains and on every high hill; *My people have been scattered* all over the face of the earth, and there is no one who searches for them, and no one who *inquires about them.* 7. Therefore, *O leaders,* hear the word of the Lord: 8. As I live, says the Lord God, because My *people* have become a

---

Apparatus, Chapter 34

[a] Or "subjugated them," SP. Others: "subjected them to hard labor."
[b] Or "exiled," "moved about."
[c] K: "Tg. Jonathan introduces an innovation, by the addition which he appends to the verse: Therefore, you wicked leaders, return to the Torah, so that in the future I may have compassion upon you. Pay

heed to the teaching of the Torah, and hear the word of the Lord." No other version of the Tg. carries this.
[d] Or "rest."
[e] R, K, and SP. RB translates the Hebrew literally, "you trample with your feet." The former version is more in keeping with Targumic exegesis, hence my preference for it.

prey, and *have been handed over for destruction to all the kingdoms of the nations for want of a leader,* and *My leaders have not searched for My people,* and *the leaders provided for themselves but did not provide for My people;*[4] 9. therefore, *O leaders,* hear the word of the Lord.[c] 10. Thus says the Lord God: Behold I am *sending My wrath* against *the leaders,* and I will *demand an accounting* for *My people* at their hand; and, I will put a stop to their *leadership of the people, and the leaders shall no longer provide* for themselves. I will rescue *My people from their hand,* and *they shall not be handed over to them for destruction.*[5] 11. For thus says the Lord God: Behold, *I am about to reveal Myself,* and I will search for My *people* and seek them out. 12. As a shepherd seeks out his flock on the day that he is among his sheep, and sets them apart, so I will seek out *My people* and rescue them from all the places where they had been scattered on a day of cloud and darkness. 13. And I will bring them out from among the nations, and I will gather them in from the countries, and I will bring them into their land; and *I will provide for* them on the mountains of Israel, by the watercourses, and in all the inhabited places of the land. 14. I will *provide* them with good *provision;* and on the *holy* mountain[6] of Israel, shall be their restful abode. There *they shall dwell,*[d] in a place which is nice. They *shall be provided with good provision* on the mountains of Israel. 15. *I will provide for My people,* and *I will make them dwell securely,* says the Lord God. 16. I will seek those that are lost, and *those that have been exiled,* will I bring back; those that have been injured I will bandage, and those who are weak will I sustain *with hope;* but I will destroy *the transgressors and the sinners.*[7] *I will provide for My people* with justice. 17. As for you, *My people,* thus says the Lord God: Behold, I will judge between *man and man, for the transgressors and for the sinners.* 18. Is it not enough for you that you are *provided* with *good provision,* that what is left of your provision *your servants eat,* and you drink *specially prepared beverages,* and what is left of them *your servants drink?*[e8] 19. And My *people* must eat the *food left over by your servants,* and must drink *the drink left over by your servants.* 20. Therefore, thus says the Lord God to them: Behold *I am about to reveal Myself,* and I will judge

Notes, *Chapter 33 continued*

[10]MT: "as people come."

[11]MT: "for they act with lust in their mouths."

[12]MT: "lustful songs." *Tg.* reads *'ugabim* for MT's *'agabim.*

Notes, *Chapter 34*

[1]MT: "shepherds." *Tg.* takes this entire chapter with its poetic pastoral imagery as metaphor, and translates it in terms of applied meaning.

[2]MT: "sheep."

[3]MT: "and they became food for all the beasts of the field, and they were scattered."

[4]MT: "because My sheep have become a prey and food for all the beasts of the field because there is no shepherd, and My shepherds have not searched for My sheep; for the shepherds have tended themselves, and have not tended My sheep."

[5]MT: "I will make them stop tending the sheep, no longer shall the shepherds feed themselves. For I will rescue My sheep from their mouths, and they shall no longer be food for them."

[6]MT: "mountains." *Tg.* interprets the entire phrase in terms of the Sanctuary on Mt. Zion, the one mountain designated as the abode of the Shekinah. *Tg.*'s rendering implies the theological hope for a restoration of the Temple, now destroyed. LXX likewise reads sing. "mountain."

[7]MT: "the fat and the strong."

[8]MT: "you trample with your feet." Servants of the priests mistreating the populace, mentioned by Josephus, *Antiquities,* 9:2, 206. Cf. *b. Pes.* 57a.

between the rich man and the poor man.[9] 21. Because you *oppressed with wickedness and force,* and *with your strength you crushed* all of the weak ones until you scattered them abroad *among the countries,*[10] 22. I will *redeem My people* and they shall no longer be *handed over as spoil;* and I will judge *between man and man.*[11] 23. And I will set up over them one *leader* who *shall provide for them,* My servant David; he shall *provide for them* and he *shall be their leader.*[12] 24. And I, the Lord, will be their God, and My servant David shall be king among them. I, the Lord, have decreed it by *My Memra.* 25. I will make[13] a covenant of peace with them, and remove the wild beast from the land, so that they may live securely in the wilderness, and *grow old*[14] in the forests. 26. I will settle them all around *My Holy Temple,*[15] and *they shall be blessed;*[16] and I will send down for them the early rain in its season; they shall be rains of blessing. 27. The tree of the field shall yield its fruit, and the earth shall yield its harvest, and they shall be secure in their land; and they shall know that I am the Lord, when I break the mighty yoke of their servitude and rescue them from the hand of those who are enslaving them. 38. They shall no longer be the spoil of the nations, *and the kingdoms*[f] *of the earth shall not destroy them,*[17] but they shall dwell securely, with none to frighten them. 29. And I will raise up for them *a planting which shall be firm*[18] and they shall never again be *wanderers* because of famine in the land, and they shall never again suffer the humiliation of the nations. 30. And they shall know that I am the Lord their God, that *My Memra comes to their aid,* and that they are My people, the House of Israel, says the Lord God. 31. And you *My people, the people over whom My name is called, you are the House of Israel,*[19] and I am your God, says the Lord God."

CHAPTER 35

1. The word of *prophecy from before* the Lord was with me, saying: 2. "Son of Adam, *hear the prophecy* against Mount Seir and prophesy against it, 3. and say to it, Thus says the Lord God: Behold I am *sending My wrath* against you, Mount Seir, and I will raise *the striking power of My might*[1] against you and I will make you a desolation and a waste. 4. I will make your cities into a ruin, and you shall become a desolation; and you shall know that I am the Lord. 5. Because you have had an eternal hatred, and you *cut down*[2] the Children of Israel by the hand of *those who*

Apparatus, Chapter 34 continued

[f] RB. SP: "kingdom."

Apparatus, Chapter 35

[a] Lit. "end."
[b] RB and K. SP: "I hate you."
[c] CR: "you hated the blood of circumcision."

[d] Lit. "who passes by."
[e] Or "mind."

slay by the sword, at the time of their disaster, at the time *of retribution for their sins,* when their doom[a] had come. 6. Therefore, as I live, says the Lord God, *I will surely do you in,* to be slain, and *those who slay by* the sword shall pursue you; verily, you[b] have hated with a bloody hatred,[c3] and therefore *those who shed* blood shall pursue you.[4] 7. I will make Mount Seir a desolation and a waste, and I will cut off from it him who goes[d] and him who returns. 8. I will fill its mountains with its slain; on its hills and in its valleys and in its streams shall be flung those who are slain by the sword. 9. I will make you a desolation forever, and your cities shall not be inhabited; and you shall know that I am the Lord. 10. Because you thought, the two nations and the two countries shall be mine, and I shall possess them; *however, the thoughts of the heart[e] are revealed before the Lord.*[5] 11. Therefore, as I live, says the Lord God, I will act in accordance with your wrath and your fury, as you have done, out of your hatred of them; and I will reveal Myself, *by being good to them,* as I *exact punishment* from you. 12. And you shall know that before Me, the Lord, are heard all the provocations which you have uttered against the mountans of the land of Israel, saying: Their land has become desolate, they have been handed over to us, *to be destroyed.*[6] 13. And you were arrogant towards Me with *the words of* your

Notes, Chapter 34 continued

[9]MT: "between the fat sheep and the lean sheep."

[10]MT: "because you pushed with flank and shoulder, and with your horns you gored all the sick ones until you scattered them abroad."

[11]MT: "I will save My sheep and they shall no longer be a prey. And I will judge between sheep and sheep."

[12]The glaring absence of a definitive Messianic interpretation, with no designation of Messiah as such, is consistent with *Tg.* Ezek.'s non-messianic eschatology. *Tg.* simply translates MT literally, as is. Whether this means the Davidic dynasty or a David *redivivus* is not altogether certain. See Levey, *The Messiah,* pp. 78 ff; "The Targum to Ezekiel," p. 144. But cf. *IB,* p. 254 f.

[13]*w'egzar,* an exact rendering of MT *wekarati,* "I will cut a covenant."

[14]MT: *weyašnu,* "and they shall sleep," but which *Tg.* takes from the root which means to grow old. See K-B, p. 412, sub *yašan* II.

[15]MT: "My hill."

[16]*Tg.'s yehon mebarkin,* either active or passive participle, can also mean "they will offer blessing." MT: "I will make ... a blessing."

[17]MT: "and the beasts of the earth shall not devour them."

[18]MT is uncertain. *Tg.* reads *šalem,* whole, sound," instead of *lešem.* LXX reads *šalom,* "peace." So, too, S.

[19]MT: "you are My sheep, the sheep of My pasture; you are Adam." *Tg.* equates the Masoretic, *'adam* with the House of Israel, perhaps implying that Israel is the personification of Adam, of humanity *par excellence.* R. Simeon b. Yoḥai cites this v. to demonstrate that Israel is designated by God as Adam in contradistinction to the other nations of the world. *b. Yeb.* 60b-61a. LXX omits the word altogether.

Notes, Chapter 35

[1]MT: "My hand."

[2]MT: *watagger.* Hif. of *nagar,* which BDB renders "to deliver over to the sword," p. 620, sub *nagar,* the basic meaning of which is "to flow" or "to pour." *Tg.* translates *wetabebta,* from *tabab,* "to saw," "to cut." See Jastrow, II, p. 1642. But cf. *Tg.* Jer. 19:21 where the root *kebe,* "to extinguish," "to blind," is used by *Tg.* for the same Hebrew root. LXX: "you have ambushed." V: "you have shut up," reading *watasger.*

[3]This refers back to the conditional of oath, indicating an affirmative assertion, not negative.

[4]MT: "I will turn you into blood and blood shall pursue you. Surely you hate with blood, therefore blood shall pursue you." CR's "you hated the blood of circumcision," is a reflection on Esau's rejection of the covenant of Abraham, and, symbolically, a reference to Rome's hatred of the Jewish people. Cf. *Gen. R.* 63:18.

[5]MT: "and the Lord was there."

[6]MT: "to be devoured."

mouth, and you multiplied your words towards Me; it has been heard by Me. 14. Thus says the Lord God: When all the earth rejoices I will make you a desolation. 15. As you rejoiced over the heritage of the House of Israel, over the desolation of their land, so will I do unto you; you shall be a desolation, Mount Seir, and all of Edom, all of it. And they shall know that I am the Lord."

CHAPTER 36

1. "And you, Son of Adam, prophesy to the mountains of Israel, and say, O mountains of Israel, hear the word of the Lord. 2. Thus says the Lord God, Because the enemy said of you, 'Hurrah! the ancient heights have become our possession,' 3. therefore, prophesy, and say, Thus says the Lord God, Because[1] *they vaunted their superiority,* and because[1] *they thought* to ruin you and to make you desolate from all sides, so that you might become the possession of the rest of the nations, and you have become the talk on the tip of the tongue, and popular gossip; 4. therefore, O mountains of Israel, hear the word of the Lord God: Thus says the Lord God to the mountains and to the hills, to the streams and to the valleys, to the desolate ruins and to the deserted cities, which have become an object of derision and mockery to the rest of the nations round about; 5. therefore, thus says the Lord God, Surely *by My Memra have I decreed My fiery punishment*[2] against the other nations and against the Edomites all of them, who gave the land *of the abode of My Shekinah*[3] to themselves as a possession with wholehearted glee, and with recklessness of soul, to drive her off[4] and to despoil her. 6. Therefore, prophesy about the land of Israel, and say to the mountains and to the hills, to the streams and to the valleys, Thus says the Lord God, Behold, I have *decreed by My Memra* in My wrath and in My fury, because you have suffered the humiliation of the nations; 7. therefore, thus says the Lord God: I swear *by My Memra* that the nations round about *who have despoiled you,* shall themselves suffer their humiliation. 8. But you, O mountains of Israel, your produce shall be abundant and your fruit you shall bear for My people; *My redemption*[a] is soon to come. 9. For, behold, *I am about to reveal Myself to you,* and I will turn *by My Memra, to do you good,*[5] and you shall be tilled and sown. 10. I will multiply people[6] upon you, the whole House of Israel, all of them; and the cities shall be inhabited and the ruins shall be rebuilt. 11. I will multiply people and cattle upon you, and they shall become numerous and *expansive;*[7] and I will cause you to be inhabited as in former times, and I will be as good to you as from the very beginning. And you shall know that I am the Lord. 12. I will *multiply*[8] people upon you — My people Israel — and they shall possess you, and you shall be their inheritance; and

Apparatus, Chapter 36

[a] SP. RB: "the day of My redemption."

you shall never bereave them of children. 13. Thus says the Lord God: Because they say to you, 'You *kill*[9] people, and you have bereaved your own nation of children,' 14. therefore, you shall no longer *kill* people, and you shall never again bereave your own nation of children,[10] says the Lord God. 15. And I will never again let you hear the humiliation by the nations, and you shall no longer suffer the reproaches of the nations, and your nation shall never again be bereaved of children[11] says the Lord God." 16. The word of *prophecy from before* the Lord was with me, saying: 17. "Son of Adam, the House of Israel, dwelling on their land, defiled it with their ways and their deeds; like the uncleanness of a menstruous woman was their way before Me. 18. So I poured out My wrath upon them, for the *innocent* blood which they had shed upon the land, and for *the worship of* their idols with which they had defiled it. 19. I *exiled* them among the nations and scattered them through the countries; in accordance with their *evil* ways and their *corrupt* deeds I *exacted payment from them.*[12] 20. And they came in among the nations to which they *had been exiled,* because they profaned My holy name, in that men said of them, '*If these are the people of the Lord, how is it then that they have been exiled from the land which is the abode of His Shekinah?*'[13] 21. But I had consideration for My holy name, which the House of Israel had profaned among the nations to which they *had been exiled.* 22. Therefore say to the House of Israel, Thus says the Lord God: It is not for your sake that I am acting, O House of Israel, but for My holy name, which you have profaned among the nations to which you *had been exiled.* 23. I will sanctify My great name, which has been profaned among the nations, which you have caused to be profaned among them, and the nations shall know that I am the Lord, says the Lord God, when I will be sanctified through you before their eyes. 24. For I will *draw you near* from among the nations, and I will gather you in from all the countries, and I will bring you into your own land. 25. And *I will forgive your sins, as though you had been* purified by the waters of sprinkling[14] and *by the ashes of the heifer sin-*

Notes, Chapter 36

[1]Note how *Tg.* renders poetic *ya'an beya'an* by providing two reasons, one reason for each "because."

[2]MT: "surely, in My fiery jealousy I have spoken."

[3]MT: "My land."

[4]MT: *migrašah,* the root of which also has the meaning of "divorce." *Tg.* renders it by a word that has the identical meaning in Aramaic. *IB* suggests emendation, *morašah,* based on MS, "possession."

[5]MT: "I am for you, and I will turn to you."

[6]MT: *'adam,* which *Tg.* renders *'enaša',* both of which in this context are inclusive of male and female. For the equation of *'adam* with Israel, cf. Ezek. 34:31 *supra.*

[7]MT: *ufaru,* generally understood as being fruitful, but rendered in *Tg.* by forms of the verb *puš,* "to expand," "to be enlarged." See Jastrow, II, p. 1149 sub *puš.* Cf. *Tg.* Onq. Gen. 1:22, *passim.*

[8]MT: "I will cause men to walk upon you."

[9]MT: "you devour people."

[10]*Tg.* follows Q. *tešakeli.*

[11]*Tg.* follows Q. Others follow Ket, "cause to stumble." LXX omits the phrase.

[12]MT: "I judged them."

[13]MT: "these are the people of the Lord, yet they had to leave His land."

[14]MT: "I will sprinkle clean water upon you." R. Akiba cites this v. in what I consider to be an assertion against Christian baptism. God Himself purifies Israel, *m. Yoma* 8:9. Cf. *S.S. R.* 1:19, where Torah is the purifying element. Cf. also *Lev. R.* 15:9; *Pes. R.* 14:15.

offering,[15] and you shall be cleansed of all your defilements, and from all your idols I will cleanse you. 26. And I will give you a *faithful*[b] heart, and I will put a *faithful*[c] spirit[16] *deep* inside of you;[d] and I will *demolish*[e] *the wicked heart, which is as hard* as stone, from your flesh; and I will give you a heart *that is faithful*[b] *before Me, to do My will.*[17] 27. And My *holy* spirit will I put *deep* inside of you[d] and I will act so that you shall walk in My statutes and keep My laws and observe them. 28. You shall dwell in the land which I gave to your fathers, and you shall be a people before Me, and I will be your God. 29. And I will redeem you from all your defilements, and I will *bless*[18] the grain and make it abundant, and I will not impose famine upon you. 30. I will make abundant the fruit of the tree and the harvest of the field, so that you shall no longer bear among the nations the disgrace of famine. 31. Then you shall remember your evil ways, and your improper deeds and you shall have regrets; and you shall be aware of your sins and your abominations. 32. Let it be known to you that it is not for your sake that I act, says the Lord God; be ashamed and humbled because of your ways, O House of Israel. 33. Thus says the Lord God: On the day that I cleanse you from all your sins, I will cause the cities to be inhabited, and the ruins shall be rebuilt. 34. And the land that was desolate shall be tilled instead of being the desolation that it had been in the eyes of every passerby. 35. And they shall say: 'This land *of Israel,* that was desolate, has *returned* to be like the garden of Eden; and the cities that were ruined and desolate and shattered are now powerful, inhabited cities.' 36. And the nations that are left all around you shall know that I, the Lord, have rebuilt the places that were shattered, and have made the desolate places live again; I, the Lord, have *decreed it by My Memra,* and I will fulfil it. 37. Thus says the Lord God; Also this I will let the House of Israel request of *My Memra* to do for them: I will make them numerous with people, and *prosperous with cattle.*[19] 38. Like the *holy people,*[20] like the *people who are cleansed and come* to Jerusalem at the time of the *Passover* festivals,[21] so the cities of the *land of Israel* which were ruined, will be filled with people, the *people of the House of Israel,*[22] and they shall know that I am the Lord."

CHAPTER 37

1. The *spirit of prophecy from before the* Lord rested upon me, and He took me out by means of the spirit of *prophecy, which had rested upon me from before* the

Apparatus, Chapter 36 continued

[b] Or, "worshipful," "reverent," "fearful."
[c] AP: "new."

[d] Lit. "in your intestines."
[e] Lit. "break."

Apparatus, Chapter 37

[a] Or "You are the Lord God; it is revealed before You."

[b] Or "air," "wind," "spirit."
[c] Lit. "a bone to its fellow."

Lord, and He set me down in the midst of a valley; it was full of *human* bones.[1] 2. He led me all around them, and behold, there were very many on the face of the valley, and behold, they were very dry. 3. He said to me, "Son of Adam, can these bones live?" And I said, "O Lord God, *before You it is revealed.*"[a2] 4. Then He said to me, "Prophesy over these bones and say to them, O dry bones, hear the word of the Lord. 5. Thus says the Lord God to these bones, Behold, I will put breath[b] into you, and you shall live.[3] 6. And I will put sinews upon you, and I will bring up flesh upon you, and form skin over you. And I will put breath[b] into you, and you shall live; and you shall know that I am the Lord." 7. So I prophesied as I had been commanded; and as I was prophesying, there was a noise, and behold, a rattling commotion, and the bones came together, one bone to another.[c] 8. And I looked, and behold, there were sinews on them, and flesh had come up, and skin had formed over them from above, but there was no breath in them. 9. He said to me, "Prophesy to the breath,[b] prophesy, O Son of Adam, and say to the breath, Thus says the Lord God: Come O breath, from the four winds, and *enter*[4] these slain, that they may live." 10. So I

Notes, Chapter 36 continued

[15]See Num. 19:17.

[16]MT: "a new heart" "a new spirit." *Tg.* recognizes the allegorical implication of the Hebrew and its poetic nuance, and renders it in terms of Yahwistic religion. Cf. *Ex. R.* 15:6. The "heart of stone" is taken by the Rabbis to mean the *yeser hara'*, the evil impulse or inclination. *Ex. R.* 41:7; *b. Suk.* 52a. Cf. *Tg.* Ezek. 11:19, 18:31, *supra.*

[17]MT: "I will take the heart of stone out of your flesh, and I will give you a heart of flesh."

[18]MT: "I will summon."

[19]MT: "like sheep."

[20]MT: "like the sheep of the holy sacrifices."

[21]MT: "like the sheep of Jerusalem during her festivals." *Tg.* interprets the unspecified feasts as the Passover, possibly because of the preponderance of sheep in the prophetic picture, hence an association with the paschal lamb. The purification may revert back to v. 25.

[22]MT: "flocks of men."

Notes, Chapter 37

[1]*Tg.* makes it clear that the dry bones are human bones, presumably the bones of Israelites whose identity is not specified. Rashi's explanation is that the bones are presumed to be those of the Israelites slain as they left Egypt before the appointed time. Cf. *Pirq. d'R. El.,* 48. *b. Sanh.* 92b has a number of conjectures as to the identity of the dry bones, including the idea that they were the bones of those Jews who worshipped the idol in the plain of Dura, Dan. 3:1 ff., whom Nebuchadnezzar had slain. The Ezekiel resurrection is considered to be a temporary measure, for, according to R. Eliezer, those who were revived arose, praised God, and then died again. For a discussion of the concept of a second death, see M. McNamara, *The New Testament and the Palestinian Targum,* pp. 117-124; *S-A,* p. 182 f. *Tg.* Ezek. makes no mention of a second death, but cf. *Tg.* Is. 22:14; 65:6, 15; *Tg.* Jer. 51:39, 57. A full treatment of the Jewish doctrine of the resurrection and of this chapter is found in *Pirq. d'R. El.,* chs. 33, 34.

The most rational explanation of Ezek. ch. 37 is that of R. Judah b. Ilai, *b. Sanh.* 92b. "In truth it is an allegory," meaning that it symbolically represents the restoration of the Jews as a people and as a national entity possessing its land once again. This would explain why this chapter of Ezekiel was designated the *haftarah* for the Sabbath of Passover, in that the restoration of Israel promised by God parallels the Exodus in its miracle of divine intervention in history and God's redemption of His people *b. Meg.* 31a.

The Church Fathers cite this chapter as Scriptural proof of the validity of the resurrection of the dead. Justin Martyr points to it as a prophecy to be fulfilled by Christ in the Second Coming at the end of time, *First Apologia,* 52. Tertullian points to the passage as reflecting Ezekiel's doubt concerning the revival of the dead, contrasted with the Christian acceptance of the doctrine as a literal truth, rather than an allegory, *On the Resurrection of the Flesh,* 30. For the liturgical use of this passage in the Christian Church see *ICC,* p. 398.

[2]MT: "O Lord God, You know."

[3]LXX: "I will bring upon you the breath of life." Cf. Gen. 6:17.

[4]MT: "and blow into."

prophesied as He had commanded me and the breath entered them and they lived, and they stood up on their feet, an exceedingly numerous host.[5] 11. Then He said to me, "Son of Adam, these bones are the whole House of Israel. Behold, they say, 'Our bones are dried up, our hope has been cut off, destruction is ours.'[6] 12. Therefore prophesy, and say to them, Thus says the Lord God: Behold I am opening your graves, and I will raise you up from your graves, O My people, and I will bring you into the *land* of Israel.[7] 13. And you shall know that I am the Lord, when I open your graves and when I raise you up from the *midst* of your graves, O My people.[8] 14. And I will put My spirit into you, and you shall live; and I will make you dwell upon your land; and you shall know I, the Lord, have decreed it *by My Memra,* and I will fulfil it, says the Lord." 15. The word of *prophecy from before* the Lord was with me saying: 16. "You, Son of Adam, take for yourself one *tablet,*[9] and write on it, 'For *the tribe of* Joseph, which is *the tribe of* Ephraim, and the whole house of Israel, their *brothers.'*[10] 17. Bring them close to one another, to you, as one *tablet,* so that they may be one in your hand. 18. And when the children of your people shall say to you, saying: 'Will you not show us what these mean to you?' 19. *prophesy* to them, Thus says the Lord God, Behold I am bringing near *the tribe of* Joseph, which is *the tribe of* Ephraim, and the tribes of Israel, their *brothers;* and I will join them to him, *the tribe of* Judah, and I will make them *one people,* and they shall be one *before Me.*[11] 20. And the *tablets* upon which you shall write, shall be in your hand before their eyes. 21. Then *prophesy* unto them, Thus says the Lord God: Behold, I am bringing near the Children of Israel from among the nations where they *have been exiled,* and I will gather them in from all around, and I will bring them into their own land. 22. And I will make them one nation in the land, on the *holy* mountain of Israel; and they shall all have one king as their king; and they shall no longer be two nations, nor shall they be divided into two kingdoms any more. 23. They shall no longer be defiled by their idols and by their detestable things and by all their *rebellions;* and I will deliver them from all their habitations in which they sinned; and I will cleanse them, and they shall be a people *before Me,* and I will be their God. 24. And My servant David[12] shall be king over them; and they shall all have one *leader,*[13] and they shall walk in My laws, and they shall keep My statutes and observe them. 25. And they shall dwell on the land which I gave to My servant, to Jacob, in which your fathers dwelt; and they and their children and their children's children shall dwell upon it forever; and David My servant shall be their *king*[14] forever. 26. I will make a covenant of peace with them, it shall be an everlasting covenant with them; and I will *bless*[15] them and make them numerous, and I will place My sanctuary in the midst of them forever. 27. *I will make My Shekinah dwell among them,*[16] and I will be their God, and they shall be a people *before Me.* 28. And the nations shall know that I the Lord, sanctify Israel, when My sanctuary is in midst of them forever."

Apparatus, Chapter 38

[a] SP. RB, AP, CR: "I will swing you around."   [b] Or "rings."

CHAPTER 38

1. The word of *prophecy from before* the Lord was with me, saying: 2. "Son of Adam, *hear the prophecy* against Gog of the land of Magog,[1] the great chief of Meshech and Tubal, and prophesy against him. 3. And say, Thus says the Lord God: Behold, I am *sending My wrath* against you, O Gog, great chief of Meshech and Tubal. 4. I will turn you around[a] and I will put chains[b] in your jaws and lead you

Notes, Chapter 37 continued

[5]There is a Rabbinic contention that Ezekiel revived the dead, as the agent of God. *b. Sanh.* 92b. *Lev. R.* 27:4 places Ezekiel on a par with Elijah and Elisha in this respect. "That which is destined to be has already occurred (Eccl. 3:15). If a man should say to you that in the future the Holy One blessed be He will restore the dead to life for us, say to him, this has already taken place through Elijah (1 K. 17:17 ff.), and through Elisha (2 K. 4:32 ff.), and through Ezekiel (ch. 37)." Implicit in this may be an anti-Christian polemic, countering the argument of John 11:1 ff. S.H. Levey, "The Targum to Ezekiel," *HUCA* vol. 46, p. 149 f.

[6]MT: "our hope is lost, we are cut off." *Tg.* departs from MT by reversing the verbs in its paraphrase. *IB* suggests a word division other than the difficult *nigzarnu lanu*, read *nigzar nulenu*, "our thread is cut off." Cf. also its comments on the use of the Masoretic phrase in the Zionist hymn *Hattiqwah*, "our hope is not lost," and Jer. 31:17. *IB*, p. 269.

[7]MT: "the soil of Israel."
The resurrection of the dead will take place in the land of Israel. The deserving who are buried elsewhere God will transport to the land of Israel by means of underground tunnels. *Gen. R.* 96:5. *Tg.* Is. 45:8 refers to the opening of the ground that the dead may live again.

[8]R. Johanan adduces from this v. that God Himself will effect the resurrection of the dead, without entrusting it to any mediating agent. *b. Ta'an.* 2a, b. Cf. *Gen. R.* 73:4.

[9]MT: "wood," "stick."

[10]MT: "his associates."

[11]MT: "I am going to take the stick of Joseph, which is in the hand of Ephraim, and of the tribes of Israel, his associates, and I will place them next to his, the stick of Judah, and I will make them into one stick, and they shall be one in My hand."

[12]*Tg.* renders the MT literally, and again steers clear of any Messianic designation. Cf. Ezek. 34:23 and n. 5 thereto, *supra*.

[13]MT: "shepherd."

[14]MT: "prince."

[15]MT: "I will give them."

[16]MT: "My dwelling place shall be over them."

Notes, Chapter 38

[1]The Gog and Magog apocalypse which appears here and in ch. 39 is based on early traditions which cannot accurately be traced or ascertained. For a critical analysis of the problem and possible theories, see *ICC* pp. 406 ff. and *IB* p. 272 f.

In the Jewish tradition, these chapters in Ezekiel provide the earliest treatment and the source upon which all subsequent projections are based. Magog is mentioned in Gen. 10:2 as a descendant of Japheth, together with Meshech and Tubal who are mentioned in v. 3. In the Targumic sources, *Tg.* Ps.-J. on Ex. 40:11 refers to the final struggle of Gog against Israel, and to the Messiah son of Ephraim who will vanquish him and his hordes. Fr. *Tg.* on Num 11:26 reads: "Two men remained in the camp, the name of the one Eldad and the name of the other Medad and the Holy Spirit rested upon them ... and the two of them prophesied together, saying, At the end, the very end of days Gog and Magog and their armies shall go up against Jerusalem, but they shall fall by the hand of the King

forth, with your entire army, horses and horsemen, all of them *attired to perfection,*[2] a great host, armed with bucklers and shields, all of them wielding swords. 5. Persians, Cushites, and Putites are with them, all of them *armed* with shields and helmets.[3] 6. Gomer and all of his armies, *the country of Germamia,*[4] at the farthest ends of the north, and all of their armies, many people who are with you. 7. Gird yourself and be prepared, you and all your armies who have gathered around you; and be a guard for them. 8. After many days you shall appoint your armies; at the culmination of the years, you shall go against the land *whose people had* returned to it from *those who slay* by the sword; who had been gathered in from many nations upon the mountains of *the land of* Israel, which had been a continual wasteland; and they had been *recovered*[c] from among the nations, and now dwell securely, all of them. 9. You shall rise like a *riot;*[d5] and you shall come like a cloud which *rises* and covers the earth, you and all your armies, and the many people who are with you. 10. Thus says the Lord God: And it shall be that time, that *impure* thoughts will come into your mind, and you will plot evil schemes.[6] 11. And you will say, 'I will go up against the land which abides tranquilly in open cities; I will go against the *people who are* quiet and dwell securely, all of them dwelling without a wall, and who have no bars and gates;' 12. to take spoil, and to carry off booty; *to gather your armies*[7] against the ruins which have now become inhabited, and against a people that have been gathered in from among the nations, who have *prospered* with herds and property, dwelling on the *stronghold*[8] of the earth. 13. Sheba and Dedan and the merchants *of the sea* and all of its *kings*[9] shall say to you, 'Have you come to take spoil? Have you *gathered your armies* to carry off booty, to take away silver and gold, to capture herds and property, to carry off great booty?' 14. Therefore, prophesy. O Son of Adam, and say to Gog, Thus says the Lord God, At that time, when My people Israel are dwelling securely, you will know *the punishment of My might.*[10] 15. And you will go from your place, from the farthest ends of the north, you and the many peoples who are with you, all of them riding horses, great armies and numerous people. 16. You will go up against My people Israel, like a cloud that *rises and* covers the earth. It shall happen at the end of days, that I will bring you to the land *of the abode of My Shekinah,*[11] in order that the nations may know *the punishment of My might,*[12] when I sanctify Myself through you, and *they see your punishment,* O Gog.[13] 17. Thus says the Lord God: Are you he, of whom I spoke in former days through My servants, the prophets of Israel, who prophesied in those days, *many* years *before this,* that I would bring you against them? 18. But it shall be at that time, on the day of Gog's coming against the land of Israel, says the Lord God, My wrath shall be kindled, *and My fury.*[14] 19. And when My *punishment is revealed,*[15] when the fire of My wrath is kindled, I have decreed *by My Memra,* that surely on that day there shall be a great earthquake in the land of Israel. 20. The fish of the sea, and the birds of the sky, and the beasts of the field, and all the creeping things that creep on the ground, and all human beings who are on the face of the earth shall tremble before Me; the mountains shall be demolished, and *the towers*[16] shall be torn down, and every *high* wall shall be *piled in rubble* on the ground. 21. I will summon him *to*

Apparatus, Chapter 38 continued

[c] Lit. "uncovered."
[d] Or "storm." RB: "in a storm."

[e] RB. SP omits "Israel."

fall by the sword on the mountains *of Israel,*[e] *My people,*[17] says the Lord God. A man's sword shall be against his brother. 22. I will *punish him* by pestilence and by *killing;*[18] torrential rain, hailstones, fire and sulphur will I rain upon him and his armies and upon the many peoples that are with him.[19] 23. Thus I will magnify and sanctify Myself; *and I will reveal My might*[20] in the eyes of many nations, and they shall know that I am the Lord."

CHAPTER 39

1. "And you, Son of Adam, prophesy against Gog, and say, Thus says the Lord God: Behold I am *sending My wrath,* against you, O Gog, great chief of Meshech and Tubal.[1] 2. I will swing you around, and lead you *astray,* and I will take you up

Notes, Chapter 38 continued

Messiah. For seven full years the Children of Israel shall use their weapons of war for kindling, without having to go into the forest to cut down the trees." This prophecy is also referred to in *b. Sanh.* 17a and *Num. R.* 15:19. See S.H. Levey, *The Messiah,* pp. 15 ff. Jewish tradition maintained that Ps. 2 is a reference to Gog and Magog. *b. Ber.* 7b.

The apocalyptic reference to Gog and Magog is borrowed by the author of Revelation, which was probably Jewish in origin. Rev. 20:7 ff. Cf. M. McNamara, *The New Testament and the Palestinian Targum to the Pentateuch,* pp. 233 ff.

[2]MT: "in gorgeous attire."

[3]The weapons mentioned in the *Tg.* seem to reflect familiarity with the weapons used by the Romans. See *S-A,* p. 97.

[4]MT: *"bet togarmah."* Cf. *Tg.* Ezek. 27:14. See M. McNamara, *Targum and Testament,* p. 194, sub Germania.

[5]MT: *kaššo'ah,* "like the storm." Note the use of the term in modern Hebrew to designate the Nazi Holocaust.

[6]Sing. in MT.

[7]MT: "to turn your hand."

[8]MT: *tabbur,* "navel" or "center," or "highest point." See BDB p. 371. *Tg.* renders the term *tuqfa,* "stronghold," which Kimhi explains geographically as a reference to the land of Israel being located higher than other countries. The Aramaic word also has the meaning of "the Omnipotent One" or "Almighty," and its use here might have theological overtones. Jastrow, II. p. 1655f. Cf. *Tg.* Jud. 9:37. For the idea of Jerusalem as the navel of the world, see *Tanh. Qedošim,* 10; *Mid. Adonai Behokmah Yasad Ares* in Jellinek, *Bet Ha-Midraš,* V, p. 63; Cf. *Eccl. R.* 1:9. LXX and V: "navel."

[9]MT: *kefireha,* "its young lions." LXX and S read *kefareha,* "its villages."

[10]*Tg.* uses the exegetical complement to expand upon MT which says simply "and you shall know."

[11]MT: "My land." *Tg.* employs a circumlocution to negate the idea that God may be territorially limited to one land, even if that be the land of Israel, which is rendered as the abode of the Shekinah.

[12]MT: "that the nations may know Me."

[13]God cannot be seen directly by the nations, but they can observe His intervention on the historic scene.

[14]MT: "My wrath shall rise in My nostrils." *Tg.*'s rendering avoids the anthropomorphism.

[15]MT: "in My jealousy."

[16]MT: "the steep places," "cliffs."

[17]MT: "My mountains." *Tg.* negates territorial limitation of God. In general the MT of this v. is unclear.

[18]MT: "and I will enter into judgment with him with pestilence and with blood."

[19]*Pes. R.* 17:8 cites this v. in demonstrating that the plagues of Egypt will in the future be visited upon Rome, and in so doing identifies Gog and Rome. Cf. *infra,* *Tg.* Ezek. 39:16.

[20]MT: "I will make Myself known."

Notes, Chapter 39

[1]For Midrashic interpretation, see *Mid. Teh.,* 150:1.

from the farthest ends of the north, and bring you against the mountains of Israel. 3. Then I will cast away your bow from your left hand, and pull down your arrows from your right hand. 4. On the mountains of the land of Israel shall your *corpse be flung,* you and all your armies, and the many peoples that are with you; I have handed you over to the fowl, to every bird that flies and the beasts of the field, to be destroyed. 5. *Your corpse shall be flung* on the open field, for *I have decreed it by My Memra,* says the Lord God. 6. I will *kindle* a fire in Magog and among the inhabitants of the islands who dwell securely, and they shall know that I am the Lord. 7. And My holy name I will *reveal* in the midst of My people Israel; and never again will I allow My holy name to be profaned; and the nations shall know that I am the Lord, the Holy One; *I have made My Shekinah dwell* in Israel. 8. Behold, it is coming, and it shall be fulfilled, says the Lord God; it is the day that I *have decreed by My Memra.* 9. Then those who dwell in the cities of the land of Israel shall go out, and use for heating and store up for kindling, the weapons, bucklers and shields, bows and arrows, wooden staves and spears, and they shall use them for kindling for seven years.[2] 10. And they shall not take wood from the field, nor cut it from the forests, because they shall use the weapons for kindling, and they shall despoil those who despoiled them, and take booty of those who plundered them, says the Lord God. 11. It shall be at that time, I will give to Gog a *proper*[3] place for a burial ground in Israel, in the Valley of the Pass,[4] east of the sea *of Gennesaret*[5] *and it is near the two mountains;*[6] there they shall bury Gog and all of his *noisy* horde; and they shall call it the Valley of Gog's *Noisy Horde.* 12. The House of Israel shall bury them for seven months in order to cleanse the land. 13. All the people of the land shall bury them; and it shall make them famous on the day that I reveal My glory, says the Lord God. 14. And they shall appoint men to traverse the land continually, *a mobile group, burying those that remain above ground,*[a7] to cleanse it; at the end of seven months they shall begin to search. 15. And if one of those who traverse the land shall pass along the road, and see a human bone, he shall erect a marker[b8] beside it until those who bury it shall have interred it in the Valley of Gog's *Noisy* Horde. 16. *There,*[9] *too, shall be flung the slain of Rome,* the city *of many boisterous crowds;*[10] thus they shall cleanse the land. 17. And you, Son of Adam, thus says the Lord God, Say to the fowl, to every bird that flies, and to all the beasts of the field, 'Assemble and come, close in from all around, on *the slain*[c] that *I am slaying* for you, a great *killing*[11] on the mountains of Israel, and you shall eat flesh and drink blood. 18. You shall eat the flesh of mighty men, and you shall drink the blood of the princes of the earth, *kings, rulers, and governors* all of them *mighty men, rich in possessions.*[12] 19. And you shall eat fat till you are sated, and you shall drink blood till you are intoxicated, *from the flesh of the slain that I slay for you.*[13] 20. And you shall be sated on the *mountains of My people*[d14] with the flesh of horses, and charioteers,[e] mighty men, and all valiant warriors,' says the Lord God. 21. And I will set My glory among the nations, and all the nations shall see *My punishment* which I have

Apparatus, Chapter 39

[a] My reconstruction. SP and RB (following MT): "burying the people who pass by, those that remain on the face of the earth."

[b] RB and AP. SP: "an order," "a will."

[c] Most versions. SP: "My slaying."

[d] SP. RB: "Israel."

[e] Lit. "chariots."

[f] Most versions. SP: "before Me."

executed, and My *might*,[15] which I have placed among them. 22. And the House of Israel shall know that I am the Lord their God from that day onward. 23. And the nations shall know that the House of Israel were exiled because of their sins, because they dealt falsely with *My Memra*, so that *I removed My Shekinah*[16] from them, and delivered them into the hand of their enemies, and they were slain by the sword, all of them. 24. I *have inflicted punishment upon* them[17] according to their uncleanness and their *rebellions;* and *I removed My Shekinah*[16] from them. 25. Therefore thus says the Lord God: Now I will bring back the exile of Jacob, and have mercy upon the whole House of Israel; *and I will inflict the punishment of My might upon the nations, because they have profaned* My holy name.[18] 26. They shall bear their humiliation and all their perfidies which they have committed *before My Memra*[f] when they dwell securely in their land, with none to make them afraid; 27. when I bring them back from among the nations, and gather them in from the countries of their enemies, and have sanctified Myself through them before the eyes of many nations. 28. And they shall know that I am the Lord their God, that I exiled them among the nations *because they sinned before Me,* and *when they repented,* I gathered them in to their land and will never again leave any of them out there. 29. And never again will *I remove My Shekinah*[16] from them, for I have poured out My *holy* spirit on the House of Israel, says the Lord God."

Notes, Chapter 39 *continued*

[2]See note 1 to ch. 38, *supra.*

[3]*kašar,* "ritually permitted," "worthy." Gog and Magog will have limited punishment and will not be condemned to eternal perdition, according to R. Akiba. *m. 'Ed.* 2:10.

[4]MT: "the Valley of the Travellers." Emendation yields "Valley of Abarim."

[5]*Tg.* identifies the unspecified sea in MT as the sea of Gennesar (Kinnereth, sea of Galilee), probably a case of mistaken identity. It could be an erroneous gloss. Jer. 22:20 would indicate Abarim as the southern part of the land, the region of the Dead Sea. Cf. *S-A,* p. 120; M. McNamara, *Targum and Testament,* p. 194, sub "Gennesar."

[6]*Tg.* does not identify the two mountains. If Gennesar is integral to the text of the *Tg.* then the mountains might be the heights above Galilee. If Gennesar is a marginal gloss, then the reference could be to the bluffs overlooking the Dead Sea, or the mountains of Abarim.

[7]I have transposed several words in the *Tg.* to arrive at this rendering, because the text as it stands is unclear. Reading: *'am de'adan meqabrin.* MT is uncertain.

[8]Simeon b. Pazzi cites this as the Halakic source for the use of gravestones. *b. M.K.* 5a.

[9]This entire v. in MT is difficult. The different versions render it in diverse ways. *Tg.* reads *šam* for Masoretic *šem.*

[10]MT: *hamonah,* "the crowded one," which *Tg.* renders as Rome, thus identifying and equating Gog with Rome. This has significant eschatological overtones, implying that the final eschatological war of Gog and Magog will actually be with Rome. Cf. *Pes. R.* 17:8; S.H. Levey, *The Messiah,* p. 86; P. Churgin, *Targum Jonathan to the Prophets,* p. 26. Gog-Magog was taken as an eschatological symbol by the Rabbis, even as a reference to Sennacherib. *b. Sanh.* 94a.

[11]MT: "sacrifice."

[12]MT: "rams, lambs, goats, bulls, all of them fatlings of Bashan," which *Tg.* understands as metaphors for different classes of men.

[13]MT: "from My sacrificial feast which I am preparing for you."

[14]MT: "at My table."

[15]MT: "My judgment which I have executed, and My hand ..."

[16]MT: "I hid My face from them."

[17]MT: "I have done to them."

[18]MT: "and I will be jealous for My holy name."

CHAPTER 40

1. In the twenty-fifth year of our exile,[1] at the beginning of the year,[2] on the tenth day of the month, in the fourteenth year after the city had been breached, on that very day, *the spirit of prophecy from before* the Lord rested upon me, and He brought me in there. 2. In the vision *of prophecy from before the Lord which rested upon me,* He brought me into the land of Israel and He set me down upon a very high mountain, and upon it there was something like the structure of a city, on the south. 3. He brought me there, and behold, there was a man,[3] whose appearance was like that of bronze. In his hand were a linen cord and a measuring rod, and behold, he was standing at the gate. 4. And the man spoke to me, "Son of Adam, observe with your eyes, and heed with your ears, and concentrate[a] on all that I show you, for it was in order to show it to you that they[4] have brought you[b] here. Relate all that you see to the House of Israel." 5. And behold, there was a wall all around the outside of the Temple;[c] and in the hand of the man there were measuring rods, each one of which was six long cubits, the long cubit being a cubit and a hand-breadth;[5] and he measured the thickness[6] of the structure, one rod, and the height, one rod. 6. Then he entered[7] the gate which faced[d] eastward, and he climbed its steps;[8] then he measured the threshold of the gate, one rod deep.[9] 7. The cell was one rod long and one rod wide; and between the cells there was *a wall*[10] *of* five cubits; and the threshold of the gate next to the vestibule of the gate, on the inside, was one rod. 8. Then he measured the vestibule of the gate from within, one rod. 9. Then he measured the vestibule of the gate, eight cubits, and its supports[e] two cubits; and the vestibule of the gate[f] was from within. 10. And there were cells by the gate on the east, three on this side and three on that side, all three being the same size;[g] and the supports on either side were the same size. 11. Then he measured the width of the entrance to the gate, ten cubits, and the length of the gate, thirteen cubits. 12. There was a marked off area of one cubit in front of the cells on the one side, and a marked off area of one cubit on the other side; and each cell was six cubits on either side. 13. Then he measured the gate, from the roof of the cell to its other roof; its width was twenty five cubits, with one door opposite the other. 14. He made the supports sixty cubits *high,* and the support of the courtyard gate was *one cubit* round about.[11] 15. And the front of *the middle gate,*[12] which was before the vestibule of the inner gate, was fifty

---

Apparatus, Chapter 40

[a] Lit. "and set your mind."
[b] AP: "you were returned."
[c] Lit. "the house."
[d] Lit. "which opened towards."
[e] Or "buttresses."
[f] Most versions. SP: "and the ground." Probably a

scribal error.
[g] Lit. "having the same measurement."
[h] Or "closed," "shuttered."
[i] Or "architectural capital."
[j] SP, following MT. Other versions: "middle."

cubits.[13] 16. The cells and their supports inside the gate round about had windows which narrowed;[h14] and the vestibules likewise had windows round about inside; and on top of each support there was a *crown*.[i15] 17. Then he brought me into the outer court, and behold, there were chambers, and a pavement had been built for the court, round about; there were thirty chambers on the pavement. 18. And the pavement, on the side of the gates, ran the length of the gates. This was the lower pavement. 19. Then he measured the width from in front of the lower[j] gate, which was before the inner court, from the outside, one hundred cubits, to the east and to the north. 20. Then he measured the length and the width of the gate of the outer court which faced to the north. 21. It had three cells[16] on the one side and three on the other side; and its supports and its vestibules were the same size as those of the first gate; its length was fifty cubits, and its width was twenty-five cubits. 22. Its windows, its vestibules, and its crowns were the same size as those of the gate which faced to the east; and they ascended it by seven steps; and its vestibules were in front of them. 23. And there was a gate to the inner court opposite the gate which faced to the north and to the east, and he measured from gate to gate, one hundred cubits. 24. Then he led me southward, and behold, there was a gate which faced to the south; and he measured its supports and its vestibules, and they were the same size as the

Notes, Chapter 40

[1]"Our exile" refers to the captivity of 597 B.C.E., in which Ezekiel was carried off; 14 years after the destruction of the city in 586, hence the year was 572 B.C.E. Cf. *b. 'Arak.* 12a; Rashi and Kimhi to this v.

[2]MT: *bero'š haššanah*, which *Tg.* renders literally. Rosh Hashanah in the sense of New Year festival is of late vintage. LXX: "in the first month," which could be Nisan. *b. 'Arak.* 12a sees it as Tishri, the tenth of which was the beginning of the jubilee. Lev. 25:9 ff. Later, Yom Kippur.

[3]An angelic being who serves as interpreter and architectural guide. Cf. Zech. chs. 1, 2; Rev. 21:10-27.

[4]MT: "you have been brought," a passive grammatical construction which *Tg.* renders as an active, referring to "they," the divine powers that control the destiny of the prophet. The Targumic rendering also precludes the possibility that the man in question was God Himself.

[5]For a critical analysis of the "long" cubit, see *ICC,* p. 431 and *IB,* p. 285.

[6]*putya'*, for MT's *rohab*, basic meaning, "width,' but may mean "depth," "breadth," "thickness," etc., depending on context. In this instance it would be the thickness, since it refers to the structure. Jastrow, II, p. 1149, limits the meaning to width, but probably with different shades of meaning.

[7]MT: "and he came to." *Tg.*'s rendering agrees with LXX.

[8]LXX read "and he entered by seven steps," corresponding to vv. 22 and 26. According to Rashi there were twelve steps, quoting *m. Mid.* 2:3.

[9]*Tg.* translates the Hebrew text literally, word for word; the meaning of both the Hebrew and the Aramaic is not entirely clear.

[10]An exegetical complement. *Tg.* supplies what it feels is missing in MT.

[11]V. 14b in MT is unintelligible. So is the *Tg.* as it stands. I have followed SP, but eliminated one word *w'al* to arrive at my translation. LXX has a different reading for the entire v.

[12]MT: "the entrance gate." Cf. *y. 'Er.* 22c where both "entrance gate" and "middle gate" are listed among the seven names of the eastern gate. Cf. *Tg.* Jer. 26:10, where "new gate" is translated "eastern gate."

[13]Rashi maintains that the height of this gate was fifty cubits. Kimhi takes violent issue with Rashi on this score. Rashi's misconception may be based on a misreading of the *Tg.* on this passage, *gaboah* for *gawa'ah*. According to *m. Mid.* 2:3, the height of the gates was 20 cubits, not fifty.

[14]*Num. R.* 15:7 cites this v. to prove that the windows were narrow within and widened outwardly, so that the sacred light which issued from the Temple could spread out to the world. But cf. *Tg.* 1 K 6:4, where the comparable phrase in MT is rendered: "And he made for the Temple windows which were wide on the inside and narrow on the outside ..." LXX, both here and in 1(3)K, reads "secret windows." V: "oblique" or "slanting" windows. S: "slanted on the inside and small on the outside."

[15]MT: "palm trees,' or "palm decorations."

[16]*Tg.* follows Q, rendering pl. of all elements in vv. 21 and 22.

others. 25. Both it and its vestibules had windows round about, like the other windows, the length fifty cubits and the width twenty-five cubits. 26. Its stairs were seven steps, and its vestibules were in front of them; and it had crowns on its supports, one on this and one on that side. 27. And there was a gate on the south of the inner court; and he measured from gate to gate on the south, one hundred cubits. 28. Then he brought me into the inner court by the south gate; and he measured the south gate; its size was the same as the others. 29. Its cells, its supports and its vestibules were the same size as those others; and both it and its vestibules had windows round about; the length was fifty cubits and the width was twenty-five cubits. 30. There were vestibules round about, twenty-five cubits long and five cubits wide. 31. Its vestibules were towards the outer court; and there were *crowns* on its supports; and its stairs were eight steps.[17] 32. Then he brought me into the inner court to the east; and he measured the gate; it was the same size as those others. 33. Its cells, its supports, and its vestibules, were the same size as those others. Both it and its vestibules had windows round about; the length was fifty cubits and the width was twenty-five cubits. 34. Its vestibules were towards the outer court, and there were *crowns* on its supports on both sides; and its stairs were eight steps. 35. Then he brought me to the gate that faced to the north, and he measured it; it was the same size as those others. 36. It had cells, supports and vestibules; and it had windows round about; the length was fifty cubits and the width was twenty-five cubits. 37. Its supports were towards the outer court, and there were *crowns* on its supports, on both sides; and its stairs were eight steps. 38. A chamber opened by the supports of the gates; there they *would prepare*[18] the burnt offering. 39. And in the vestibule of the gate there were two tables on either side, on which to slaughter the burnt offering, and the sin offering and the guilt offering. 40. And on the outside, as one goes up to the entrance of the north gate, there were two tables; and on the other side of the vestibule of the gate there were two tables. 41. There were four tables on this side and four tables on that side flanking the gate, eight tables in all,[k] where they would be slaughtering *between* them. 42. The four tables for the burnt offering were of hewn stone, one cubit and a half long, one cubit and a half wide, and one cubit high; on them they were to lay the instruments with which they would slaughter the burnt offering and the holy sacrifices. 43. And hooks[19] of one hand-breadth, were affixed to the pillars of the *slaughtering* chamber, inside the vestibule round about; and on the tables was the flesh of the sacrifices. 44. Outside the inner gate were the chambers *of the Levites*[20] in the inner court, which was on the side of the east gate, facing north. 45. And he spoke with me: This chamber which faces to the south, is for the priests[21] who have charge of the service of the Temple. 46. And the chamber which faces to the north is for the priests who have charge of the altar; these are the sons of Zadok,[22] who, from among the sons of Levi, may come near to *the service of*

Apparatus, Chapter 40 continued

[k] Lit. "between them."

Apparatus, Chapter 41

[a] Or "dwelling," "tent."
[b] Lit. "house."

[c] Lit. "chamber over chamber."

the Lord, to minister before Him, 47. And he measured the court; the length was one hundred cubits and the width was one hundred cubits; it was square; and the altar was in front of the Temple. 48. Then he brought me into the vestibule of the Temple, and he measured the support of the vestibule, which was five cubits on either side; and the width of the gate was three cubits on this side and three cubits on that side. 49. The length of the vestibule was twenty cubits and the width eleven cubits; and there were steps[23] by which they would go up to it; and there were columns by the supports, one on this side, and one on that side.

CHAPTER 41

1. Then he brought me into the Sanctuary, and he measured the supports; the width was six cubits on this side and six cubits on that side; this was the width of the *tabernacle.*[a1] 2. And the width of the door was ten cubits, and the shoulders of the door were five cubits on this side, and five cubits on that side; and he measured its length, forty cubits, and its width, twenty cubits. 3. Then he entered the inner room, and he measured the support of the door, two cubits; the door itself, was six cubits, and the width of the door, seven cubits. 4. He measured its length, twenty cubits, and the width in front of the Sanctuary was twenty cubits; and he said to me, "This is *the locus[b] of* the Holy of Holies." 5. Then he measured the wall of the Temple, six cubits; and the width of the side-chamber, four cubits, round about, encircling the Temple all around. 6. And the side-chambers, one above the other,[c] were thirty-three, in sequence of eleven; fixed to the walls inside the side-chambers round about, were beams resting on brackets, so the beams would not extend into the walls of the Temple. 7. And a wide, *winding staircase* rose higher and higher above the side-

Notes, Chapter 40 continued

[17]This differs from the description in *m. Mid.* 3:5, which declares that the Second Temple had fifteen circular stairs here.

[18]MT: "they would wash."

[19]MT: *wehašfattayim,* a word of uncertain meaning. Other ancient versions read *usefatam,* "and their edge." See BDB, p. 1052. *Tg.'s* rendering reflects *m. Mid.* 3:5, which describes the slaughter chamber of the Temple as having eight short pillars, topped with cedar-wood, into which were fixed iron hooks on which to hang the slaughtered animals to be skinned.

[20]MT: "chambers of the singers." The Levites were the choristers in the Temple. Cf. *m. Tam.* 7:3, 4. LXX: "two chambers," reading *štayim* rather than *šarim.*

[21]Rashi identifies these as the singing Levites, probably on the basis of *Tg.* on v. 44.

[22]It is generally accepted that the reference to the sons of Zadok at this point is an editorial intrusion. This theme will be discussed *infra,* Ezek. 44:15.

[23]LXX: "ten steps." V: "eight steps." According to *m. Mid.* 3:6 there were twelve steps.

Notes, Chapter 41

[1]MT: "the tent."

chambers, for it encompassed the Temple, continuing higher all around on the inside. Thus, the Temple was wider from above. And thus they would ascend by the staircase from the bottom story to the top story by way of the middle story.[2] 8. I saw the Temple's height all around; the side-chambers were complete, measuring a rod, six extended cubits. 9. The thickness of the outer wall of the side-chamber was five cubits, and a space was left open on the inside of the Temple's side-chambers. 10. And between the chambers there was a width of twenty cubits, round about, encircling the Temple. 11. As to the entrance of the side-chamber by the open space, one gate faced north, and one gate faced south, and the width of the open space was five cubits round about. 12. The structure which was in front of the balcony to the west was seventy cubits wide, and the wall of the structure was five cubits thick round about, and its length was ninety cubits. 13. He measured the Temple; the length was one hundred cubits; and the balcony, the structure and the walls, one hundred cubits long. 14. And the width in front of the Temple and the balcony to the east, was one hundred cubits. 15. He measured the length of the rear of the structure which was in front of the balcony,[3] and its corners on both sides, one hundred cubits. The inside of the Sanctuary, and the vestibules by the courtyard, 16. the thresholds, the narrowing[d4] windows, and the supports round about all three of them, opposite the threshold, were overlaid with boards of cedarwood round about, from the ground to the windows, and the narrowing windows 17. to the top of the door, to the inner Temple and the outside. And upon every wall round about, inside and outside, their *sketched patterns*[5] 18. were engraved with cherubim and *crowns,* a *crown* between cherub and cherub; and every cherub had two faces: 19. the face of a man *was fashioned* for the *crown* on the one side, and the face of a lion *was fashioned* for the *crown* on the other side, engraved on the entire Temple round about. 20. From the ground to the top of the door, cherubim and *crowns* were engraved; so, too, for the wall of the Sanctuary. 21. As for the Sanctuary, its doorposts were square, and, as for the appearance of the Holy *of Holies,*[e6] its appearance was like the appearance *of glory.*[f7] 22. Opposite the altar was a wooden table, its height three cubits, and its length two cubits; and it had corners, and its length and its walls were of wood. And he spoke to me, "This is the table which is before the Lord." 23. There were two doors for the Sanctuary and for the Holy *of Holies.* 24. And there were, *mother* doors,[8] two swinging doors, two for the one door, and two doors for the other. 25. There was engraving on them; on the doors of the Sanctuary, cherubim and *crowns,* like that which was engraved on the walls; and there was *a threshold*[9] of wood in front of the vestibule on the outside. 26. And there were narrowing windows and *crowns* on this side and that side, on the corners of the vestibule, and on the side-chamber of the Temple and *the thresholds.*

Apparatus, Chapter 41 continued

[d] Lit. "closed," "shut."

[e] Lit. "the place of atonement."

[f] RB: "His glory." MM: "like the sweet taste of glory."

CHAPTER 42

1. Then he took me out to the outer court, by way of the gate which faces north, and he brought me into the chamber which was in front of the balcony and in front of the structure on the north. 2. Along the length, which was a hundred cubits, there was a door which faced north, and the width was fifty cubits. 3. Opposite the twenty cubits[1] of the inner court, and facing the pavement which opened into the outer court, there were balconies[2] facing balconies at three levels. 4. And in front of the chambers there was a walkway of ten cubits, and the width inside the passage was one cubit, and their gates faced north. 5. The upper chambers were narrower than the lower and middle levels of the building, because the balconies took space away from them. 6. For they were on three levels, and they had no columns like the columns of the court; hence they were narrower than those that were on the lower and middle levels from the ground. 7. And the outer wall, opposite the chambers towards the outer court which was in front of the chambers; its length was fifty cubits. 8. For the length of the chambers of the outer court was fifty cubits, while those facing the Sanctuary were a hundred cubits. 9. Below these chambers was an entrance from the east, through which they entered from the outer court. 10. Along the width of the wall of the court, eastward, in front of the balcony which was in front of the building, there were chambers, 11. with a passage in front of them, which had the appearance like the chambers which opened to the north, and were similar in length, so also their width, and like all their exits, and like their general appearance, and like their entrances, 12. and like the doors of the chambers which faced south. There was a

Notes, Chapter 41 continued

[2]The MT is obscure and virtually impossible to disentangle. Cf. *IB*, p. 293. The same applies to other vv. in this chapter. A "winding staircase" is mentioned in *m. Tamid* 1:1. *Tg.*'s rendering is incorporated in *JPS* (N), *ad loc.*, p. 745

[3]MT: Q reads *we'attiqeha*. K-B translates "passage," or, questioningly, "gallery." p. 101. *Tg.* renders the word *zewi*, which Jastrow describes as "a projection of a wall formed by abruptly reducing its thickness, so as to give space for a balcony." I, p. 386.

[4]See *supra, Tg.* Ezek. 40:16 and note 14 thereto.

[5]MT: "measurements."

[6]MT: "and the face of the holy" or "in front of the holy." *Tg.* renders it "place of atonement," which is equated with the "Holy of Holies," the inner sanctum. Cf. Jastrow, I, p. 658, sub *kapori* and *kaporet*.

[7]MT: "and the appearance was like the appearance." *Tg.* senses that MT is laconic, and by exegetical complement, adds what it believes to be missing. The v. seems to reflect the mystic awesomeness of the glory of God.

[8]MT: "and the doors had two doors." The meaning is unclear. Perhaps it means superior doors.

[9]MT: *'ab*, an architectural term the meaning of which is uncertain. Cf. BDB, p. 712.

Notes, Chapter 42

[1]As in MT, "cubits" is implied but unwritten.

[2]See *supra* Ezek. 41:15 and note 3 thereto.

door at the head of the passage, the passage in front of *the platform of the Levites,*[3] to the east, as they entered. 13. And he said to me, "The northern chambers and the southern chambers which are in front of the balcony, they are the sacred chambers where the priests, who approach to serve before the Lord, shall eat the most sacred offerings; there they shall put down the most sacred offerings, and the meal offerings, the sin offerings, and the guilt offerings, for the place is holy. 14. When the priests enter, they shall not go out of the holy place to the outer court, unless they leave there, their garments in which they minister, for they are holy; and they shall put on other garments and then *mingle* with the people." 15. When he finished the measurements of the inner Temple, he led me out by way of the gate which faced east, and he measured it round about. 16. He measured the east side with the measuring rod, five hundred rods, by the measuring rod, round about. 17. He measured the north side, five hundred rods by the measuring rod, round about. 18. The south side he measured, five hundred rods, by the measuring rod. 19. He turned to the west side and measured, five hundred rods, by the measuring rod. 20. He measured it on the four sides; it had a wall round about it, the length, five hundred and the width, five hundred, to separate between the holy and the non-holy.

CHAPTER 43

1. Then he brought me to the gate, the gate that faced east. 2. And behold, the glory of the God of Israel *was revealed* in the east,[1] and the voice of *those blessing His name*[2] was like the sound of many waters, and the earth *shone*[a] from the *radiance* of His glory. 3. And the vision was like the vision which I had seen; like the vision which I had seen when I *prophesied*[b] concerning the destruction of the city;[3] and the vision was like the vision which I had seen by the river Chebar; and I bowed down upon my face. 4. The glory of the Lord *was revealed* in the Temple[4] by way of the gate which faced east. 5. The Spirit lifted me and brought me into the inner court, and behold, the Temple was filled with the glory of the Lord. 6. And I heard someone speaking with me from the inside,[5] and there was a man standing beside me. 7. And He said to me, "Son of Adam, this is the place *of the abode* of My throne *of glory,* and this is the place of *the abode where My Shekinah dwells,* for I will make My *Shekinah dwell there,*[6] in the midst of the Children of Israel forever; and the Children of Israel shall no longer defile My holy name, neither they nor their kings, *with their idols*[7] and the shrines[c] of the corpses of their kings, 8. by placing their threshold beside the threshold of My *Holy Temple,* and *their buildings* beside My *Temple*

Apparatus, Chapter 43

[a] Most versions. BM: "was lit up."
[b] Lit. "in my prophesying."
[c] SP, following MT. RB(2): "when they die," reading *bemotam.*

[d] Lit. "show," "tell."
[e] Lit. "decrees."
[f] Lit. "holy of holies."
[g] RB. SP: "from the place where they ascended it."

Court, with only a wall of *My Holy Temple* between *My Memra* and them.[8] They defiled My holy name with their abominations which they committed, so *I destroyed them*[9] in My anger. 9. Now let them put their *idols* and the corpses of their kings far away, *so as not to sin* before Me, and I will *cause My Shekinah to* dwell among them forever. 10. You, Son of Adam, describe[d] the Temple to the House of Israel, so that they may humble themselves for all that they have done *when they see it,* then make known to them and write down before their eyes, the form of the Temple and its design, and its exits and entrances, and its entire form, all of its ordinances, and its entire framework, and *everything to which it is entitled;* and write it down before their eyes, that they may observe all of its framework and all of its regulations,[e10] and perform them. 12. This is the divine law[11] concerning the Temple on the top of the mountain; everything within its boundaries round about is most holy.[f] Behold, this is the divine law of the Temple. 13. These are the dimensions of the altar in long cubits, where the cubit is a cubit and a handbreadth: the base[12] a cubit, and the width a cubit, and a rim around its edge round about, one span; this is the measurement of the altar. 14. From the base on the ground to the lower ledge, two cubits, and the width, one cubit; and from the smaller ledge to the larger ledge, four cubits; and the width, one cubit. 15. The altar,[13] four cubits; and from the altar and upward, four horns. 16. The altar shall be square on all four of its sides, twelve cubits in length by twelve cubits in width. 17. And the ledge shall be fourteen cubits in length, by fourteen cubits in width, on its four sides; and the rim surrounding it round about, one-half cubit, and its base, one cubit round about.[14] The steps[g] *by which they*

Notes, *Chapter 42 continued*

[3]MT: "the approach facing the fenced area of *haginah.*" The last word is unintelligible as it stands. *Tg.* reads *neginah,* "music," "song," and interprets it as referring to the Temple singers, the Levites.

Notes, *Chapter 43*

[1]MT: "coming from the way of the east."

[2]MT: "and His voice." Kimhi interprets the phrase as referring not to God but to glory, "and its sound." The idea that the sound was that of those blessing God's name, a reference to the angelic beings, is unique to the *Tg.*, and in keeping with the doctrine of the Merkabah. Cf. 3:12 and note 5 thereto, *supra.*

[3]MT: "when I came to destroy the city." V and MSS read: "when He came ..."

[4]MT: "entered the House."

[5]MT: "from the House."

[6]MT: "this is the place of My throne, and the place of the soles of My feet, where I will dwell." The Hebrew is a poetic description, similar to Is. 66:1, but *Tg.* finds this too anthropomorphic, and interprets the picture accordingly. It refers of course to the Temple, which Jer. 17:12 calls the Throne of Glory. The intimations of Merkabah are subtle. The restoration of the earthly Temple, here depicted by Ezekiel, is, according to the Rabbis, the successful replication in the future, of the celestial abode of God in the Merkabah tradition. R. Johanan insists that the earthly Jerusalem is a counterpart of the heavenly Jerusalem. *b. Ta'an.* 5a. Cf. Rev. 21:1 ff.

[7]MT: "by their harlotry."

[8]MT: "by placing their threshold with My threshold, and their doorposts with My doorposts, with only a wall between Me and them."

[9]MT: "I consumed them."

[10]MT: *torotaw,* (Q), "its divine laws." *Tg.: gezerateh,* "its decrees," "its regulations."

[11]MT: "this is the Torah of ..." *Tg.* uses customary designation of Torah, *'orayta'.*

[12]MT: "the bosom."

[13]MT: *wehahar'el,* "and the *har'el,*" literally, the mountain of God; also referred to as *'ari'el,* later in this v. and v. 16. *Tg.* renders all of these as "the altar." For a critical analysis see *IB,* p. 303 f.

[14]There is a discrepancy in the dimensions of the altar, between Ezekiel and the Rabbinic sources. Cf. *m. Mid.* 3:1, but then the latter is a description of the reality of the Second Temple, and Ezekiel is a projection of what it might be.

ascend it shall face east." 18. Then He said to me, "Son of Adam, Thus says the Lord God, These are the regulations concerning the altar, on the day of its construction, for offering upon it the burnt offering, and for sprinkling upon it the blood *of the holy sacrifices.* 19. You shall give a young bull for a sin offering to the priests, the Levites, who are of the family[h] of Zadok, who may approach for *My priestly service,* to serve before Me, says the Lord God. 20. And you shall take of its blood and put it on its four horns and on the four corners of the ledge, and upon the rim round about, and you shall cleanse it and make atonement for it. 21. Then you shall take the bull of the sin offering, and burn it in *its proper place*[15] in the Temple, outside the Sanctuary. 22. And on the second day, you shall offer an unblemished he-goat as a sin offering; and you shall cleanse the altar, as they cleansed it with the bull. 23. When you have finished cleansing it, you shall offer an unblemished young bull from the herd, and an unblemished ram from the flock. 24. And you shall offer them before the Lord, and the priests shall put salt on them, and offer them up as a burnt offering before the Lord. 25. Every day for seven days you shall provide a goat for a sin offering; and also they shall provide a young bull from the herd and a ram from the flock, unblemished. 26. For seven days they shall make atonement for the altar, and cleanse it, and *offer up its sacrifices.*[16] 27. When they have completed the days, on the eighth day and onward, the priests shall offer your burnt offerings and your *holy sacrifices,*[17] on the altar; and your sacrifices shall be favorably accepted,[18] says the Lord God."

CHAPTER 44

1. Then he brought me back towards the outer gate of the Sanctuary, which faces east; and it was closed. 2. And the Lord said to me: "This gate must remain closed; it must not be opened; and no one shall enter by it, for the Lord,[a] the God of Israel, *has been revealed above it,*[b1] and it must remain closed. 3. *It shall be for* the prince.[2] The prince, only he may sit in it, to eat bread before the Lord; he shall enter by way of the vestibule of the gate, and shall go out by the same way." 4. Then he brought me in by way of the north gate, which is in front of the Temple; and I looked, and behold, the Temple of the Lord was filled with the glory of the Lord, and I bowed down on my face. 5. Then the Lord said to me, "Son of Adam, take note, observe with your eyes

Apparatus, Chapter 43 continued

[h] Lit. "the seed."

Apparatus, Chapter 44

[a] Most versions. AP: "for the glory of the Lord."
[b] Most versions. BM 1474: "entered by it," but another version: "was revealed above it."
[c] Lit. "sons of the nations."

and listen with your ears to everything which I speak with you, concerning all the regulation[3] of the Temple of the Lord, and everything *which is proper* for it;[4] note well the entrances to the Temple, as well as all the exits of the Sanctuary.[5] 6. And you shall say to the rebellious *people,*[6] to the House of Israel, Thus says the Lord God: Too many for you, are all your abominations, O House of Israel, 7. by your bringing of foreigners,[c] *wicked* of heart and uncircumcised of flesh,[7] to be in My Sanctuary, to desecrate My Temple, when you offer up My *sacrifice,*[8] the fat and the blood *of My holy sacrifices;* and they have altered My covenant with all your abominations. 8. You have not kept watch on My holy things,[9] but you *appointed others* to be guardians for you of the holy watch of *My Memra* in My Sanctuary." 9. Thus says the Lord God: "No foreigners, *wicked* of heart and uncircumcised of flesh, shall enter My Sanctuary,[10] even all the foreigners who are among the Children of Israel. 10. Only the Levites who removed themselves from *My worship* when Israel went astray, who strayed from following *My worship,* straying after their idols, they shall receive punishment for their sins. 11. They shall serve in My Temple, appointed over the Temple gates, and performing the services of the Temple. They shall slaughter the burnt offering and the *holy* sacrifice of the people; and they shall stand before them to serve them. 12. Because they had been serving them in the presence of their idols, and had been a sinful stumbling-block to the House of Israel, therefore I have sworn *by My Memra* concerning them, says the Lord God, that they shall receive punishment for their sins. 13. They shall not approach for *My worship,* to serve *before* Me,[11] and to come near to all of My holy things, or to the Holy of Holies; but they

Notes, Chapter 43 continued

[15]MT: "the appointed area."

[16]MT: "and they shall fill its hands." Rashi on Ex. 28:41 says that this is an idiomatic expression which means sanctification or consecration. *Tg.* takes it in the sense of being ready for its sacred function, the offering up of the sacrifices.

[17]MT: "your peace offerings." The term is invariably rendered "holy sacrifices" by *Tg.*, both in Ezek. and elsewhere. Cf. *Tg.* Onq. and Ps.-J. on Ex. 20:21; 24:5; Lev. 3:1; 19:5; *Tg.* Neb. on Josh. 8:31; and numerous instances throughout Scripture, this rendering is without exception. Lit., "slaughter of the sacred," as opposed to ordinary slaughter.

[18]MT: "and I will accept you favorably." Note *Tg.*'s translation in the passive, maintaining God's transcendence.

Notes, Chapter 44

[1]MT: "has entered by it."

[2]Rashi thinks this refers to the High Priest, Kimḥi and Mezudat David, to the future King Messiah.

[3]See *supra,* ch. 43:11 and note 10 thereto.

[4]MT: "concerning all the ordinances of the House and all its laws."

[5]*Tg.*'s translation is identical with that of LXX. V is similar. The Rabbinic commentaries follow suit, *ad loc.* Modern exegetes take the passage as referring to persons who may or may not enter, requiring emendations. Cf. *IB,* p. 308.

[6]MT: "say to the rebellion."

[7]MT: "aliens, uncircumcised of heart and uncircumcised of flesh." While *Tg.* seems to go along with MT as referring to actual foreigners, the Rabbinic sources take this entire passage as referring to unqualified or disqualified Jewish priests, alienated from God by their deviant conduct. *b Sanh.* 83b, 84a: *Lam. R.* 1:36. Cf. also Rashi and Kimḥi on this v. Cf. Jer. 4:4, 9:6. See *IB,* p. 308 f. on Gentiles in the Temple of Herod.

[8]MT: "My bread."

[9]Probably a reference to the twenty-four divisions, or watches, during which Israelites kept guard at the Temple services, while the priests and Levites functioned. Cf. *m. Ta'an.* 4:2.

[10]In quoting this v., R. Ḥisda adds "to serve me" as part of the quotation. *b. M. K. 5a.*

[11]MT: "to serve Me as priests."

shall suffer their humiliation, for the abominations which they have committed. 14. But I have appointed them watchmen guarding the Temple, for all of its service, and for everything that must be done in it. 15. But the priests, the Levites,[d] the sons of Zadok,[12] who kept the watch of My Sanctuary when the children of Israel strayed from *My worship,* they shall approach for *My worship,* to serve *before* Me, and *they shall serve at My altar,*[13] to offer up *before Me* the fat and the blood *of the holy sacrifices,* says the Lord God. 16. They shall enter My Sanctuary, and they shall approach My table of the *Display-bread,*[14] to minister before Me, and they shall keep the watch of *My Memra.* 17. And when they enter the gates of the inner court, they shall wear linen garments; no woolen *cloak* shall be upon them when they serve at the gates of the inner court and within. 18. Turbans of linen shall be upon their heads, and linen trousers on their loins; they shall not gird[e] *their loins; they shall gird their hearts.*[15] 19. And when they go out *of the court of the Sanctuary* to the outer court, *to mingle* with the people,[16] they shall put off their garments in which they serve and lay them in the sacred chambers; and they shall put on other garments, so that they should not *mingle* with the people in their vestments. 20. They shall not shave their heads nor let their hair grow wild; they shall only trim the hair of their heads. 21. No priests shall drink wine when they enter the inner court. 22. A widow and a divorced woman, they shall not marry, but they may marry a virgin descended from the House of Israel; and a widow, who is a widow of *other* priests, they may marry.[f17] 23. They shall teach My people the difference between the sacred and the unconsecrated, and they shall make known to them the distinction between the unclean and the clean. 24. In matters of judicial litigation, they shall rise to judge; they shall judge according to the judgments *of My will;* they shall keep My Torah and My statutes concerning all My festivals; and My Sabbaths they shall keep holy. 25. He shall not enter where there is a dead person, thereby defiling himself; except that they may defile themselves for a father or mother, for a son or daughter, for a brother or an unmarried sister.[g] 26. After his purification, they shall count seven days for him. 27. And on the day of his entry into the Sanctuary, into the inner court, to serve in the Sanctuary, he shall offer his sin offering, says the Lord God. 28. Their share of inheritance[h] shall be the *residue of My sacrifice;*[18] but you shall give them no possession in Israel; *the gifts that I give them, these are*[18] their possession. 29. The meal offering and the sin offering and the guilt offering they shall eat; and everything in Israel which is set apart as sacred, shall be for them. 30. And the first of everything; the first fruits of every kind, and all contributions which you set aside, shall be entirely for the priests; and your first batch of bread you shall give to the priests, so that a blessing may rest upon your home. 31. The priests shall not eat anything of bird and of cattle that has died a natural death or has been torn by wild beasts."[19]

Apparatus, Chapter 44 continued

[d] MM: "and the Levites."

[e] K uses a cognate verb *zrz.*

[f] A and RB. SP: "and a widow who is a widow, other priests may marry."

[g] Lit. "a sister who has not been with a man."

[h] RB. SP omits "inheritance."

Apparatus, Chapter 45

[a] RB: "they."

[b] Or "graded field."

CHAPTER 45

1. "When you*ª* *divide*[1] the land as an inheritance, you shall set aside a gift *before* the Lord, a sacred portion of the land, the length twenty-five thousand cubits long, and the width, ten thousand;[2] it shall be sacred within its entire boundary round about. 2. Of this, there shall be for the Sanctuary, a square five hundred cubits by five hundred cubits round about, and fifty cubits of open space for it, round about. 3. And from this measurement, you shall measure off a length of twenty-five thousand cubits and a width of ten thousand,[2] and within it shall be the Sanctuary, Holy of Holies. 4. It is a sacred portion of the land; it shall be for the priests who serve in the Temple, who approach to serve *before* the Lord, so that they might have a place *left* for houses, and a *precinct*[b3] by the Sanctuary. 5. And an area of twenty-five thou-

Notes, Chapter 44 continued

[12]The Zadokite priesthood prevailed during the First Temple and were restored to their dominant priestly position upon the return from the Babylonian Exile. They were presumed to be the descendants of Zadok the son of Eleazar, son of Aaron. Cf. *ICC*, p. 482 f. For a brilliant analysis of the Sons of Zadok in the Qumran sources, see B.Z. Wacholder, *The Dawn of Qumran*, pp. 99 ff.

[13]MT: "and they shall stand before Me."

[14]*lehem apaya*, a literal Aramaic translation of the Hebrew *lehem panim*, "the bread of the face," or "bread of the Presence," or "showbread." Cf. *Tg.* Onq. on Ex. 25:30; but Ps.-J. on the same v. translates the phrase "the bread of the inside;" however, on Num. 4:7, Ps.-J. translates like Onq. *Tg.* here uses the exegetical complement to expand on MT, which merely refers to "My table" unspecified.

[15]MT: "they shall not gird themselves with anything that makes them perspire." *Tg.*'s rendering could be halakic, reflecting *b. Zeb.* 18b, which asserts that the belt of the priest must be worn at the level of the elbow, i.e., around the heart, to avoid perspiration. Cf. Rashi to this v. It may also be a homily, asserting the peaceful nature of the priestly role, in contrast to those who gird their loins with the sword.

[16]MT: "to the outer court, to the outer court of the people."

[17]This is one of the verses in Ezekiel which contradict the Mosaic Law, in this instance Lev. 21:7, which says nothing about the priest marrying the widow of another priest, nor the prohibition against the priest marrying a widow. R. Naḥman attempts to resolve the difficulty, asserting that the first part of the v. refers to the High Priest, compatible with Lev. 21:13 f., while the second part of the v. refers to the ordinary priest. *b. Kid.* 78a, b. Rashi on this verse in Ezek. follows the Talmud. Kimhi tends to interpret the v. as applying to all priests, and that the prohibition against marrying widows is a legislation for the future, which will be more stringent, even for ordinary priests. He continues: Ezekiel does not have to mention the prohibition against the priest marrying a prostitute or a woman who has been defiled (who has lost her virginity), because these are already covered by the Torah itself (Lev. 21:7).

[18]MT: "I am their inheritance."

[19]MT: *nebelah uterefah*. These are prohibited for all Israelites (Ex. 22:30; Deut. 14:21), why then single out the priests? "Rabina said, It was necessary to impress this upon the priests. Since priests are permitted to eat a bird offering whose head has been torn off at the neck (Lev. 1:15), they might be misled into thinking that they may also eat *nebelah* and *terefah*, it was therefore imperative to alert them that they may not. R. Johanan said, Elijah will explain this passage in the future." (That is, the problem cannot be resolved). *b. Men.* 45a.

Notes, Chapter 45

[1]MT: "when you cast lots for."
[2]LXX: 20,000
[3]MT: "holy (ground)." *Tg.* probably read *umigraš* for *umiqdaš*.

sand cubits length and ten thousand width, shall be for the Levites, the servants of the Temple, for a possession, twenty chambers.[4] 6. And as property of the city, you shall give an area of five thousand cubits width and a length of twenty-five thousand, facing that which is set aside for the Sanctuary; it shall belong to the whole House of Israel. 7. And to the prince shall belong a portion on both sides of that which is set aside for the Sanctuary and the city property, from a westerly direction west, and from an easterly direction east; and the length shall correspond to one of the portions[5] extending from the western border to the eastern border. 8. This land shall be for the prince as a possession in Israel; and My princes shall no longer oppress My people, but they shall give the land to the House of Israel according to their tribes. 9. Thus says the Lord God: Enough for you, princes of Israel! Put away violence and robbery, and practice true justice and righteousness; cease *your taxation*[6] of[c] My people, says the Lord God. 10. You shall have *accurate* scales,[d] and *accurate measures,*[7] and *accurate baths.* 11. The *measure* and the *bath* shall have the same volume, for *you; an amount of three seahs, being the equivalent* of one-tenth of a kor[8] *in the liquid* measure of the *bath;* and one-tenth of a *kor dry measure* of the *kor;* this shall be its measurement. 12. The *sela* shall be twenty *meah.*[9] *A third of a mina*[10] *shall be* twenty *sela. A silver mina shall be* twenty-five *sela. One fourth of a mina shall be* fifteen *sela. All of them together equals sixty.* And you shall have a *large mina for Temple purposes.*[11] 13. This is the contribution which you shall make: one-sixth of a *measure* from a *kor* of wheat, and one-sixth of a *measure* from a *kor* of barley. 14. And that which is proper to take from the oil by *liquid* measure, one-tenth of a *bath* from a *kor;* one-tenth of a *kor* is a *bath,* for there are ten *baths* to the *kor.* 15. And one sheep from every flock of two hundred, which is proper to take from the *fatlings* of Israel; for meal offerings, and for burnt offerings, and for the *holy sacrifices,* to make atonement for them, says the Lord God. 16. All the people of the land shall make this contribution for the prince in Israel. 17. And the prince shall be responsible for the burnt offerings and the meal offerings and the libations during the pilgrimage festivals, the new moons, and the Sabbaths, during all the appointed festivals of the House of Israel. He shall do[12] the sin-offerings and the meal offerings and the burnt offerings, and the *holy sacrifices,* to make atonement for the House of Israel. 18. Thus says the Lord God: In the first month, on the first day of the month, you shall take a bullock of the herd, unblemished, and you shall cleanse the Sanctuary.[13] 19. The priest shall take of the blood of the sin offering and put it on the doorpost of the Temple, and on the four corners of the ledge of the altar, and on the doorpost of the gate of the inner court. 20. And so shall you do on the seventh day of the month for any one who has sinned through error or folly; thus you shall make atonement for the Temple.21. In *Nisan,*[14] on the fourteenth day of the month, you

Apparatus, Chapter 45 continued

[c] Lit. "from the midst of."
[d] Lit. "scales that are true," or "honest."

[e] Or "in exchange for,"

Apparatus, Chapter 46

[a] Or "kneel," "worship."

[b] Lit. "perfect."

shall have the Passover, the pilgrimage festival for seven days; unleavened bread shall be eaten. 22. On that day the prince shall present *as a substitute*[e] for himself and *substituting* for all the people,[15] a bull for a sin offering. 23. And during the seven days of this festival, he shall present burnt offerings before the Lord; seven bulls, and seven rams without blemish, every day, for seven days, and a he-goat as a sin offering, daily. 24. And he shall present a meal offering of a *measure* for each bull and a *measure* for each ram and a full *hin* of oil for each *measure*. 25. In the seventh month,[16] on the fifteenth day of the month, on the pilgrimage festival, he shall do as on these seven days, like the sin offering, like the burnt offering, like the meal offering, and like the oil."

CHAPTER 46

1. Thus says the Lord God: "The gate of the inner court that faces east shall be closed on the six week-days, but on the Sabbath day it shall be opened, and on the day of the new moon it shall be opened. 2. The prince shall enter by way of the vestibule of the gate from the outside, and he shall stand at the door-post of the gate; and the priests shall sacrifice his burnt offering and his *holy sacrifices;* and he shall bow down[a] at the threshold of the gate and then go out; but the gate shall not be closed until the evening. 4. The burnt offering which the prince presents before the Lord on the Sabbath day shall be six lambs without blemish[b] and a ram without

Notes, Chapter 45 continued

[4]LXX reads: "for cities to live in."

[5]According to Rashi and Kimhi, tribal portions.

[6]MT: "your evictions." *Tg.* reflects a common mode of oppression, in this instance exegetically implying confiscation of property and eviction for non-payment of taxes.

[7]MT: "a just *ephah.*" *Tg.* translated *ephah* by *mekilta* wherever it occurs in the Prophets, with one exception, Is. 5:10, where it is rendered by its quantitative equivalent, "three *seahs.*" Cf. *Tg.* Onq. Lev. 19:36, where *ephah* is translated as it is here. Cf. *b. Men.* 77a; *m. Men.* 7:1. Cf. *S-A,* p. 96.

[8]Here, too, *Tg.* equates *homer,* with the more familiar Aramaic *kor.* LXX: *"gomor."* V: "core."

[9]MT: "the *shekel* shall be twenty *gerahs.*"

[10]MT: *maneh,* Aramaic *manya'.*

[11]The MT is difficult and its meaning is uncertain. *Tg.* supplies what it believes to be missing in the Hebrew, by its exegetic complements. The total of sixty is in accord with the Mesopotamian mina of sixty shekels, with which *Tg.* would be familiar. The Talmud testifies that the Temple mina was double that of the ordinary. *b. B.B.* 90a, b. For a critical analysis, see *IB,* p. 317 f.

[12]The Aramaic, like the Hebrew has the verb "to do." It is unclear from these texts if the prince is an active participant in the sacrifices, or merely provides the wherewithal for them. Rashi is of the opinion that in this context "prince" means High Priest, but he did hear from Menaḥem that it refers to the king. However, Cf. 46:2 *infra.*

[13]The sacrifices mentioned here for the specific purposes indicated, are unknown in the Mosaic legislation, hence a discrepancy that might have a bearing on why Ezekiel was almost withdrawn from public use. Nonetheless, this section constitutes the *haftarah* for *Šabbat Haḥodesh.* Cf. *b. Meg.* 30a, b.

[14]MT: "in the first month."

[15]MT: "on behalf of himself and of all the people." *Tg.*'s rendering is unique and significant. Cf. *Tg.* Onq. and Ps.-J. on Lev. 9:7.

[16]*Tg.* does not name the month, as in v. 21, but it is obviously Tishri.

blemish. 5. And the meal offering shall be a *measure* for the ram, and for the lambs, the meal offering shall be as much as he desires;[c] and a *full hin* of oil for each *measure*. 6. On the day of the new moon, it shall be a bullock from the herd without blemish, and six lambs and a ram, which shall be without blemish. 7. He shall present a meal offering of a *measure* for the bull and a *measure* for the ram,[1] and for the lambs, as much as he desires; and a *full hin* of oil for each *measure*. 8. When the prince enters, he shall go in by way of the vestibule of the gate and he shall go out by the same way. 9. When the people of the land enter to bow down before the Lord at the appointed feasts, the one who enters to worship by way of the north gate shall go out by way of the south gate; and the one who enters by way of the south gate shall go out by way of the north gate; he shall not return by way of the gate by which he entered, but he shall go out straight ahead of him.[2] 10. And the prince shall be among them; when they enter he shall enter, and when they go out he[d] shall go out. 11. On the pilgrimage festivals and on the appointed feasts, the meal offering shall be a *measure* for the bull, and a *measure* for the ram, and for the lambs, as much as he desires, and a *full hin* of oil for each *measure*. 12. When the prince shall present a free-will offering, either a burnt offering or *holy sacrifices* as a free-will offering before the Lord, one shall open for him the gate which faces east, and he shall present his burnt offering and his *holy sacrifices*, as he would present them on the Sabbath day. Then he shall go out, and one shall close the gate after his departure. 13. A year old unblemished lamb shall you provide as a daily burnt offering before the Lord; you shall provide it every single morning. 14. And you shall provide a meal offering with it every single morning, one sixth of a *measure*, and one third of a *hin* of oil with which to mix the flour; it is the regular meal offering *before* the Lord, an eternal statute. 15. They shall provide the lamb and the meal offering and the oil every single morning as a regular burnt offering." 16. Thus says the Lord God: "If the prince shall give a gift to *one*[3] of his sons, it is his inheritance and it shall belong to his sons, it is their possession by right of inheritance. 17. But if he shall give a gift, from his inheritance, to one of his servants, it shall be his until the year of the *jubilee*,[4] and then it shall revert to the prince. However, his inheritance shall belong to his sons. 18. The prince shall not take away any part of the inheritance of the people, by robbing them of their possessions. He shall provide an inheritance for his sons from his own possessions, so that not one of My people shall be driven[e] from his property." 19. Then he brought me in through the entrance which was by the side of the gate, to the holy chambers of the priests, which faced north; and behold, there was a place at their western extremity. 20. And he said to me, "This is the place where

Apparatus, Chapter 46 continued

[c] Lit. "as much as his hand can grasp."
[d] RB(1), CR and MSS., using Q. SP and others read "they," using Ket.

[e] Lit. "scattered," "dispersed."

Apparatus, Chapter 47

[a] Most versions. SP: "to the east," probably a scribal error.

[b] Or "deep."

the priests shall boil the guilt offering and the sin offering; where they shall bake the meal offering, so as not to take them out to the outer court, *to mingle*[5] with the people." 21. Then he brought me out to the outer court, and took me past the four corners of the court, and behold, there was a court at the corner of each court, a court at the corner of each court. 22. In the four corners of the court there were *fenced-in courts,*[6] forty cubits in length and thirty in width; all the four courts had the same measurement. 23. And there were tiers of stone *made for them* round about, for all four of them, and a place arranged for cooking was at the bottom of the tiers round about. 24. Then he said to me: "This is the place arranged for cooking where those who serve at the Temple shall boil the *holy* sacrifices of the people."

CHAPTER 47

1. Then he brought me back to the door of the Temple, and behold, there was water coming out from under the threshold of the Temple to the east, for the Temple faced east, and the water was coming down from below, by the right side of the Temple, south of the altar.[a] 2. Then he took me out by way of the northern gate, and led me around by way of the outside, to the outer gate, by way of the gate which faces east, and behold, the water was coming out from the south side. 3. When the man went out *from* the east, he had a measuring line in his hand, and he measured a thousand *cubits* by the cubit, and then led me across the water, water up to the ankles. 4. Then he measured a thousand, and led me across the water, water up to the knees. Again he measured a thousand and led me across the water, water up to the loins. 5. And he measured another thousand, and it was a river which I was unable to cross for the water was overpowering,[b] water that one had to swim across, a river

Notes, Chapter 46

[1]This is one of the vexing discrepancies between Ezekiel and the Mosaic Law which Hananiah b. Hezekiah b. Garon labored so diligently to reconcile. *b. Šab.* 13b, *Hag.* 13a, *Men.* 45a. Only one Tannaitic reference gives us a clue as to the methodology of that reconciliation. It is found in *Sifre* on Deuteronomy, portion *ki tese*, 294:14, ed. L. Finkelstein, p. 313; *Yal. Šim.* Ezek. *v*383, 45. "R. Eleazar b. Hananiah b. Hezekiah b. Garon says, An ephah for a bull, and an ephah for a ram, and an ephah for a lamb, are then the measures (quantities) for the bulls, the lambs, and the rams all the same quantity? But isn't it written (Num. 29:3, 4), three tenths for the bull, two tenths for the ram and one tenth for the lamb? Rather, this teaches that there was a large ephah and there was a small ephah, both of which were called ephah." According to this version, the reconciliation is attributed to R. Eleazar, son of the famed Hananiah. According to the version in Tosafot, *b. Men.* 45a, bottom, caption *weki midat parim*, Hananiah himself was the author of the statement.

[2]R. Helbo in the name of R. Huna uses this v. as a proof-text that a person who enters the synagogue to pray, may leave by the door other than the one by which he entered, even though it may appear that he is using the synagogue for a short-cut. *b. Ber.* 62b.

[3]MT: "to a man."

[4]MT: *šenat hadderor*, "the year of release," or "liberty." Cf. Lev. 25:10.

[5]MT: "to consecrate the people."

[6]MT: *qeturot*, The meaning of the Hebrew is uncertain. It may be an Aramaism, the rendering in the *Tg.* is of the same root. Cf. BDB, p. 883 sub *qtr* II. Cf. also *m. Mid.* 2:5, where the same root is used with the meaning of "without a roof." But cf. Jastrow, II, p. 1353.

which was impossible to ford. 6. And he said to me, "Have you seen, O Son of Adam?" Then he carried ^{c} me and brought me back to the bank of the river. 7. When I came back, behold, on the bank of the river were very many trees on this side and that side. 8. And he said to me, "These waters go out to the eastern region and down to the plain,^{1} and enter into the sea;^{d} they spread to the Great Sea, and the waters become purified.^{e2} 9. And it shall be that every living creature that swarms, in every place where the waters of the river enter, shall live; and there will be very many fish, for these waters enter there and they are purified; and everything shall live in whatever place the waters of the river enter. 10. There shall *be a place* to stand upon for fishermen, from En-gedi to En-eglaim; it shall be for fishermen to spread their nets; their fish shall be of various kinds, and very plentiful, like the fish of the Great Sea. 11. Its swamps and its *reservoirs*^{3} shall not be purified, they shall be left for salt *mines*. 12. Along the river, many trees shall spring up^f on its bank, from this side and that side, every kind of tree for food. Its leaves shall not wither, and its fruit shall not cease. It will produce fruit every single month, because its waters issue from the Temple. Its fruit shall be for food, and its leaves for healing." 13. Thus says the Lord God: "This^4 is the boundary line by which you shall assign the inheritance of the land among the twelve tribes of Israel. Joseph shall receive two portions. 14. And you shall assign possession of it, every man the same as his brother, for I swore *by My Memra* to give it to your fathers; and this land shall *be divided* among you as an inheritance. 15. This is to be the boundary line of the land: on the north, from the Great Sea, by way of Hethlon to the entrance of Zedad, 16. Hamath, Beruth,^{g} Sibraim, which is between the border of Damascus and the border of Hamath, *the pond of the Agebeans,*^{5} which is on the border of Hauran. 17. So the boundary shall be from the Sea to Hazar-enon,^{6} on the northern border of Damascus northward, and the border of Hamath; this shall be the northern side. 18. On the east side, between Hauran and Damascus, and between Gilead and the land of Israel, the Jordan. You shall measure from the border on the Eastern Sea;^{7} this shall be the eastern side. 19. The southern side shall be from *Jericho*^{8} to the Waters of Strife *of Reqam,*^{9} an inheritance, to the Great Sea; this shall be the southern side, to the south. 20. On the western side, the Great Sea, from the border to a point opposite the entrance to Hamath. This shall be the western side. 21. You shall divide this land for yourselves among the tribes of Israel. 22. And it shall be, that you shall divide it as an inheritance for yourselves, and for the *proselytes who have converted* among you,^{10} and who have begotten children among you. They shall be to you as the native-born Children of Israel. They shall share with you in the inheritance, in the midst of the tribes of Israel. 23. And whatever tribe it may be, in the midst of which the *proselyte shall convert,*^{10} there you shall give him his inheritance," says the Lord God.

Apparatus, Chapter 47 continued

^{c} Or "led."
^{d} Or "west."
^{e} Lit. "healed."

^{f} lit. "rise."
^{g} RB: "Berotah"

CHAPTER 48

1. "These are the names of the tribes: From the northern end, at the border, in the direction of Hethlon, to the entrance of Hamath, as far as Hazar-enan, bordering on Damascus, north, to the border of Hamath; he shall have from the eastern side westward,[1] Dan, one portion. 2. Bordering on Dan, from the east side to the west side, Asher, one portion. 3. Bordering on Asher, from the east side to the west side, Naphtali, one portion. 4. Bordering on Naphtali, from the east side to the west side, Manasseh, one portion. 5. Bordering on Manasseh, from the east side to the west side, Ephraim, one portion. 6. Bordering on Ephraim, from the east side to the west side, Reuben, one portion. 7. Bordering on Reuben, from the east side to the west side, Judah, one portion. 8. Bordering on Judah, from the east side to the west side, shall be the portion which you shall set apart, twenty-five thousand cubits in width and in length, equal to one of the tribal portions, from the east side to the west side; and the *precinct* of the Sanctuary shall be in the middle of it. 9. The portion which you shall set apart *before* the Lord shall have a length of twenty-five thousand cubits and a width of ten thousand.[2] 10. And for these, the holy portion shall be set apart;

Notes, Chapter 47

[1]MT: "the Arabah." Cf. *Tg.* Onq. Deut. 11:30.

[2]v. 8b is difficult. The ancient versions have different readings other than MT, although LXX and V come close to the Hebrew text that we possess. The Dead Sea is probably intended, and S characterizes that as "putrid waters." *Tg*'s rendering, including the reference to *yama' raba'*, the Great Sea, usually the Mediterranean, can only be understood against the background of Rabbinic legend concerning the river which will flow from the future Temple, a Midrash found in *t. Suk.* 3:3 ff.; *Pirq. de R. El.,* ch. 51; *Yal. Šim.* on Ezek. #383 (47). The relevant features of that Midrash, which connects Zech. 14:8 with this passage in Ezekiel, are, that the river will separate into three branches, one flowing into the Sea of Tiberias (Galilee); one flowing into the Sea of Sodom (the Dead Sea); and the ultimate destination being the Great Sea (Mediterranean), encompassing the entire world.

Tg.'s mitafqin, "spread," could be a misinterpretation or a misreading of the word *mefakkim* "the water shall ooze (and bubble)," in this Midrash, a play on the biblical word in Ezek. 47:2.

[3]MT: "its marshes."

[4]MT: *geh,* a scribal error for *zeh,* which is the Targumic reading.

[5]MT: *ḥaṣer hattikon,* lit. "the inside court." The place, whether by its Hebrew or Aramaic name, has never been correctly identified. Cf. *S-A,* p. 119; *IB,* p. 330.

[6]*Tg.* transliterates MT. The identity of the place is obscure.

[7]*Tg.* follows MT. The reference is to the Dead Sea.

[8]MT: "Tamar." Jericho was known as the city of palm trees, Deut. 34:3; 2 Chron. 28:15. Cf. *S-A,* p. 119 f.

[9]MT: "the waters of Meribot Kadesh." *S-A* maintain that *Tg.*"s rendering, *Rekem,* is a case of mistaken identity, p. 120.

[10]MT: "the strangers who reside among you."

Notes, Chapter 48

[1]MT: "the sea." *Tg.* makes certain that its rendering is not misunderstood, by the term *ma'raba',* whereas the usual rendering for west is *yama'.*

[2]*Tg.* follows MT. Some emend to read "twenty thousand."

for the priests, to the north, twenty-five thousand cubits; and to the west, a width of ten thousand; and to the east a width of ten thousand; and to the south, a length of twenty-five thousand; and *the precinct* of the Sanctuary of the Lord shall be in the middle of it. 11. It shall be for the priests, who are consecrated, of the sons of Zadok, who kept the watch *of My Memra,* who did not go astray when the Children of Israel went astray, as the Levites had gone astray. 12. They shall have it as a portion set apart, of the land that was set apart as most holy, bordering on the Levites. 13. And the Levites, alongside the border of the priests, shall have a portion twenty-five thousand cubits in length and ten thousand in width. The entire length shall be twenty-five thousand cubits, and the width ten thousand. 14. They shall not sell any of it, nor exchange it, nor transfer this choice land, for it is sacred *before* the Lord. 15. The remaining five thousand cubits in width by twenty-five thousand, is non-sacred, for the city, for dwellings and for open space, and *the precinct of* the city shall be in the middle of it. 16. And these shall be its dimensions: on the north side, four thousand five hundred cubits; and on the south side, four thousand five hundred; and on the east side, four thousand five hundred; and on the west side, four thousand five hundred. 17. And the city shall have open space to the north, two hundred and fifty cubits; to the south, two hundred and fifty; to the east, two hundred and fifty; and to the west, two hundred and fifty. 18. What remains, by the side of the portion which has been set apart as sacred, ten thousand in length to the east, and ten thousand to the west, shall be alongside the holy portion. Its produce shall be for food for those who work in the city. 19. Those who work in the city, from all the tribes of Israel, shall cultivate it. 20. The entire portion which is set part, shall be twenty-five thousand cubits by twenty-five thousand, a square; you shall set it apart as the sacred portion, up to the city's property. 21. And what remains on this side and that side of the sacred portion and of the property of the city, shall belong to the prince. Alongside the twenty-five thousand cubits, set apart as sacred, to the eastern border, and to the west alongside the twenty-five thousand cubits on the western border, alongside *one* of the tribal portions, shall belong to the prince. The sacred portion and *the precinct of* the Temple building, shall be in the middle of it. 22. And part of the property of the Levites and part of the property of the city shall be in the middle of that which belongs to the prince. That which is between the border of Judah and the border of Benjamin shall belong to the prince. 23. As for the remaining tribes: from the east side to the west side, Benjamin, one portion. 24. Bordering on Benjamin, from the east side to the west side, Simeon, one portion. 25. Bordering on Simeon, from the east side to the west side, Issachar, one portion. 26. Bordering on Issachar, from the east side to the west side, Zebulun, one portion. 27. Bordering on Zebulun, from the east side to the west side, Gad, one portion. 28. Bordering on Gad, in a southern direction, the boundary shall be from *Jericho,*[3] the Waters of Strife of *Rekam,*[4] an inheritance, to the Great Sea. 29. This is the land which you shall divide as an inheritance among the tribes of Israel, and these are their portions,

Apparatus, Chapter 48

[a] RB and AP. SP: "their measurement."
[b] Lit. "round about.
[c] SP. R, K and other versions: "the name of the city

shall be designated (or proclaimed) from the day when the Lord makes His Shekinah dwell there."

says the Lord God. 30. These shall be the exits of the city: on the north side, the measurement[a] shall be four thousand five hundred cubits. 31. And the gates of the city, named for the tribes of Israel, three gates facing north, the gate of Reuben, one; the gate of Judah, one; the gate of Levi, one. 32. On the east side, four thousand five hundred cubits, three gates: the gate of Joseph, one; the gate of Benjamin, one; the gate of Dan, one. 33. On the south side, their measurement four thousand cubits, three gates: the gate of Simeon, one; the gate of Issachar, one; the gate of Zebulun, one. 34. On the west side, four thousand five hundred cubits, their gates, three: the gate of Gad, one; the gate of Asher, one; the gate of Naphtali, one. 35. Its circumference[b] shall be eighteen thousand cubits. And the name of the city, *designated* from the day *that the Lord makes His Shekinah rest upon it,*[5] shall be: The Lord is there."[c6]

Notes, Chapter 48 continued

[3]MT: "Tamar." Cf. 47:19 and note 8 thereto, *supra.*

[4]Cf. 47:19 and note 9 thereto, *supra.*

[5]MT: "from the day." *Tg.* expands with an exegetic complement.

[6]MT: "and the name of the city from that day on, shall be, 'The Lord is there.'" The ancient versions vary in their rendering of this v. LXX omits "Lord" altogether, though some MSS. follow the MT. V also adheres strictly to MT. S: "the Lord named it" or "the Lord is its name," reading *šemah* for MT's *šamah.* It is interesting that R. Samuel b. Naḥmani, quoting R. Joḥanan, also reads it *šemah, b. B.B.* 75b. Cf. *Mid. Teh.* 21:2. There is some mysticism and mystery and the esoteric in the versions of *Tg.* cited by Rashi, Kimḥi and others: "and the name of the city shall be designated (or explained) from the day when the Lord makes His Shekinah dwell there." According to this version, the name of the city is not specified at all, but Yahweh will name it in the future when it is restored. What the name of it will be remains a mystery. This, too, could be associated with Merkabah. Cf. S.H. Levey, "The Targum to Ezekiel," p. 145.

Bibliography

Bacher, W., "Targum," JE, XII, pp. 57 ff. "Synagogue," XI, 619 ff.

Blank, S. H., *Jeremiah, Man and Prophet*, Cincinnati, 1961.

Blau, L., "Shekinah," *JE*, XI, p. 259 f.

Bowker, J., *The Targums and Rabbinic Literature*, Cambridge, 1969.

Braude, W. G., *The Midrash on Psalms*, 2 vols., New Haven, Conn., 1959.

_____, *Pesikta Rabbati*, 2 vols. New Haven, 1968.

Brown, Driver, and Briggs, *Hebrew and English Lexicon of the Old Testament*, Oxford, 1952.

Buttenwieser, M., *The Prophets of Israel*, N.Y., 1914.

Cassuto, M. D., *Sefer Yeḥezkel*, Tel Aviv, 1959.

Charles, R. H., *Apocrypha and Pseudepigrapha of the Old Testament*, vol II, Oxford, 1963.

Churgin, P., *Targum Jonathan to the Prophets*, New Haven, Conn., 1927.

Cooke, G. A., *The Book of Ezekiel*, International Critical Commentary, Edinburgh, 1960.

Eichrodt, W., *Ezekiel*, Philadelphia, 1952.

Friedlander, G., *Pirke de Rabbi Eliezer*, N.Y., 1965.

Ginzberg, L., "Adam Kadmon," and "Book of Adam," *JE*, I, pp. 179 ff. "Anthropomorphism and Anthropopathism," I, pp. 621 ff.

Greenberg, M. *Ezekiel, 1-20*, Anchor Bible, Garden City, N.Y., 1983.

Grossfeld, B., and Aberbach, M., *Targum Onkelos to Genesis*, N.Y., 1982.

_____, "Targum to the Prophets," *EJ*, IV, pp. 846 ff.

Hasting's *Dictionary of the Bible*, IV, N.Y., 1902.

Hayward, R., *Divine Name and Presence: The Memra*, Totowa, N.J., 1981.

Herford, R. T., *Christianity in Talmud and Midrash*. Clifton, N.J., 1966.

Herscher, U. D., "Johanan B. Zakkai: Acrobatics at Yavneh," unpublished minor, Hebrew Union College—Jewish Institute of Religion, Los Angeles, 1973.

Hertz, J. H., *The Authorised Daily Prayer Book*, N.Y., 1959.

Howie, C. G., *The Date and Composition of Ezekiel*, J. B. L. Monograph Series, VI, Phila., 1960.

Jastrow, M., *A Dictionary of the Targumim, etc.*, 2 vols., London and N.Y., 1903.

Kaufmann, Y., *The Religion of Israel*, tr. by M. Greenberg, Chicago, 1960.

Klein, M. L., "The Preposition *qdm*: a pseudo antianthropomorphism in the Targum," *JThS*, 1979.

_____, "The Translation of Anthropomorphisms and Anthropopathisms in the Targumim," *Congress Volume*, Vienna, 1980.

Koehler, L., and Baumgartner, W., *Lexicon in Veteris Testamenti Libros*, Leiden, 1958.

Kohler, K., *Jewish Theology*, N.Y ., 1928.

_____, "Memra," *JE*, VIII, pp. 464 f. "Merkabah," VIII, pp. 498 ff.

Komlosh, Y., *HaMikra B'or HaTargum* (TheBible in the Light of the Aramaic Translations), Tel Aviv, 1973.

_____, "'*Al Šitato Šel Targum Yonatan L'Sefer Yehezkel*" (Concerning Targum Jonathan's Method for the Book of Ezekiel), *Yeda' 'Am*, 17, Tel Aviv, 1974.

Lauterbach, J. Z., *Mekilta de Rabbi Ishmael*, 3 vols., Philadelphia, 1949.

Levey, S. H., "The Date of Targum Jonathan to the Prophets," *VT*, 1971.

_____, *The Messiah: An Aramaic Interpretation. The Messianic Exegesis of the Targum*, Cincinnati, 1974.

_____, "The Targum to Ezekiel," *HUCA*, 1975.

Levy, J., *Chaldäisches Wörterbuch über die Targumim*, Darmstadt, 1966, 2 vols. in one.

_____, *Neuhebräisches und Chaldäisches Wörterbuch*, 4 vols., Leipsig, 1876.

Maimonides, M., *Moreh Nebukim*, Jerusalem, 5720, and an English translation by Pines.

_____, *Mishneh Torah*, N.Y., 5716.

May, H. G., and Allen, E. L., *The Book of Ezekiel*, The Interpreter's Bible, VI, Nashville, 1980.

McNamara, M., *The New Testament and the Palestinian Targum to the Pentateuch*, Rome, 1966.

_____, *Palestinian Judaism and the New Testament*, Wilmington, Del., 1983.

_____, *Targum and Testament, Aramaic Paraphrases of the Hebrew Bible: A Light on the New Testament*, Shannon, Ireland, 1972.

Moore, G. F., *Judaism in the First Centuries of the Christian Era*, Cambridge, Mass., 1927. 2 vols.

Neusner, J., *A Life of Rabban Yohanan ben Zakkai*, Leiden, 1970.

Orlinsky, H. M., *Pseudo-Ezekiel and the Original Prophecy and Critical Articles*, N.Y., 1970.

————————, "Introductory Essay: On Anthropomorphisms and Anthropopathisms in the Septuagint and Targum," in Zlotowitz, B. M., *The Septuagint Translation of the Hebrew Terms in Relation to God in the Book of Jeremiah*, N.Y., 1981.

Rivkin, E., "The Meaning of Messiah in Jewish Thought," *Union Seminary Quarterly Review*, vol 26, no. 4, 1971.

Scholem, G. G., *Major Trends in Jewish Mysticism*, N.Y., 1954.

————————, *Jewish Gnosticism, Merkabah Mysticism, and Talmudic Tradition*, N.Y., 1965.

Smolar, L. and Aberbach, M., *Studies in Targum Jonathan to the Prophets*, N.Y. and Baltimore, 1983, (with a reprint of Churgin).

Stenning, J. F., *The Targum of Isaiah*, Oxford, 1953.

Urbach, E., *The Sages — Their Concepts and Beliefs*, Jerusalem, 1975.

Wacholder, B. Z., *The Dawn of Qumran, the Sectarian Torah and the Teacher of Righteousness*, Cincinnati, 1983.

Yadin, Y., *Megilat Hammiqdaš*, 3 vols., Jerusalem, 5737.

Zeitlin, S., "The Origin of the Synagogue," *Proceedings of the American Academy of Jewish Research*, 1931, pp. 72 ff.

MT   The Masoretic Text of the Hebrew Scriptures (Kittel).
      (Targum's departures from MT are in italics.)

TRANSLATIONS OF EZEKIEL FROM THE HEBREW

THE ANCIENT VERSIONS

LXX   Greek, Septuagint, Göttingen. 1952.

S   Syriac, Peshitta, London, 1823-1826.

Tg.   Aramaic, Targum(im).

V   Latin, Vulgate, Rome, 1959.

ENGLISH TRANSLATIONS

The Anchor Bible, Ezekiel 1-20, Garden City, N.Y., 1983.

The ArtScroll Tanach Series, Yechezkel, 3 vols., N.Y., 1977.

The Complete Bible: An American Translation, Chicago, 1960.

The Jewish Publication Society (New Series), *The Prophets*, Philadelphia, 1978.

The New American Bible, N.Y., 1970.

The New English Bible, Oxford, 1970.

The Holy Bible, Revised Standard Version, N.Y., Toronto, Edinburgh, 1953. Also included in *The Interpreter's Bible*, vol. VI, Nashville, 1956.

Indexes

I. THE HEBREW SCRIPTURES

II. NEW TESTAMENT

III. PSEUDEPIGRAPHA

IV. ANCIENT VERSIONS
(All references are to Ezekiel)

V. OTHER TARGUMIM

VI. RABBINIC LITERATURE

VI. THE RABBIS
(Alphabetically)

VII. MEDIEVAL JEWISH COMMENTARIES on Ezekiel

VIII. MODERN COMMENTARIES on Ezekiel

IX. MODERN AUTHORS

X. SUBJECT INDEX